P9-DCV-659

WORLD WAR II

Personal Accounts

PEARL HARBOR TO V-J DAY

WORLD WAR II

Personal Accounts

PEARL HARBOR TO V-J DAY

A Traveling Exhibition Sponsored by
The National Archives and Records Administration

CURATOR OF THE EXHIBITION AND CATALOG EDITOR
Gary A. Yarrington

ESSAY BY
James Stokesbury

PUBLISHED BY
THE LYNDON BAINES JOHNSON FOUNDATION
AUSTIN, TEXAS
1992

Printed in the United States of America.

Published by the Lyndon Baines Johnson Foundation
P.O. Box 1234, Austin, Texas 78701

ISBN 0-911333-95-9

This exhibition commemorates the fiftieth anniversary of the United States involvement in World War II.
It is sponsored by, and travels under the auspices of, the National Archives and Records Administration, Washington, D.C.—Dr. Don W. Wilson, Archivist of the United States.

The exhibition was created and designed by the Lyndon Baines Johnson Library and Museum, Austin, Texas.

The exhibition is made possible, in part, by a grant from the USAA Foundation.

Educational outreach materials made possible by a grant from:
Amon G. Carter Foundation, Fort Worth, Texas
Carl B. & Florence E. King Foundation, Dallas, Texas

Additional funding provided by:
Consumers Power Foundation, Jackson, Michigan
Lyndon Baines Johnson Foundation, Austin, Texas
National Archives Trust Fund Board
Potomac Electric & Power Company, Washington, D.C.

Library of Congress Cataloging-in-Publication Data

World War II : personal accounts—Pearl Harbor to V-J Day: a traveling exhibition sponsored by the National Archives and Records Administration / curator of the exhibition and catalog editor, Gary A. Yarrington : essay by James Stokesbury.
p. cm.
ISBN 0-911333-95-9 (National Archives and Records Administration)
1. World War, 1939-1945—United States—Exhibitions.
I. Yarrington, Gary A. II. Stokesbury, James. III. United States. National Archives and Records Administration. IV. Title: Personal accounts—Pearl Harbor to V-J Day.
D733.U6W67 1992
940.54'0973'07473—dc20 92-9108
CIP

FRONTISPIECE

The appearance of the mailman holds the promise of a "letter home" from a loved one overseas.

Alfred Eisenstaedt, LIFE Magazine © Time Warner Inc.

ABOUT THE COVER

Pictured: Ens Gaylord E. Barber, Lt (jg) William C. Bieluch, Lt Col Alfred F. Birra, Col Clifford Bluemel, 1st Lt Sven G. Carlson, 1st Lt Richard E. Cole, Fire Controlman Clifford M. Dunn, Jr., Electricians Mate Second Class A. J. Ehlert, Maj George Fisher, Artilleryman Arthur A. Fredette, 1st Lt Austen H. Furse, Chief Radioman Walter Germann, Henry Mason Geselbracht, Jr., Craftsman Gordon Hansford, S Sgt Vernon D. Hasley, Fireman First Class Edward Joseph (Bud) Heidt, Fireman First Class Wesley John Heidt, Ens Thomas Ray Jones, Lt Gen Tadamichi Kuribayashi, S Sgt Charles F. Logue, Pvt Norman Maffei, 1st Lt Hiram E. Mann, S1c Richard Thomas Mariner, Pfc Richard Minear, Seaman Marshall Nichols, Pfc DD Roche, Lt Col J. Earl Rudder, Obergefreiter Kuno Schmitt, Pfc Peter Sisoy, Cpl Leonard J. Travaline, Radioman First Class Raymond M. Tufteland, Cpl Robert E. Turner, 1st Lt Carl G. Weeks, 2d Lt Lucy Wilson
Medals: American, Purple Heart, Bronze Star, Combat Infantryman badge; French, Croix de la Liberation; German, Iron Cross, first class; Japanese, Order of the Rising Sun, eighth class
Photography by Dennis Fagan and Patrick Keeley

EXHIBITION ITINERARY

San Antonio Museum of Art
San Antonio, Texas
Dec 7, 1991 - April 5, 1992

Lyndon B. Johnson Library
Austin, Texas
Apr 18, 1992 - Aug 23, 1992

Dwight D. Eisenhower Library
Abilene, Kansas
Sept 19, 1992 - Jan 4, 1993

Herbert Hoover Library
West Branch, Iowa
Jan 30, 1993 - April 11, 1993

Harry S. Truman Library
Independence, Missouri
May 5, 1993 - Aug. 15, 1993

Gerald R. Ford Museum
Grand Rapids, Michigan
Sept 11, 1993 - Jan 3, 1994

Jimmy Carter Library
Atlanta, Georgia
Jan 29, 1994 - May 1, 1994

IBM Gallery of Science and Art
New York City, New York
May 24, 1994 - Aug 27, 1994

John F. Kennedy Library
Boston, Massachusetts
Sept 24, 1994 - Jan 2, 1995

Ronald Reagan Library
Simi Valley, California
Jan 28, 1995 - Apr 9, 1995

National Archives
Washington D.C.
May 6, 1995 - Nov 11, 1995

CONTENTS

THE WHITE HOUSE

WASHINGTON

March 26, 1990

During the Second World War, we and our Allies were engaged in nothing less than a life-and-death struggle for our freedom and security. Totalitarian regimes intent on regional hegemony and world domination posed a grave threat to all free and sovereign nations. In an extraordinary response to that threat, millions of Americans -- people of every age, race, and walk of life -- rallied to defend the cause of liberty and human dignity. Their bravery and selflessness, demonstrated day after day in acts of personal sacrifice, both great and small, led the way to victory.

As a veteran of what President Franklin Roosevelt called "the most tremendous undertaking in American history," I salute the National Archives for commemorating the 50th anniversary of U.S. participation in World War II. This nationwide program of events will reach millions of Americans, giving a record of that war with the authenticity, clarity, and detail that only the National Archives can provide.

It will be a fitting tribute to our parents and grandparents, to our Nation's veterans, to all those on the homefront, and to those who gave their lives in defense of liberty and justice during World War II. The exhibitions, film programs, lecture series and publications to be produced through the National Archives will help young and old alike to understand the purpose and magnitude of that conflict and the great price paid for victory.

With so many changes sweeping through Europe and elsewhere in the world, we do well to reflect upon the history of World War II. We must also draw the proper lessons from those perilous times -- the first of which is that freedom must never be taken for granted. I wish the National Archives every success in conveying these important lessons to the American people.

G Bush

N. Nav. 48
(Mar. 1929)

Page 494

UNITED STATES SHIP FINBACK — Saturday (Day) 2 (Date) September (Month), 1944

ZONE DESCRIPTION Minus 10

REMARKS

0 to 2
Underway on course 000°(T) making standard speed on two main engines.
G. L. REDMOND,
Lieutenant, U.S. Naval Reserve.

2 to 4
Underway as before.
J. R. PEAT,
Ensign, U.S. Navy.

4 to 6
Underway as before.
J. L. LAWRENCE,
Lieutenant, U.S. Naval Reserve.

6 to 9
Underway as before. 0800 changed course to 070°(T).
H. D. SPRATLIN,
Lieutenant Commander, U.S. Naval Reserve.

9 to 12
Underway as before. Steering various courses and speeds on life guard station. 1156 rescued Lt.(jg) George H. W. BUSH, File No. 173464, U.S. Naval Reserve, from rubber life boat.
W. H. PARKMAN,
Ensign, U.S. Naval Reserve.

12 to 15
Underway as before.
G. L. REDMOND,
Lieutenant, U.S. Naval Reserve.

15 to 18
Underway as before. 1504 changed course to 110°(T). 1505 changed course to 095o(T) and submerged. 1530 sighted downed aviator in life boat. Made approach on boat and took boat in two with periscope. 1651 changed course to 270°(T). 1717 surfaced with four main engines on the line. Took aboard Ensign James W. BECKMAN, File No. 301442, U.S. Naval Reserve. 1723 changed course to 250°(T), commencing constant helm. 1740 changed course to 270°(T).
J. R. PEAT,
Ensign, U.S. Navy.

18 to 20
Underway as before. 1855 changed course to 335°(T) and changed to two engine speed.
J. L. LAWRENCE,
Lieutenant, U.S. Naval Reserve.

20 to 22
Underway as before. 2015 investigating possible radar contact, various courses and speeds. 2031 resumed two engine speed on base course 335°(T). 2126 slowed to two-thirds speed.
L. HEYWORTH, Jr.,
Lieutenant, U.S. Navy.

22 to 24
Underway as before.
W. H. PARKMAN,
Ensign, U.S. Naval Reserve.

Approved: R. R. WILLIAMS, Lt. Comdr., USN, Commanding.
Examined: H. D. SPRATLIN, Lt. Comdr., U.S.N.R., Navigator.

(Original (ribbon) copy of this page to be sent to Bureau of Navigation monthly)

Page from the deck log of the USS *Finback* dated September 2, 1944

National Archives and Records Administration

Lt (jg) George Bush was assigned to the USS *San Jacinto*, an aircraft carrier in the Pacific. On September 2, 1944, his plane was hit by antiaircraft fire while on a bombing mission over the Bonin Islands. Even though his plane was burning, Bush attempted to hit his target before bailing out. Three hours after landing in the ocean, he was rescued by the submarine *Finback*.

FOREWORD

Archivist of the United States

"World War II: Personal Accounts—Pearl Harbor to V-J Day" is a deeply moving, highly personal exhibition of unique documents. These diaries and letters, written by GIs and generals, offer a kaleidoscope of emotions—isolation, fear, discomfort, euphoria—that are at once individual and universal. Reading these accounts stirs further recollections of the war years, whether of our own experiences or those recounted by our parents or grandparents.

"World War II: Personal Accounts—Pearl Harbor to V-J Day" is one of many nationwide programs produced by the National Archives and its nine presidential libraries and twelve regional archives to commemorate the fiftieth anniversary of U.S. participation in World War II. These activities provide an unprecedented opportunity for us to share our unique resources with the country.

The National Archives is the permanent repository of the records of the federal government, including the papers and records of the ten most recent presidents. Among our holdings are millions of documents and photographs that touch on World War II and the largest collection of documentary film footage in the world relating to the war. This material reflects every aspect of the war—the home front (including rationing, war bonds, and the War Production Board), information and propaganda, military strategy, and diplomatic initiatives. The scope of our holdings stretches beyond the American war effort and includes personal accounts of German and Japanese soldiers as well as official archives contained within captured German records.

"Personal Accounts" draws on these rich resources, highlighting some of the most famous documents, photographs, and three-dimensional objects: the correspondence between British Prime Minister Winston Churchill and President Franklin Roosevelt, the draft of Roosevelt's famous Day of Infamy speech, Hitler's last will and testament, Eva Braun's personal photograph album, and the German and Japanese surrender documents. These materials complement the moving accounts of soldiers, sailors, airmen, and nurses who fought bravely, but anonymously, to preserve our freedom.

The overwhelming response by veterans in donating their personal effects to this exhibition and of the private sector in supporting it recalls the "can-do" spirit and patriotism of the 1940s. This exhibition is a paragon of the public-private partnership that is crucial to the successful educational efforts of cultural institutions today. Without the cooperation of veterans across the country and grants from the private sector, this exhibition would not have been possible. The United Services Automobile Association (USAA) Foundation, whose headquarters is in San Antonio, Texas, provided major funding for the design and fabrication of this exhibition. The Lyndon Baines Johnson Foundation, Austin, Texas; the National Archives Trust Fund Board; the Amon G. Carter Foundation, Fort Worth, Texas; the Carl B. & Florence E. King Foundation, Dallas, Texas; the Potomac Electric & Power Company, Washington, D.C.; the American Legion; the Consumers Power Foundation, Jackson, Michigan; and Donovan Leisure Newton and Irvine, New York, New York, have all contributed generously to this exhibition and catalog and to many other National Archives World War II educational events and publications.

We look forward to this same spirit of cooperation throughout the commemorative period as the exhibition travels across the country. It is my hope that millions of Americans will participate in these activities and take time to reflect on the sacrifices and hardships endured by Americans both at home and abroad during World War II. "World War II: Personal Accounts—Pearl Harbor to V-J Day" is not just a tribute to veterans; it is much more. It is an opportunity, perhaps the last one, to preserve the memories of missions past, both at home and abroad, and to make them available to millions of children, grandchildren, and great-grandchildren.

Don W. Wilson

Secretary of the Army

On December 7, 1991, America commemorated the attack on Pearl Harbor and the beginning of U.S. military involvement in World War II. We remembered "a date which will live in infamy" and recalled the heroism of those who stood in harm's way on that tragic morning fifty years ago. We also paused to reflect on an era that in many ways seems far removed from today—a world in which simple beliefs fit a less complicated time.

Some of us may question the utility of the commemorations. We ask, "What insights can such a time period offer our more sophisticated age?" or "Why should we resurrect the emotions of a bygone era?"

This publication and the exhibition it describes provide some answers to those questions. They demonstrate that World War II was both an intensely private and a profoundly public event that holds many lessons for those who now confront the challenges of a dangerous, unstable world.

On the personal level, World War II was replete with intensely human experiences. It introduced many to the hard lessons of growing up—lessons still meaningful today.

Randall Jarrell, for example, captured the hardship of falling into adulthood in his famous poem, "Death of the Ball Turret Gunner":

From my Mother's sleep I fell into the State,
And I hunched in its belly till my wet fur froze.
Six miles from earth, loosed from its dream of life.
I woke to black flack and the nightmare fighters.

Many of us were awakened during that period—some in airplanes like the one Jarrell recalls, others at sea in gray armadas, and still others on the bloodstained beaches of Normandy or in the malaria-ridden jungles of New Guinea. We awakened to the fact that there are principles worthy of supreme sacrifice and that, in times of dire need, free men and women of good will can accomplish seemingly impossible deeds.

As a public activity, the war touched whole generations of Americans. Eight million World War II GIs are still alive today. They have deeply ingrained memories of their wartime experience. They understand that heroism was not necessarily a hallmark of service, but devotion to country and principle surely were. They know the power derived from national unity and appreciate the value of shared sacrifice in a just cause.

World War II was also a watershed for America. It was one of the defining events of this century because it steeled American resolve in the pursuit of freedom and brought our nation to a position of global leadership.

This National Archives exhibition has captured the individual and collective experiences of those who lived through the war as well as its historical significance. As "World War II: Personal Accounts—Pearl Harbor to V-J Day" appears across our country, I hope it will touch the lives of millions of young people—schoolchildren, teenagers, and those who have little or no knowledge of World War II. The personal diaries, letters, films, photographs, and memorabilia featured in "Personal Accounts" offer important insights into this period and reveal how World War II has molded today's world. More important, they bring to life those principles and lessons for which so many sacrificed so much.

I hope Americans of all ages will take advantage of this remarkable exhibition to join in the commemoration of World War II and the American warriors who fought so bravely in it. I hope each of you will find in the exhibition some simple truths that enrich your life and enable you to hold the contributions of our World War II veterans more dear.

M. P. W. Stone

♦ ♦ ♦

The Department of the Army was appointed Executive Agent to plan and coordinate the Department of Defense 50th Anniversary of World War II Commemorative Program, December 17, 1990.

PREFACE

"World War II: Personal Accounts—Pearl Harbor to V-J Day" goes beyond the mere unfolding of the major events of the war. Over one hundred letters and diaries, enhanced by photographs and personal possessions, tell the story of individuals caught up in a critical moment—for themselves and for the world. This exhibition is the centerpiece of the National Archives' national celebration of the fiftieth anniversary of U.S. participation in the Second World War.

During these years of commemoration, many of those who served their country on the battlefront or on the home front will recall their own memories, painful and joyous, and share them with those who are too young to remember the war. The vast majority of us who are "ordinary" citizens do not often consider our actions to be of "historic" importance. This exhibition and catalog prove otherwise. The letters, diaries, and pictures shed light on the individual's contribution to the greater world struggle, and there are countless more stories waiting to be told.

This catalog first presents a historical essay by noted World War II historian James L. Stokesbury. The essay helps readers gain a better understanding of the sequence and significance of the events between December 7, 1941, and V-J Day. The documents, pictures, and objects then are arranged as they appear in the exhibition, with each section focusing on a major campaign or event of the war. It is the hope of all those who worked on the exhibition and the catalog that you will carry away a sense of wonder, pride, and appreciation of the achievements and experiences of those who here share with us a part of their lives.

HISTORICAL ESSAY

WORLD WAR II: AN OVERVIEW

Prologue: December 7, 1941

0755 on the morning of December 7, 1941; Pearl Harbor, on the island of Oahu, in the territory of Hawaii, temporary home of the U.S. Fleet; a beautiful Sunday morning, with fleecy little clouds rolling across the blue sky. Along Battleship Row, just off Ford Island, quartermasters stood at the jack- and flagstaffs of the great ships, ready to make morning colors. Below, the messdecks were filled with sleepy sailors, coming off watch, going on, or recovering from a night ashore. The scene was repeated with variations on land, at Schofield Barracks and at the army air force stations about the island, where bored sentries guarded the airplanes that had been lined up closely to protect them from saboteurs.

Higher commanders had been warned that some sort of move was afoot. The Imperial Japanese Fleet had been lost by radio intelligence; some units had been spotted in the Gulf of Siam, and the American government expected an aggressive move by Japan. To the extent that they had worked out the possibilities, they thought the Japanese were about to move against the British bastion of Singapore. They were wrong.

At Pearl Harbor, specks appeared in the sky to the northwest; a distant drone grew rapidly. Watching soldiers and sailors thrilled to the spectacle of masses of aircraft, which they of course assumed to be American; the United States, after all, was not at war—it was instead an island of sanity and normality in a world gone crazy. Unchallenged but admired, the planes swept on.

Over the harbor and its beautiful battleships and cruisers, over Wheeler Field and Schofield Barracks, the formations broke apart and the planes came screaming down, strafing and bombing; low-flying torpedo planes skimmed across the waters of the harbor, aiming their deadly loads at the battleships. Within minutes the fleet was a shambles; *Oklahoma* rolled over, *West Virginia* settled in the mud; *Arizona* took a bomb right down her stack that blew the ship apart. Hundreds of men were swimming in the scummy water, or worse, trapped below decks with no hope of rescue. On the airfields, the neatly parked planes were burning piles of rubber and aluminum as aircraft flaunting the red circle of Japan strafed up and down the rows. At 0758 the first actual warning went out, followed two minutes later by the message: "Air raid on Pearl Harbor. This is no drill."

The island was still reeling under a second and third attack when the news reached San Francisco, from where it was immediately relayed to Washington. On the east coast of the United States it was afternoon. Senior U.S. government officials, who were in fact waiting for a delayed communication from the Japanese special envoy then in the capital, were shocked and stunned. Soon after two o'clock their time, they issued a message of their own: Execute unrestricted air and submarine warfare against Japan. Suddenly, without warning, for the second time in a quarter century, the United States was at war.

The pall of smoke rising into the sky over Oahu marked one of those seminal turning points in American history, a period to one era and the beginning of another. There is probably not one American alive today, who had reached the age of reason by 1941, who does not remember exactly where he was and what he was doing when he heard the news of Pearl Harbor. The event marked the passage from peace to war, from isolation and neutrality to active participation in the most immense conflict in world history. It was a galvanic shock whose effects are still being worked out fifty years later, and generations still to be born would lead different lives because of it. World War II, just beginning on that day for Americans, would call the country to greatness, and to that call America would return a resounding answer.

The Background of the War

The seeds of World War II were sown in the aftermath of World War I, or The Great War, as it used to be called. That conflict, waged between 1914 and 1918, pitted the Central Powers of Germany, Austria-Hungary, Turkey, and Bulgaria against a coalition of the Allies, including France, Great Britain and her empire, Russia, Italy, and eventually the United States, as well as a host of lesser belligerents. By the end of it, both sides were exhausted, and only the late entry, and enormous untapped wealth, of the United States permitted the Allies to win. By late 1918 only the United States could continue; the victors were as depleted and war-weary as the vanquished.

The peacemaking process that took place in Paris in 1919 was supposed to be a general and genuine meeting that would satisfy all of the world's states and resolve the complex issues and ambitions that had caused the war. But by the time the ostensible winners had finished quarreling over the spoils, there was no room for the nominal losers, and they were simply forced to sign an imposed peace treaty, which they perceived, rightly or wrongly, as bitterly unfair, and on which they blamed all their subsequent troubles and frustrations.

The United States, its President Woodrow Wilson feeling disgusted, soiled, and cheated by the whole process, never even bothered to sign the peace treaty, and the country retreated from Europe into a profound isolationism. The prevalent view among Americans was that they had been tricked into fighting the war, cheated into paying for it, and then robbed of a just peace by grubby European politicians who would never learn to mend their ways and therefore deserved any trouble that they got into. It was a simplistic view that was not entirely accurate, and it dogged American foreign policy for the next two decades.

Much of the rest of the world was in dire condition. The costs of the war, in money, resources, and above all lives, were horrendous; the world and its separate states lurched from crisis to crisis through the twenties and into the thirties. The western democratic states of France and Britain managed to survive, hollow shells of their former greatness, but they were among the few who did. The Russian Empire had collapsed during the war itself, to be replaced by revolution, civil war, and finally a one-party state led by the Communists. In central Europe the war had created a belt of fragile states with long historical memories and little political experience: Finland; the three little Baltic republics of Latvia, Lithuania, and Estonia; Poland, a large weak country with a tragic past and a more tragic future; and out of the wreckage of the Dual Empire, Austria, Hungary, Czechoslovakia, Yugoslavia, and finally the older but no more stable Bulgaria, Rumania, and Greece.

These were all weak though perhaps viable states; but there were far more potentially dangerous states around than they. Italy had sided with the Allies in 1915, had incurred enormous casualties in the war, and believed itself cheated by the peace process. Torn between the extremes of the political left and right, Italy in 1922 succumbed to the first of the great dictators of the period, when Benito Mussolini, head of a militant right-wing political party known as the Fascists, came to power and put into practice the idea of totalitarianism.

In this doctrine, fruit of nineteenth-century political philosophy, all power in the land flowed into and derived from the state; the governmental institutions of state and political party were one. The whole was exemplified and epitomized in Il Duce (The Leader). Mussolini was soon blustering to cheering crowds, boasting of Italian prowess, and advancing Italian claims to neighboring territory. The totalitarian view was simple: Might did make right, and the world belonged to those strong enough to take it. In a time of political, economic, and ideological confusion, Mussolini's strident pronouncements had a wide appeal, and he had many admirers, even in the democracies. More important, he also had imitators.

In 1918 the German Empire, the Second Reich, had collapsed. Kaiser Wilhelm had abdicated and fled to neutral Holland, and German politicians had set up a weak government, called after the place of its founding the Weimar Republic. But the state was burdened by signing the Treaty of Versailles, by the reparations payments imposed on it by the Allies, and above all by the fact that the Germans believed they should have won the war, and would have, had they not somehow been betrayed by some ill-defined villain. The republic was surrounded by sharks who tore at it from right and left, and who tore at each other—a political feeding frenzy that finally killed it.

Most significant, because most successful, of these sharks were the Nazis, the National Socialist German Workers' Party, led by a demonic former Austrian named Adolf Hitler. An embittered bum before the war, convinced of his own genius but too erratic to do anything to fulfill it, Hitler had fought bravely as an enlisted man on the Western Front in a German infantry regiment. After the war, he drifted into politics in Munich in Bavaria and discovered a gift for inspired demagoguery. Through the early twenties he slowly built a following. He went to prison for an attempted coup and wrote a turgid autobiography, *Mein Kampf*, in which he blamed all his and Germany's troubles on Jews, capitalists, foreigners, Versailles, everyone but himself, and offered his prescription for the revival of the country.

His party languished during the relative prosperity of the mid-twenties, but with the Depression of the thirties he began to gain strength. Other people's misery was his advantage. The discontented, the frustrated, the unemployed, of whom there were millions in Germany, rallied to his impassioned speeches. The Nazis had a simple answer to opposition—brute force, and street riots and beatings were a common feature in German politics of the period.

By late 1932, the Weimar Republic was near collapse, governing by decrees and deserted by many of its supporters. Outside his own party, Hitler was no one's first choice for power, but he was almost everyone's second choice, and on January 30, 1933, he was given the office of Chancellor of the Republic. With a grant of dictatorial powers for ninety days, he then destroyed the state of which he was leader.

Like Italy before it, but much more efficiently and ruthlessly, Germany became a totalitarian, one-party state; it was, in the phrase of the day, *Ein Reich, Ein Volk, Ein Führer* (One State, One People, One Leader). Hitler brilliantly and viciously suppressed all opposition, from other political parties, from labor unions, from intellectuals, from the churches, and even within his own party. The Jews were his particular scapegoat, and he inculcated and fostered a virulent anti-Semitism that had been growing in central Europe for a half century. Those Jews who were lucky enough to get out began fleeing the country, but thousands remained, victims of increasingly repressive legislation.

With all Germany marching in lock step, Hitler proclaimed the Third Reich; the First and Second had passed away, but this new one was to be The Thousand Year Reich, strong, confident, and militant, disdainfully casting aside the limits imposed by the Versailles Treaty. There was soon a new German air force, the Luftwaffe; German battleships were laid down in German shipyards, military conscription was introduced, there was full employment, the currency stabilized. Germany was strong and happy once again, its young men singing their way through cross-country marches and goose stepping proudly before their Führer.

Around the world there were also other strains of martial music. Japan was another Allied power in World War I, like Italy dissatisfied with its share of the peace treaty. Opened to western influence a mere seventy years, Japan had quickly adopted and adapted western technology and organization, and produced a unique blend of western skills and eastern attitudes. In the 1890s Japan had defeated China; in the 1900s, Russia; and in World War I, the few Germans in the Far East. The Japanese had occupied Korea, much of Manchuria, and the western Pacific islands. By the 1920s, with military leaders dominating foreign policy, they set their sights on China.

There was not much to stop them. China was in one of its periodic agonizing fits of collapse and rebirth, and its nascent government, under a successful warlord named Chiang Kai-shek, could barely keep itself afloat. In 1922, in a series of naval treaties, the United States and Great Britain had agreed not to fortify anything east of Singapore or west of Pearl Harbor, leaving the western Pacific, and all their holdings in it—Hong Kong, concessions in China, the Philippines, Guam—hostages to Japanese good will.

Hardly anyone in the western world understood the Japanese; they were assumed to be friendly and well-disposed people; imitation, after all, is the most sincere form of flattery, and the Japanese were openly imitative. They imitated British naval technology, American aircraft design, and German military organization. True, they were not behaving well in China, in which there was a strong American missionary interest, but then no one was behaving well in China, and no one understood China either.

As the dictatorships became more overtly aggressive, the democracies fell into progressive disarray. There was a supranational organization, the League of Nations, set up in the aftermath of World War I, but the United States had refused to join it, and its feeble attempts at some sort of collective security were impotent in the face of determined opposition. The League had no coercive power, and no provision for any. Any state that disliked its judgment or condemnation, on the rare occasions when it offered any, simply ignored it. When in 1932 the League mildly chastised Japan for invading Manchuria, the Japanese just walked out. In 1935, when Italy invaded Ethiopia, the latter's Emperor Haile Selassie made an agonized plea for support. The Canadian delegate, who suggested the League actually do something, was quickly disavowed by his own government. Eventually economic sanctions were voted against Italy—a list that carefully avoided anything the Italians actually needed—and Ethiopia was soon overrun. France and Britain were left to look to their own devices.

France had a string of alliances in central Europe, designed to protect her from Germany but actually involving her in any move the Germans might make. Britain, under an antimilitary prime minister, Neville Chamberlain, had no armed force to speak of except the Royal Navy. Communist Russia was beyond the pale. The United States, safe behind two great oceans, simply wanted to be left alone. Amid all this confusion, Adolf Hitler was free to move, and in 1936 he began a march of first political and then military conquest.

In March of 1936 Hitler, having put his internal house in order, made his first external move. The Rhineland, a strip of territory fifty kilometers wide along the Franco-German border, had been disarmed by the Treaty of Versailles. Germany was permitted neither to garrison nor fortify it, thus giving France both an advantage over, and protection from, Germany in the event of a military crisis. On March 7, Hitler moved troops into the Rhineland. It was a huge bluff; the Germans had no tanks, no aircraft to speak of, no heavy weapons. But no one dared call the bluff. The French, who had configured their army solely for defense, believed all the German propaganda and would not move without the support of the British. The British shrugged their shoulders: the territory was German, after all. The British and French presented a note of protest and let it go at that. Hitler got away with it.

Two years went by while civil war raged in Spain, and Japan invaded China proper, and the Powers twisted and turned. In March of 1938 Hitler was ready again. He invaded and annexed Austria, again in violation of the Versailles Treaty and his own pledges. By now the Germans did have tanks, of a sort, and armored cars, and airplanes, but there was little opposition from the Austrians—"It was roses all the way," one soldier wrote home—and none from anyone else, just the usual ineffective notes of protest, and scurrying about to consult.

Next came the Sudetenland, the mountainous western district of Czechoslovakia, ethnically largely German and given to the new state at the end of World War I. This might be different; Czechoslovakia had an army and an alliance with France, and the Soviet Union was also concerned by any move of Germany to the east. By mid-summer of 1938, it looked as if there would be war within days.

Instead, Prime Minister Chamberlain intervened; after two futile conferences, he and Hitler, with Premier Edouard Daladier of France and Mussolini from Italy, met in Munich. While the Czechs waited in an anteroom, Britain and France agreed to give Hitler everything he wanted and even to do his dirty work for him. They told the Czechs to agree or else; the Czechs agreed. Hitler got the Sudetenland, and the rump of Czechoslovakia became indefensible. Frenzied crowds, cheering madly, greeted Chamberlain and Daladier upon their return home. Hitler wanted, he said, nothing more. It was "peace in our time," said the relieved and happy Chamberlain.

He was wrong again. In March of 1939 Hitler moved once more and took over the rest of Czechoslovakia. The scales fell from Chamberlain's eyes, and he responded with an ironclad guarantee to Poland, obviously next on the list: If Hitler invaded Poland, Britain would fight.

Unfortunately, Poland was even less defensible than Czechoslovakia, and if she were to be defended, either the French would have to attack from the west, which they were not configured to do, or the Soviet Union would have to be brought into the alliance. The Poles, though, hated the Russians more than they feared the Germans. In August, Hitler again stole a march on everyone. He signed a nonaggression pact with his worst enemy, Russia, and he and the Russian dictator, Joseph Stalin, agreed to divide the corpse of Poland between them. Faced with that, Britain and France announced they would stand by their guarantees; no one believed them. President Roosevelt pleaded for calm and restraint; no one listened. It was too late for all that.

On September 1, 1939, without warning, German armed forces flooded across the frontier of Poland, striking any targets before them. Britain and France, still trying to avoid the unavoidable, gave Hitler an ultimatum: Stop or else. He ignored it. On September 3, a tired Chamberlain rose in the House of Commons to announce that Great Britain was at war with Germany. A few hours later France, too, declared war. The political and diplomatic posturing was over at last. Now the real agony began.

The Early Campaigns

The campaign the Germans unleashed on Poland reintroduced concepts all but forgotten during World War I—mobility and maneuver—and gave the world a new name, *Blitzkrieg*, or "lightning war." The Poles had lined up their infantry along the frontier, expecting to reinforce with their reserves and their horsed cavalry, widely thought to be the best in the world. They never had a chance. In the first hours of the war, German aircraft struck at road and communication centers, tanks and trucked infantry smashed through the frontier positions, and Polish mobilization broke down before it was completed. Though the Poles fought bravely and even fanatically, and caused the Germans some bad moments, the matter was never really in doubt. Within a week the Germans were approaching Warsaw; in another they had completed a second pincer around the remaining Polish forces. On September 17 the reeling Poles were hit again, as the Red Army crossed their eastern border and moved to clean up the remnants. Embattled Warsaw surrendered on the twenty-seventh, and by the first week of October, Poland had once again disappeared from the map of Europe.

Poland's western allies, after declaring war on her behalf, did nothing. The French mobilized and manned their great fortress belt, the Maginot Line, where they sat for the next nine months. The British sent a minuscule British Expeditionary Force to France, two divisions strong—or weak—and it drilled along the frontier, and also did nothing. Blitzkrieg in Poland was thus succeeded by "phony war" in the west, and everyone waited, in an atmosphere of tired cynicism, for someone to make a deal.

There was activity over the winter. The Soviets, scared by German success, looked to their own borders and forcibly took over the Baltic states, Latvia, Lithuania, and Estonia. They then turned on Finland and demanded cessions along the frontier there. The Finns refused, and the two went to war, David against Goliath, with all the world rooting for David. Though the Finns won some substantial battles, and even drove the Reds back in places, weight eventually told, and by mid-March of 1940 the Russians had what they wanted.

Britain and France considered intervention in the north, not because they liked the Finns better than they did the Poles, but because such a move would have placed them in northern Norway and Sweden, the source of much of German iron ore. Their moves in this direction led Hitler to the same thoughts, and as usual at this stage of the war, he moved more effectively than they did. On April 8, again without warning, German troops and naval and air units invaded Denmark and Norway. The former collapsed in five hours. The Norwegians tried to fight, and did substantial damage to German shipping, but the southern part of the country was quickly overrun, largely because of German control of the air. In the north it was a little different; the British could operate here without aerial threat, and they landed troops in central Norway and virtually wiped out a German naval squadron up around Narvik. Gradually, however, German command of the air was extended north, and by early June it was all over. At the price of a crippled surface navy, the Germans had secured their northern flank.

Probably the most important immediate result of the campaign was that it caused Prime Minister Chamberlain to fall in Great Britain, and his replacement was the fiery Winston Churchill, the very epitome of the bulldog politician and warrior. For all his quirks, Churchill was to prove the one indispensable man for the Allies in World War II.

He came to power just in time to preside over disaster. On May 10 the Germans opened their long-awaited campaign in the west. Here the Dutch, Belgians, French, and British had fitfully prepared to resist, but the former two clung to neutrality, and the French remained mired in outdated tactics and ideas. The Allies had more men than the Germans, but little coordination; more tanks, but poorer armored doctrine. They were four World War I armies facing one modern one, and they were smashed in a matter of days; it was the greatest military collapse since Napoleon had overrun Prussia in two weeks in 1806.

The Germans drove into the Low Countries, breaking the Dutch and Belgians and sucking the French and British into coming to their rescue. When the Allied maneuver elements were committed in Belgium, the Germans drove through the Ardennes Forest to the south of them, broke the front wide open, and sent the Allies reeling back toward the seacoast. The French government responded to the crisis by collapsing, their military leaders threw up their hands in despair, and in a terrible six weeks the greatest army in the world was laid low. The Dutch surrendered, the Belgians gave up, the British struggled clear of the wreckage to the sea, and in what many considered a miracle, a quarter of a million men of the British Expeditionary Force were evacuated from the little port of Dunkirk, along with another hundred thousand French.

The Germans quickly turned south, Paris was declared an open city, and the French government fled to Bordeaux. The hero of World War I, Marshal Philippe Pétain, came to power and immediately asked for an armistice. Mussolini in Italy, unable to resist the chance for cheap glory, declared war on the Allies. Fighting stopped on June 15; the Low Countries, northern and western France were all occupied, and a puppet French government was left at Vichy to collaborate with the Germans' New Order. Only Britain was left.

It was a Britain determined to fight on, but lacking almost everything with which to fight. The army had lost all its weapons and equipment in France. But there was still the Royal Navy, and there was also the Royal Air Force, fifty squadrons of fighter aircraft held back from France and now ready for their supreme test.

The Germans might conceivably have jumped the Channel on the run, but they were disorganized by victory and needed time to get ready. Not until July did they start working up invasion preparations, and in the middle of the month they started what Churchill immediately christened the "Battle of Britain." In this, the first full-scale aerial campaign in history, the Germans fought for air control over the Channel, and the Royal Air Force came forth to deny it. Though the numbers involved were surprisingly small—a couple of thousand pilots and planes on either side—it was an epic the whole world watched with bated breath. Day after day the Germans came over, and day after day the R.A.F. sent its young men up to meet them. Both sides made mistakes that might have cost them the battle, but the Germans made more of them, and as a beautiful summer turned toward autumn, it was increasingly clear the British had won. The Germans turned to night bombing, to the attempted destruction of London and other cities, but they could not break the British. It was indeed, as Churchill said of them, "their finest hour."

That was certainly the view in the United States, and American opinion was an enormously important factor in the way the war developed. President Roosevelt had announced his country's neutrality as soon as the war was declared, but the attitudes and policies of the greatest industrial power on earth were bound to be of consequence. The problem was, Americans were deeply and irrevocably divided on the issue of the war. The vast majority of them wanted nothing to do with it. Congress in 1935-37 had passed a series of neutrality acts designed to keep the country from being sucked into the vortex of a war. As the war flared in Europe, Roosevelt took hesitant steps to build up the lamentable U.S. armed forces—the army ranked behind those of Rumania and Bolivia in the thirties—but everything he did was interpreted as a move to war, and subject to intense debate. Only slowly and belatedly were American arms refurbished, and each step was accompanied by bitter argument.

Yet the perception slowly grew that the Allies had to be supplied, that Britain must survive, and that only the United States could help. The Neutrality Acts were gradually eroded into a policy of cash-and-carry, in which belligerents were permitted to buy American goods if they paid cash and carried them in their own ships, a policy that favored the Allies with their command of the sea. That worked until the British went broke, which they threatened to do in late 1940. The cash-and-carry was transformed into lend-lease, in which the president, after designating a certain country's condition as vital to American interests, could "loan" war goods and services to that country. Gradually the United States was supplying huge amounts of guns, ammunition, foodstuffs, and other supplies to Britain, then to other countries in the war as well. All of this, of course, was achieved at the price of America's own rearmament. Then came the conscription issue.

Albeit reluctantly, Congress had voted money for defense, first millions and then billions of dollars, to transform the country into "the arsenal of democracy." But the armed forces needed men as well as weapons, and the only way to get them was through conscription. The argument was vicious, opponents charging that Roosevelt, running for a third term of office, was a would-be dictator, that he was bent on war, that he was going "to plow under every fourth American boy." Yet the tide of events was inexorable, and slowly, reluctantly, Americans recognized the fact. Selective Service became law in September of 1940, and soon the first of what would become fourteen million servicemen were donning khaki and navy blue and learning their close-order drill.

At the same time, the war was already having positive effects on the American economy. The Depression had hit the United States terribly hard in the early thirties, and all of the innovations of Roosevelt's New Deal had not brought a return of prosperity. Not until the war was well along would American productivity return to pre-Depression levels. But there was an undeniable quickening of pace as the first rearmament orders trickled in. British and French trade and military missions had placed orders for aircraft, shells, boots and uniforms, food, and trucks, and from Massachusetts to California factories reopened, then geared up, then went to double shifts, then built new plants. President Roosevelt threw out a figure of "fifteen thousand planes a year"; it seemed insane in 1940, but however unrealistic, it meant jobs. The U.S. Navy laid down carriers, cruisers, and destroyers; trucks and tanks began rolling out of plants in Michigan and Ohio, and the giant American industrial capacity began to flex its muscles. America might not yet be on the march, but it was starting to move.

♦ ♦ ♦

The war blundered on. After the fall of 1940, Hitler could not get at the British, nor they at him. Mussolini solved the problem for them by opening up the war in the Mediterranean. From his colony of Libya he attacked British-held Egypt, and all through 1941 the armies swept back and forth across the North African desert, aiming for Suez in the east or Tripoli in the west, Italians and then Germans on the one side, British and Commonwealth troops on the other, fighting each other to a standstill.

Hitler turned his attention eastward too, to the Soviet Union, his longtime foe and late ally. He decided to settle with Russia once and for all. To clear his flanks he undertook another lightning campaign, into the Balkans, and drove the British out of Greece, where they had intervened unwisely to rescue their allies, as handily as he had done out of France. It was probably the low point of Churchill's stewardship.

Then, on June 22, 1941, he invaded the Soviet Union. The Russians, in spite of warnings from Britain and the United States, were caught totally by surprise. It looked like Poland and France all over again, except on an immensely large scale. Literally millions of troops, thousands of tanks and aircraft, swept eastward, destroying all in their path. Some Russian units fought fiercely, some collapsed ignominiously. Stalin disappeared for a week, prostrated by the betrayal of his erstwhile ally, and it looked as if the Germans would be masters of Russia by fall.

But, as in the Battle of Britain, the Germans began to make mistakes. They paused to regroup, and to argue about what they should do next. They wore out their armor running back and forth along the front, and the field commanders resisted Hitler's orders when they did not agree with them. The fall days slipped by. Still the Germans advanced, but the Russians rallied, and the British offered help, and the Americans offered help too. Slowly, almost imperceptibly, the tide began to shift. By early December the Germans were getting close to Moscow. To an objective observer, it still looked as if they were going to win, though the margin was growing ever slimmer.

♦ ♦ ♦

At that point, the Japanese attacked Pearl Harbor. Invading China in 1937, they had progressively overrun the coastal and eastern part of the country. But they could not make the Chinese give up; there were just too many of them, and the leaders of Japan became increasingly frustrated. Events in Europe led them to fish in troubled imperial waters, and they took over Indochina after the French collapse and made threatening moves against the British and Dutch holdings in southeast Asia and the Indies. The Americans, and the U.S. possession of the Philippines, stood in their way, and as Japan became ever more greedy, the American attitude progressively hardened. Japan was basically a second-rate industrial state with few resources, and her strength lay more in isolation and the weakness of her neighbors than in real power. By mid-1941, the Americans had put sufficient economic pressure on Japan that she must either get out of China or go to war to capture what she could not buy. The Americans thought the Japanese would, sensibly, do the former; after all, a Japan who could not defeat China could not defeat the United States.

The Japanese decided instead to do the latter. If they could destroy American power in the Pacific, they would have a free hand to seize and exploit the territories they needed. They could then create a defensive perimeter against which the Americans might batter in vain until they gave up and went home. Instead of giving in, the Japanese planned and carefully launched the strike at the one major obstacle in their way, the U.S. Fleet in Pearl Harbor. On December 7 they carried out one of the great tactical surprises of modern military history.

It was the worst possible mistake they could have made. In the space of one terrible morning, the sleeping giant sprang awake and to arms, all inhibitions gone, all doubts cast aside. With that terrible stroke, the war was decided.

1942: The Year of Crisis

By rational calculation, the war might have been won for the Allies with Pearl Harbor and the U.S. entry into the conflict. Unfortunately, human affairs do not proceed by wholly rational calculation, otherwise there would be no need for wars. It was to take three and a half years of pain, suffering, and expense for the equation to be worked out, and in that time, the whole world was transformed by the struggle. For much of 1942 it looked as if the Allies might actually lose the war, rather than win it. This was a year of agony before the tide began to turn at last.

In the western Pacific the wave of Japanese conquest washed over the old colonial empires. Within hours of Pearl Harbor, aircraft, ships, and troops of the Rising Sun had struck at American holdings in the Philippines and at the British in Hong Kong and

Malaya. Almost everywhere they encountered delay, confusion, terror, and a feeble response that showed how hollow the imperial powers really were.

Hong Kong fell on Christmas Day. By then the Japanese had landed in Malaya; the British had sent their capital ships out to contest the invasion, but on December 10 the battleship *Prince of Wales* and battlecruiser *Repulse* were caught and sunk by dive- and torpedo bombers, the end of the era of the battleship in naval warfare. The Japanese occupied Thailand and spread both south toward Singapore and north into Burma. British forces, more numerous than the Japanese but thoroughly outclassed by them, fell back in disarray. Singapore surrendered in mid-February, the greatest single disaster in the long annals of British military history, and Burma was gone by early May. Japanese task forces were raiding into the Indian Ocean and hitting targets on Ceylon.

From Malaya they ranged down into the East Indies, and the remnants of British, Dutch, Australian, and American naval power in the area put up a gallant but ultimately futile fight to stop them. At Macassar Strait, at the Java Sea, and in the Sunda Straits the Allies were whittled away, and by late May all southeast Asia, with its rice and its oil, its rubber and its tungsten, was under Japanese control.

Only in one place did the Japanese timetable fall apart. In the Philippines a weak American garrison and its barely organized local forces held out longer than expected. The United States had promised the Philippines eventual independence, but in the late thirties, as the world situation worsened, America had taken some steps to strengthen its forces there. Gen Douglas MacArthur, a former chief of staff of the U.S. Army, was named to command American forces in the Far East, and his air forces were materially increased. When the war began, most of the aircraft were destroyed on the ground, thanks to MacArthur's hesitation as to what to do. But he then carried out a successful withdrawal into defensive positions on the Bataan Peninsula, west of Manila on the main island of Luzon. Here the Americans held on grimly in the jungle and mountainous terrain, assured that help was on the way, though in fact no rescue was even remotely possible.

The defenders of Bataan lasted until April 9, and even after that; the island fortress of Corregidor, in the mouth of Manila Bay, was not overrun until May 6. MacArthur was gone by then, ordered out to Australia to preside over the eventual American response. The Japanese treated their American prisoners terribly, even taking into account the fact that they were swamped by the number of men they captured. The survivors of the Bataan Death March went into prison camps where, in desperate conditions, they had to wait through the long years for liberation.

Japanese Adm Isoroku Yamamoto, the genius behind Japan's amazing victories, had told his government he could give them eighteen months of conquest, time in which to create their defensive perimeter and organize their empire. But the United States, in spite of confusion and dismay, was not going to give Japan any such free time. Weak and disorganized as they were, the Americans immediately began thinking of the offensive. In April, even as the Japanese were still fighting for the Philippines, American army air force bombers, flying precariously off the aircraft carrier *Hornet*, bombed Tokyo and other Japanese cities. It was a mere pinprick; most Japanese did not even know it happened, but their leaders did, and partly because of that, partly because of the almost astonishing ease of their war so far, they decided to push out their perimeter farther than originally planned. To the southeast they extended past the East Indies and New Guinea, toward the Solomon Islands, to cut the connection between the United States and Australia; in the central Pacific, they began an operation aimed at Midway, the westernmost of the Hawaiian Island chain. Without realizing it, they were approaching equilibrium.

♦ ♦ ♦

On the other side of the world as well, the Axis Powers, as the alliance of Germany, Italy, and Japan called themselves—they were creating a new axis around which the world might turn—also appeared in the ascendant. Hitler and Mussolini celebrated the news of Pearl Harbor by declaring war on the United States on December 11, a piece of unparalleled stupidity that solved a lot of problems for American leaders. They had already agreed with the British that Germany was by far the major threat and must have priority over Japan: Roosevelt and Churchill, meeting in Newfoundland in August of 1941, had made that crucial decision, and reconfirmed it in a second meeting in Washington immediately after Pearl Harbor. But the American public, outraged by the Japanese attack, needed convincing of the wisdom of that view. Hitler's declaration helped the process along.

Not that American belligerence seemed in early 1942 to make a great deal of difference. In the Mediterranean, the Germans and Italians were fighting a supply battle against Britain, and for a time they were winning. The North African desert offered nothing, and the war there was a battle of logistics. The Axis had to supply from the tip of Italy across the Sicilian Narrow to Libya, while the British had to carry materiel from Britain, or America, usually all the way around Africa and through the Red Sea to Egypt. They also held Malta, right on the track of enemy supply routes, a bone in the throat of the Mediterranean. The Germans and Italians tried to reduce it, and at one point, the British were down to resupplying the island by submarine; it became the single most bombed place of the entire war, a dubious and hard-won distinction.

By mid-1942 the Axis, under the energetic leadership of Erwin Rommel and his German Afrika Korps, were pressing the British back beyond the Egyptian frontier. The battle had seesawed back and forth, and several British commanders had been killed or replaced when Churchill sent out Gen Sir Harold Alexander as area commander and Gen Sir Bernard Montgomery as his Eighth Army commander. They then began a massive buildup of materiel, including new American tanks and aircraft, and virtually with their backs to the wall, a mere eighty miles from Alexandria and their base area, got ready for the climactic struggle.

But what was happening in North Africa paled before the immense conflagration in Russia. In late 1941, the Germans had finally been held at the very gates of Moscow and Leningrad. The Russians had rallied and fought tenaciously, and then their old allies, Generals January and February, had come to their rescue with the coldest winter in fifty years. The German offensive had stopped dead in its tracks. With spring, however, the Germans were ready to go again; this time Hitler decided to drive for the south, to cut Russian oil supplies and, in effect, to take ground instead of men, ultimately a crucial error of the kind better soldiers than Hitler have made before.

For a few weeks it looked as if it were 1941 all over again. German spearheads broke into the open in southern Russia, and took off toward the distant Caucasus Mountains and the Caspian Sea. With almost nothing in front of them, some of the reconnaissance elements were making fifty and sixty miles a day. It looked great on a map back in East Prussia, which was where Hitler had set up his command headquarters. In fact, the Germans were opening up a long, thinly held left flank, the key to which was a Soviet city on the great bend of the Volga River, a city named Stalingrad. Gradually its name appeared more and more often on the situation reports, and more and more units were slowly sucked into the fight to control it. Almost unwittingly, both sides became increasingly obsessed with this one place.

So in all the major areas, in the Pacific, in the Mediterranean, and in Russia, the war raged on, approaching some sort of crescendo. For a while it looked as if somehow the Axis might unite somewhere in Asia, Japanese pushing west from Malay, Germans and Italians pushing east from Egypt, and southeast from the Soviet Union. Could they all meet somewhere in the Persian Gulf or the Arabian Sea? Was it possible the war might be lost after all? By mid-1942, the stage was set for dramatic events.

♦ ♦ ♦

They came first in the Pacific. In May a Japanese naval task force sailed around the eastern end of New Guinea, where Australian and American forces were fighting a desperate battle to hold off the Japanese in some of the worst terrain in the world. The Japanese were aiming for Port Moresby, a little spot on the south coast of New Guinea; if it were taken, the island would fall, and Australia would be pretty well isolated. But the Americans had broken some of the Japanese codes—just as the British had already broken some of the Germans'—and the Allies were increasingly reading enemy operational plans. With a small aircraft carrier task force, the Americans ambushed the Japanese. The resulting Battle of the Coral Sea was another milestone, the first naval battle ever fought solely with aircraft, without any of the ships engaged actually sighting each other. The Americans lost a carrier, the Japanese a smaller one, but it was a clear strategic victory for the Americans; the Japanese turned back and gave up their plan.

A month later the same thing happened on a far larger, more significant scale. In the central Pacific the Japanese mounted a huge operation directed against Midway. Virtually their entire fleet was involved, and the plan included supporting operations as far away as the Aleutian Islands. To meet them the Americans could muster but three aircraft carriers and their escorting destroyers, and a screen of submarines.

But the Japanese were overconfident, and the Americans read enough of their codes to know what was happening. Once again they ambushed the enemy. There was a lot of simple good luck involved, but there was also superior intelligence assessment, more careful planning and deployment, and more thorough use of available resources. Given equal amounts of courage and dedication, the side that works harder ought to win, and so it was. American torpedo planes made virtually suicidal attacks on the Japanese carriers; in sacrificing themselves, they also disrupted the Japanese combat air patrols over their carriers. Minutes later, American dive-bombers found their targets, and in five minutes they entirely altered the balance of power in the Pacific war. When the battle finally ended, four Japanese carriers had been sunk for one American. Seldom can a major historical event be dated so precisely, but it can be said with assurance that the Americans began to win, and the Japanese to lose, the war in the Pacific at 1025 on the morning of June 4, 1942.

For the first time now, the initiative lay with the Americans. There had long existed in American military circles plans for a war against Japan, and there were conflicting schools of thought. One wanted a rapier thrust into the heart of the Japanese Empire; the other a slow progression through successive island chains. Now, thanks to Pearl Harbor, the slow and steady approach was the only possible one. With the resources available, the Americans could fight only along the Japanese perimeter. In August they began the process; U.S. Marines landed on the island of Guadalcanal in the Solomons. Here, in this horrible island full of swamps, jungle, snakes, and insects, the two edges of empire ground away at each other, wearing down flesh and muscle and sinew and bone. Men went ashore on "the 'Canal" looking twenty and came off a few months later looking eighty.

While Imperial and American Marines savaged each other in the jungles, their two navies fought to keep the waters around the Solomons. In a series of intense naval battles, both sides committed cruisers, and destroyers, and eventually battleships. They hammered away at each other with a ferocity and tenacity seldom sustained in all the annals of naval warfare. It was the end of the year before Guadalcanal was secured, and then the Americans began the slow and painful process of leapfrogging up the Solomons, heading toward New Guinea and the Bismarck Islands and the great Japanese base at Rabaul, while to the west of them, on New Guinea itself, Australians, New Zealanders, and U.S. Army troops fought bitterly to drive the Japanese back toward the Indies.

♦ ♦ ♦

By late 1942 the American war machine was at last gearing up for major action. Before

Pearl Harbor, it had upset the entire training and mobilization process to send one meager division to occupy Iceland, but now the same men who had denounced the government's attempts at preparation were fiercely demanding action, and factories and training camps were pouring forth their products. In a congressional election year, it was essential to get troops in action in the European theater. Army planners and particularly the chief of staff, George C. Marshall, would have liked a massive build-up in England, then a cross-Channel invasion of France and a drive to Germany and the heart of Hitler's empire. Time was against them, however, and they were forced to accept the logic of Britain's peripheral Mediterranean strategy. Thus it was that the first American combat commitment in the European area came in the oddest of places, French North Africa.

The intent was that if the British drove west from Egypt, and the Americans and British landed in Morocco and Algeria and drove east, the Axis would be quickly pinched out between them. It turned out to be more difficult than anticipated.

On the night of October 23-24, 1942, General Montgomery opened the great Battle of El Alamein. Finally, on the fifth day of intense fighting, the Axis forces broke and took off in pell-mell retreat. The British swung into the pursuit, and both sides were soon racing west along the coast. Then, on November 8, Anglo-American task forces landed at Casablanca, Oran, and Algiers. After some confused fighting with the French garrisons, who quickly agreed to an armistice, they began moving east. Geography was against them, however. Their ultimate objective was Tunis, but that city was nearer to Rome than to either of the approaching Allied armies. The Germans quickly got troops across to Tunisia, and threw together a rough line that held until May of 1943. This set a pattern for the entire European war. In virtually every operation, the Allies achieved strategic surprise, but the Germans' tactical response was so flexible that the Allied advantage was evened out.

It was in the hills and gullies of Tunisia that the Americans got their first test of combat in the big leagues, and they soon found, at places such as Kasserine Pass and Hill 109, that they had a lot to learn. As Tacitus said in the days of the Roman Empire, "He who has not fought the Germans does not know war." Nonetheless, El Alamein and the invasion of North Africa marked the turning point in western Europe. Hitler ultimately lost a quarter of a million men in North Africa; before this, the Allies never won a campaign—after it, they never lost one.

The victories at Midway and in North Africa were matched in the Soviet Union by the immense fight for Stalingrad. As the fall wore on, the battle for that city took on a life of its own, the closest thing in the war to the mindless, endless slaughter of World War I. Russian soldiers sent there were told to write their last letters home because they would not be coming back. Week after week, month after month, the two sides fought over the same ruined buildings, in little squad- and platoon-sized battles that obviated the Germans' individual superiority and simply wore them down. By late October, the Germans had thinned their flanks in the open country, sucked into the vortex of battle, and it was then that the Russians struck. On November 19-20, nine Russian armies crashed through the German positions on either side of the beleaguered city, and within four days, the Germans were surrounded. Then, instead of letting them break out, Hitler insisted they form an all-around fortress defense. They lasted until January 31, 1943, when, down to their last rations and ammunition, they finally surrendered. Stalingrad was the greatest single battle of the entire war, and more Russian soldiers died there than did Americans in the whole war.

In all three major areas, then, the Pacific, and western and eastern Europe, the course of the war was reversed during 1942. From this time on it would be the Allies who were on the offensive, the Axis who had to turn and twist and try to avoid the fate they had themselves unleashed. Churchill, as usual, summed it up: It was not the end, or even the beginning of the end, but it was the end of the beginning.

Allied Initiatives

In January of 1943 President Roosevelt, Prime Minister Churchill, and their staffs and advisers met at Casablanca. This was the third of nine such wartime meetings, and the first where there was a ray of sunshine; when they met for the first time at Placentia Bay, in Newfoundland, in August of 1941, and again in December of 1941 in Washington, all they could do was hang on and hope for the best. But now, in the sun of Morocco, on territory recently liberated, if only from Vichy France, they could look forward to great things. It was fortunate that the mood was optimistic, because they had widely divergent ideas on how the war should be waged and where they should go next.

Basically, the Americans still wanted a big build-up in Britain, followed by an invasion of France. The British wanted to keep on in the Mediterranean, nibbling away at the periphery of Hitler's empire, wearing it down, and hoping it might ultimately collapse. They did not actually expect that to happen, but they wanted to delay invasion until the odds of success were overwhelmingly on their side. These differing perceptions had already dogged the alliance, and would continue to do so for another year. While they were argued out, the war of course went on. As an interim measure, the Allies agreed to invade the island of Sicily.

This decision was in response to a peculiar problem. As Malta had been a bone in the Axis throat in the Mediterranean, so was Sicily to the Allies. They were still locked in mortal struggle with the German U-boats for command of the Atlantic, suffering immense shipping losses in the longest battle of the war. From New York, Halifax, and St. John's, Newfoundland, the convoys went forth week after week, running the gauntlet of weather and submarines to deliver food and materials to Britain.

At several points the Germans came close to winning the battle, which would have meant a Britain starved into submission, and the Allies were perpetually short of cargo ships. Sustaining operations in North Africa merely added to the overall burden. But there were ways around it. They could not build any more ships than they were already doing, because it was physically impossible, and they could not sink any more U-boats than they were doing. But they could shorten their shipping routes, and if they could send supplies through the Mediterranean rather than all the way around Africa, they would lighten their shipping load considerably. Such thinking also fit in with the British idea of continuing the momentum in the Mediterranean theater and with the peculiar fixation of the British Chief of the Imperial General Staff, Lord Alanbrooke, about knocking Italy out of the war. So for a variety of superficially somewhat unrelated reasons, the Allies decided to attack the island of Sicily next. Because the British got their way, they conceded the point that an American should command the operation, and the job went to Gen Dwight D. Eisenhower, who had exercised overall command of the North African invasion, and who, if unproven as a combat leader, was emerging as a successful practitioner of the difficult art of coalition warfare.

The last Axis troops in Tunisia surrendered on May 13, 1943. Two months later, on July 10, the Allies invaded Sicily. It was the greatest armada in history to that time, more than three thousand ships carrying half a million men. With the British on the right and the Americans on the left and a Canadian corps in the middle, the troops went ashore against fairly light opposition and began working their way inland. The Germans had already decided that Sicily was untenable, and the several hundred thousand Italian troops on the island were not eager to fight. The overall German commander, Field Marshal Albert Kesselring, ordered delaying actions which gave the British a bloody nose around Mount Aetna; meanwhile the Americans, under Gen George S. Patton, broke off to the westward and made a long end run around the more open part of the island. Eventually the campaign turned into something of a race to get to Messina. British and Americans arrived in a dead heat, but the Germans beat both of them and got almost all of their supplies and equipment across the straits to southern Italy, surviving to fight again.

Meanwhile, in the month that the campaign lasted, strange things were happening in Italy. The Italian people had never had much enthusiasm for the war, in spite of Mussolini's posturing and boasting. Now they saw themselves increasingly used as the tail on the German kite, and they wanted to get out of it all as soon, and as painlessly, as possible. Opposition mounted even into the Fascist Grand Council, and finally, on July 25, Mussolini was dismissed from office by the king of Italy and arrested. His replacement, Marshal Pietro Badoglio, announced that Italy would remain faithful to her Axis partners and immediately opened secret negotiations with the Allies for a surrender. The collapse of the Fascists in Italy had the effect of further muddying the waters of Anglo-American planning for the future of the war.

♦ ♦ ♦

Progress was more straightforward on other fronts. In the Soviet Union, 1943 saw the Russians at last develop the "steamroller" effect that had been one of the fond fictions of

World War I. By now the Reds outnumbered the Germans in all categories of arms and equipment, and though they remained qualitatively inferior in tactics and communications, they ground the Germans into the dirt. Stalingrad was only the most significant of a whole series of huge battles fought through the winter of 1942-43, and by the spring of the new year, both armies were reorganizing in preparation for further gigantic struggles. Russian production was now wholly devoted to the war, and in addition they were receiving substantial aid from the United States and Britain. In Germany the country had finally geared up for full-scale war, with the organizational genius Albert Speer taking over Germany's economy. In the summer, the Red Army and the Wehrmacht savaged each other in immense battles whose scope dwarfed everyone else's efforts—in mid-1943, out of 252 divisions, the Germans had 175 in Russia. The greatest of the battles was at Kursk, where the largest tank battle of the war was fought. Both sides employed as many as three thousand tanks, and the Soviets emerged the clear victors, killing several hundreds of the Germans' new monster Tiger and Panther tanks. After their defeat in this Operation Citadel, the German armored forces were never the same again.

In the south the Reds cleared the Ukraine and then moved on toward the southwestern frontier and the Pripet Marshes. Leningrad, besieged since the early days of the war in another epic story, was finally relieved, and the Russians kept offensives going north, south, and center while the Germans used up reserves and resources running back and forth trying to stop them.

On the strength of his country's effort, Stalin was able to demand ever greater help from his British and American allies, and the question of the invasion of Europe became more and more pressing. But there were other distractions as well, for the war in the Pacific had to be kept going, and this area was especially dear to the heart of the U.S. Navy.

In fact, the war against Japan consisted of a number of converging campaigns, all interdependent but related in their objectives and their rivalry for resources. In China, the Chinese were doing little except hanging on. The few supplies that reached them got in over the Himalayas from India and through Burma, but China was a bottomless pit of misery and inefficiency in which millions of people were simply starving, and little of major significance could be accomplished. Up in the north Pacific, there was a campaign through the Aleutians, a sideshow set off by the Japanese Midway operation, but this area was so marginal that again little could be done, though the oversensitive Americans kept thousands of troops up there freezing for much of the war. In the other direction, the British were fighting a shoestring war in northern Burma, trying both to keep routes open through to China and also to lever the Japanese out of Burma itself. It was very poor country to fight over, and both sides were starved of resources at the end of long tenuous supply lines, and all through 1942, 1943, and 1944 each side tried, with much pain but little profit, to gain advantage over the other.

That left the vast spaces of the Pacific. Here, in spite of American acknowledgment that Germany must have priority, the United States actually waged two complementary—and sometimes competing—campaigns against the Japanese Empire. One of these was Douglas MacArthur's push along the coast of New Guinea, a brutal campaign in inhuman conditions that lasted eighteen months, from mid-1942 until late 1943. This fit in with another campaign, the continuation of the Solomons drive begun in Guadalcanal and ending on Bougainville, in the same time period.

But north of both of these, in the central Pacific, the U.S. Navy was determined to have its day. By the middle of the war, cruisers, carriers, destroyers, and even new battleships were coming out of American shipyards in unprecedented numbers, and the American Chief of Naval Operations, Adm Ernest J. King, was set on using them against the men who had surprised Pearl Harbor. As far as the sailors were concerned, no matter what Europe needed or the British or Russians wanted, this was the war the navy was made for.

It was late in 1943 before the navy was both ready to go and able to do so. The preceding months had been spent around the Southwest Pacific islands, in the savage fighting in the Solomons and northeast of Australia. The Americans had met the Japanese and found them worthy opponents, but techniques and materiel were perfected in the harsh school of battle, and now the navy was ready for the island chains: the Gilberts, the Marshalls, the Carolines, and the Marianas.

The basic idea was that naval task forces, built around aircraft carrier groups, would range across the ocean, seeking and destroying the Japanese fleet units. Then the Americans, using amphibious forces, would leapfrog from one island to the next, eating up the Japanese garrisons as they went and staging from one group to the next. Major Japanese bases, which initially the Americans expected to have to take, could instead be isolated and left to starve and die.

It is far easier to describe than it was to do. The first target was Tarawa, a little atoll in the Gilberts. The tiny main island of Betio, only 291 acres in all, cost the U.S. Marines thirty-three hundred casualties in four days of fierce fighting; of forty-eight hundred Japanese, less than a hundred survived. Many lessons were learned about amphibious warfare at Tarawa, all of them painful and costly. But the Americans learned them, while the Japanese did not live to do so. In early 1944 the Americans took Kwajalein and Eniwetok in the Marshalls. They destroyed and isolated the great Japanese bastion at Truk in the Carolines and swept on to the Marianas. Here, off Saipan, the Japanese fleet came out to fight, and in the Battle of the Philippine Sea the Americans chewed it to bits, downing nearly five hundred aircraft and sinking three carriers. The battle went down in American lore as "the great Marianas turkey shoot." The Central Pacific and the Southwest Pacific drives would finally coalesce in the Philippines.

All of which made the questions of what to do in Europe even more vital. Indeed, by the time the Americans reached the Philippines, those questions had already been solved, but only after long and acrimonious discussion.

◆ ◆ ◆

Even at the time of Casablanca, the timing, direction, and method of defeating Germany was too contentious to be resolved, and the invasion of Sicily, as noted, was something of a stopgap operation. Throughout 1943, the arguments became ever fiercer the closer the Allies got to the actual invasion. In May at the Trident Conference in Washington and in August at Quadrant in Quebec, the British and the Americans argued their preferences. This was in fact the single most complex strategic question of the war, complicated by the fact that not only did British and Americans essentially disagree but also by the fact that neither's perceptions quite matched the reality of their respective situations.

For American planners, who believed totally in the straight-to-the-heart thrust, a great climactic struggle on the plains of north Germany, the problem was that they lacked the army to do it. The U.S. Army was simply not big enough for the job, not at any time in the entire war, and certainly not in the early stages when they most vigorously advocated such a strategy. Much of the burden of American strategy would therefore have to be borne by British and Commonwealth forces; but the British, with their vivid memories of the agony of World War I, wished to avoid the great battle as long as possible, and though they accepted the necessity of the invasion of France and ultimately Germany, they wanted to put it off until the last minute, whereas the Americans wanted to get at it as soon as it was even marginally feasible. As the British leaders, from Churchill down, consistently pressed for action anywhere else, the Americans and especially Marshall, constantly argued for invasion and regarded any of the British suggestions as digressive; they were also suspicious of the British desire to keep or add to their empire and resented what they saw as Britain's "postwar political aims." For them, somewhat naively, winning the war was an end in itself.

Not only were there these geostrategical arguments, but there were other views as to how the war might be fought overall. The most important of these was the idea of strategic air power. During the twenties and thirties a series of air power theorists had argued that land warfare, as in World War I, was totally out of date and unnecessary. Countries should concentrate on building up an air force capable of bombing an enemy into submission immediately upon the opening of hostilities. Most countries either could not afford this, or chose to develop tactical air support of ground forces instead, but both the United States and Great Britain, with their peculiar geographical situations, tried to develop strategic bomber forces. Such forces increased and improved enormously under the impetus of the war itself, and in 1942, growing into 1943, first the Royal Air Force and then the U.S. Army Air Force mounted a campaign to destroy German industry and the will of Germany's people to continue the war.

This was incredibly expensive, in materiel and ultimately in lives. The bombers laid much of Germany in ruins, but not until the very end of the war did they achieve an intensity that promised success, and even then, the hope that Germany could be defeated from the air was not fulfilled. The question of both the efficacy, and ultimately the morality, of strategic bombing remains one of the most hotly argued of World War II.

Another possibility, with which Churchill was particularly enamored, was what he called The Fourth Arm. The first three were land, sea, and air; the fourth was the Underground, or the Resistance, in the countries overrun by Germany. To foster, supply, and organize these underground movements the British set up the Special Operations Executive (SOE), and the Americans developed the Office of Strategic Services (OSS). At his fondest, Churchill had visions of an uprising of the entire Continent that would simply sweep the Germans away. This was quite unrealistic, and Churchill knew it, but he was anxious to help the cause along wherever he could. There were underground movements in all of the occupied countries, but they spent a great deal of time fighting among themselves, especially those groups led by the Communists. Some were very good, many were not, and though they seriously annoyed the Germans in some areas where the terrain was favorable—the Balkans, the Pripet Marshes, the Massif Central in France—they were still marginal to the whole war. Only in Yugoslavia did partisans led by Marshal Tito eventually succeed in their own liberation.

Much of the resistance to Germany was fueled, of course, by the Germans themselves and the increasingly harsh rule they imposed on their conquests. As the war turned sour for them, their exactions became greater and greater. Foodstuffs and raw materials were commandeered, factories put to work for Germany, men drafted off as virtual slave labor or even conscripted into the German army. Though they were, at the start of the war, reasonably "correct" in their behavior in western Europe, in the east, and as the war went on, they got worse and worse. The Poles were brutally treated, the Russians worse still; Hitler professed to regard all Slavs as *untermenschen* or subhumans, and that was the way his minions treated them. The New Order was only for Germans, which of course ultimately helped to defeat it.

Worst of all was the treatment accorded the Jews of Europe. Much of the ideology of the Nazis were based on a rabid hatred of the Jews, whom Hitler saw as the universal villains of Europe. Everywhere they came to power, the Nazis first dispossessed, then abused, then officially persecuted the Jews. Eventually they began to kill them, first casually, then carefully. By the later period of the war, the rounding up, deportation, and execution of Jews was one of the most fundamental features of the Nazi regime, and huge resources of transport and manpower were devoted to the destruction of the Jewish people. In Germany itself, and those states most thoroughly or longest under German control, the Jews were indeed virtually wiped out. Of some millions in prewar Poland, only a few thousand survived. Some authorities have argued that killing off the Jews became the ultimate rationale for the Nazis in the later stages of the war. It is this vicious destruction that has come to be called the Holocaust, and to describe it a new word was coined: *genocide*, or the killing of a whole people.

Much of what was going on inside Europe was either not known on the outside, disbelieved, or ignored, but it served to give added point to the arguments over grand strategy. Decisions now studied at leisure in universities literally meant in 1942 or 1943 that some people would live, and others would die.

In 1943, in spite of all the American pressure, the Allies still believed they were not sufficiently powerful to invade France. The British got their way, and the cross-Channel operation was put off until 1944. Instead, they invaded Italy in pursuit of British Mediterranean strategy. Mussolini's collapse and the Italian defection from the Axis led them to seize what looked like a golden opportunity to get Italy out of the war cheaply. On September 3, 1943, British and Canadian troops crossed the Straits of Messina; on the 9th, American and British troops landed in the Bay of Salerno, just below Naples, as the Italian government and armed forces were collapsing. The hope and intention was to get southern Italy and its airfields without much fighting—even, Churchill allowed himself to hope, to get as far as Rome. But as always, German reaction was swift and strong. Troops quickly seized Italian cities and ports, and the Allies found themselves engaged in a long, frustrating battle from one river line to the next, stalled in the mud and rain of sunny Italy.

In November of 1943 President Roosevelt and Prime Minister Churchill met for the first time with Marshal Stalin, at the Teheran Conference. The meeting was successful, though not as harmonious as it appeared on the surface. The Soviets still believed they were doing most of the work, and the Anglo-Americans were still working out their divergent views. There was now no doubt the Allies were winning. How, when, and what it would all lead to still remained to be decided.

The American Way of War

In many respects that are still with us, World War II transformed American life and attitudes, both about the United States itself and about its place in the larger world. One might look at any number of changes, but surely one of the most startling, and significant in the long term, was the immense growth of the power and size of government itself.

This had of course begun before the war started, in the depths of the Depression, as more and more people demanded intervention by their government in the everyday details of their lives, to provide employment, and to provide services that were not available by other means—highways, education, regulation of business, and a whole host of things not thought the province of government, especially of central government, in earlier, simpler times. But the demands of war, first of staying out of it, then of helping the other allies, finally of waging it, increased government activity exponentially. Not only did the war have to be fought, but all aspects of the economic life of the country had to be directed toward that end, especially in a country that billed itself as "the arsenal of democracy." So prices were controlled, resources allocated, transport regulated, goods rationed, taxes collected. Washington, D.C., grew from a somewhat sleepy, rather low-key, capital to a bustling beehive where space was at a premium, traffic was jammed, building went on frantically, and there was never entirely enough of anything, especially time, and always too much of everything, especially people and paper.

The most visible aspect of change was naturally the almost unprecedented growth of the armed forces. Before the war, military service as an occupation had not enjoyed much prestige. It had of course its own rewards for those who chose it, but neither money nor public admiration were among them. The services were small. The army fluctuated around 150,000 men; most officers knew, or knew about, their contemporaries. The navy lived in a separate, watery world, the air force was not yet independent, and toward all of them the country took a generally out-of-sight-out-of-mind attitude.

Even the war in Europe did not appreciably change that. Congress and especially the isolationist wing of opinion bitterly resisted any attempts to prepare the United States for the possibility of war; in their view, preparation meant commitment, and they could not see that to be strong militarily might be a way of keeping America out of war rather than dragging her in. Nor was President Roosevelt a great deal of help to his professional military men. He thought in simplistic and grandiose political terms rather than realistic military ones. In 1940 he announced that America would build fifteen thousand warplanes a year, but he did not want to acknowledge that if America reached this goal, she would at the same time have neither bases for the planes, nor pilots to fly them, nor personnel to service them. He was as much a political opportunist as Churchill was a military one, and between them they caused their respective military people a great deal of heartburn.

But of course reality kept intruding, so there finally came the defense bills, and the taxes to support them, and the draft, and the eventual buildup of American strength. Fortunately, there were two oceans and the British Empire between the United States and its enemies, for as has always been the case in the past, America ended up creating her armed forces while fighting the war.

Though ships and planes were more exciting to readers of the popular press, it was the army that actually saw the greatest change. By 1945, when it reached its peak strength, there were 8,300,000 officers and men in the army. It was a magnificent achievement accompanied by huge difficulties. Even then, the army did not get all it wanted. Planners in 1940-41 had decided they needed a two-hundred-division army to fight on the continent of Europe, but they did not get it. They were forced by presidential decisions as to the allocation of manpower to settle for a one-hundred-division army, and they did not even get that; the United States eventually fielded only eighty-nine divisions, compared with more than three hundred for Germany.

In addition, partly because of the distances at which the war was fought, partly because of its technological complexity, the army remained surprisingly short of combat personnel; of its eight-million-plus members, only about two million were actually in combat. By the standards of previous wars, and most of its foes and allies, it was an extraordinarily "fat" army. It was also a rich army, though the troops eating cold rations in the rifle companies certainly did not feel that way. Thanks to the production miracle at home, American soldiers were more mobile, and more lavishly equipped, than any army in the world; they had some—though by no means all—of the best weapons in the world, and they had a lot of them.

It was the same in the navy, which went from 161,000 men in 1940 to 3,380,000 in 1945. The battleship navy of pre-Pearl Harbor was transformed into a huge force, concentrated mostly around the aircraft carriers. Even their numbers give a suggestion of what happened. In 1941 the U.S. Navy had 8 aircraft carriers and 17 battleships, only two of which were less than twenty years old. In 1945 it had 24 battleships, but it had 124 aircraft carriers, and American yards had built another 37 for Britain. Lesser vessels, destroyers and escorts and auxiliaries, joined the fleet by the hundreds. In the 1930s the navy built its first destroyers since World War I, 8 ships of the *Farragut* class; its first real wartime class of destroyers was the *Fletchers*—175 strong. By war's end, the U.S. Navy was as strong as all the navies of the world combined, including its great ally and rival, the Royal Navy.

Most startling of all was probably the growth of the air arm of the American forces. Unlike Britain or Germany, the United States did not have an independent air service, but the Army Air Forces had been granted coequal status with the other major army commands in a reorganization immediately before war began, a recognition by General Marshall of both the importance and distinctness of air power. Since the navy restructured its forces around the carriers, the importance of air power to it was equally obvious.

Though both services employed large amounts of tactical air power, for the airmen themselves the strategic bomber campaign was the key to victory and also to independence for their arm of service and their view of war. Eventually huge resources were devoted to this concept; for example, the three main bombing aircraft were the Boeing B-17 Flying Fortress, of which 12,700 were built; the Consolidated B-24 Liberator, 19,200; and the Boeing B-29 Superfortress, of which 3,000 saw service. More than 75,000 of the main types of fighter aircraft were produced; almost twice as many machine guns were made for aircraft as were made for the U.S. Army for use on the ground. This expenditure paid off in campaigns that reduced German, and later Japanese, cities and industry to rubble. Air power employment was considered to be relatively clean, neat, efficient, and highly sophisticated technologically—in other words, to fit perfectly with the preconceptions of American society and modern war. It was of course none of these things in any absolute sense, though it was in comparison with the infantryman sitting in a muddy hole with a rifle and a bayonet.

The U.S. Marine Corps was another specifically American development, for where most countries used marines as originally developed—as shipboard guards and occasional landing parties—the United States developed its marine corps as an elite amphibious assault force, or in more common words, as the navy's private army. Only twenty-eight thousand strong in 1940, the marines grew to half a million men by the end of the war. With logistical services from the navy, the marines had proportionately more combat personnel than the army, and a different tactical doctrine; they considered themselves special and won a glorious reputation that was both hard-earned and carefully nurtured.

The United States did not draft women during the war, but all of the services found it useful to have women's auxiliary services, and substantial numbers of young women went into uniform as drivers, typists, clerks, and service personnel. Nurses were commissioned in both army and navy, and a few women actually managed to do some of the more exciting jobs such as flying aircraft across to Britain, though there was at this time not the slightest thought that they should actually participate in combat. In all, some 333,000 women served in the armed forces during the course of the war.

Of the several things that set America's war effort apart from practically everyone else's, the most significant was probably the outburst of energy manifested in American production figures. Before 1940, the United States had a great deal of industrial potential lying undeveloped. American businessmen were reluctant to get involved with military orders, which tended to be at the mercy of a parsimonious government; there was usually a market for automobiles, but the prewar market for tanks was very spotty. Once war began in Europe, however, and even more as it came closer to America, business got interested. The demands of war initiated a boom that carried America all the way to the seventies. Unemployment dropped to zero, as the young men went off to the service and women went to work in the factories, doing jobs hitherto the exclusive preserve of the men. By 1945 the American work force numbered 73,000,000 people out of a population of about 136,000,000. With another 12,000,000 in the armed forces, that meant that practically every American who could do so was either working or in the service.

The production figures were truly amazing. Roosevelt's call for thousands of planes a year had been greeted with initial incredulity. Yet even by 1941 that figure was almost doubled, and in 1944 the United States turned out 96,318 aircraft, more than Germany and the Soviet Union together. The Americans built 49,000 Sherman tanks, where the Germans built only about 20,000 tanks in all. American industry made 14,000,000 rifles, 2,500,000 machine guns, 37,000,000 bombs, 630,000 Jeeps, and more than 400,000,000 artillery shells.

Strangely enough, this cornucopia of destruction poured forth from a land enjoying apparent peace and prosperity. For most Americans, vitally interested though they were in the war, it remained distant. Families were disrupted and separated, of course, by the exigencies of service. But no bombs were dropped, no cities razed, no armies invaded the United States. The war was in the news, on the radio every night, in the newsreels at the movies, and in the magazines and papers. But it was over there, beyond some distant horizon. Mothers and fathers, wives and sweethearts, worried and anxiously watched the mail, and virtually everyone was caught up in the great crusade that the war was perceived to be. Yet for many Americans, the fighting was there, the prosperity was here. Unless you were one of those boys lying in a swamp in New Guinea or on a hill in Italy, or torn apart in the waist of a B-17, it was a good war.

The Allies in the Ascendant

As 1943 ended, the Allied war machine began to gather increasing momentum. On all fronts the Axis were now on the defensive and were going to remain that way. The year just over had been one of bitter combat, and that, at least, was not going to change. On the vast Russian front, in the Pacific, and in the Italian mountains, the enemy still held hard.

Italy proved a particularly frustrating venture for the western Allies. The invasion of the peninsula had been taken more as an opportunistic gesture than as a soundly conceived strategic move, and what the Allies had hoped to get on the cheap they could hardly get at all. They did manage to secure the great port of Naples, thoroughly destroyed by the Germans, but winter found them stalled before the main German positions, the British Eighth Army on the Adriatic coast around Ortona, the American Fifth Army in front of the Gustav Line, anchored on the famous monastery town of Cassino.

This was country perfectly suited for defense, and offering little scope for the maneuver possibilities conferred on the Allies by air and armor superiority. The result was that the battles for Cassino—four of them eventually—became straightforward infantry slugfests of the type more usually associated with the First World War than the Second. All through the winter Fifth Army tried to break through the Gustav Line, above Cassino, below it, and in the town itself. The Fifth was the most international of Allied armies; the Germans, the terrain, and the weather combined to stop Americans, British, Australians, New Zealanders, Indians, and French. A man who was at Cassino could say without boasting that he had fought with and against the best soldiers in the world.

To get around the logjam, the Allies developed the idea of a further landing, at the little port of Anzio. On January 22, 1944, they scored a complete surprise and landed a whole corps sixty miles up the coast and a mere twenty from Rome itself. But again the Germans responded with their usual rapidity, and soon the Allies were contained and fighting desperately just to stay ashore. The Germans held the high ground, and Churchill growled that he had hoped to throw a wildcat ashore behind the Germans, but got a stranded whale instead. In March the frustrated Allies bombed into rubble both the town of Cassino and the unoccupied Benedictine monastery that dominated it, but still would not achieve a decisive success. As winter turned into spring, it was imperative that some progress be made.

The Allies were now preparing for the invasion of France, and the Italian campaign was already being downgraded because of that. There must be some dramatic action that would cause a breakthrough and distract German attention. To achieve this, the area commander, Gen Sir Harold Alexander, concentrated all his forces, U.S. Fifth and British Eighth Armies, against Cassino, leaving the Adriatic coast virtually bare. He opened an enormous World War I-style artillery barrage, and on May 11, the Allied divisions jumped off all along the line. It took a week of heavy fighting, but finally the Germans cracked; as the Allied troops filtered through the mountains on either side of Cassino, they started going back. At the same time the forces trapped at Anzio finally broke into the clear. Supposed to block the retreating Germans, they turned north instead, and by late May, everyone, Allies and Germans all mixed up together, was racing for Rome. On June 4, 1944, American and British troops almost simultaneously entered the Eternal City, the first Axis capital to fall.

That was not the end of it, because the Germans could not put together another blocking position for two hundred miles. They were up in the northern Apennines before they stopped, and here they threw together the Gothic Line. The Americans and British, disorganized both by their dash and by the withdrawal of seven divisions to invade southern France, stalled in the mountains again. From weary to exultant to weary, they were now back in the same scenario as the year before, and faced another heartbreaking winter of mountains, mud, and misery.

♦ ♦ ♦

Rome had barely fallen when it was pushed to the back pages of the newspapers, for on June 6, 1944, the Allies invaded France, and the climactic campaign of the war in the west was opened. The landings in Normandy were in many respects the high dramatic point of the war; they marked both the beginning of the end for Germany, and within the Allied coalition they also signaled the point at which the United States became the senior partner. From now on it would be American strategic thought which dominated the alliance, while the British, ever shorter of manpower and resources, were increasingly relegated to a supporting role. This was not immediately apparent, but with hindsight it is again possible to date precisely the moment of transition.

The British had been preparing this operation ever since they had been pushed off the continent at Dunkirk, and of course the invasion was an article of American military faith; disagreements had been more over timing and details than over the idea itself. So all through 1942 and 1943, all through the successive distractions of the Pacific and the Mediterranean, the Allies had been building for the invasion. The buildup went slowly and erratically at first, but by late 1943 things were changing. The U-boats were being beaten, American production was readying astounding totals, and the troops, fully mobilized and trained at last, were coming in their hordes to the British Isles. Convoy after convoy, division after division, they landed in the British ports. The roads were clogged with tanks and the ubiquitous American trucks and Jeeps, and the long columns of olive-drab-clad, heavily burdened young men wound along the English lanes. The airfields were filled with fighters and attack aircraft, and from the flat eastern fens the heavy bombers took off, day after day, night after night, to pound targets in Germany and western Europe. It was as if a mighty beast were gathering its strength for some incredible spring.

The Germans of course knew it was coming, but they did not know when, and they did not know where. Between breaking the German codes on the one hand and planting misleading information on the other, the Allies managed to convince Hitler they were going to cross at the most narrow, logical, place, the Pas de Calais. Instead, they planned to invade the beaches of Normandy, well to the southwest and a hundred miles across the Channel. To do so they developed swimming tanks, an underwater pipeline to deliver fuel, portable harbors, every kind of gadget that ingenuity could conceive including, ironically, the kind of toy clickers that children used at parties, so American paratroopers could locate each other in the darkness.

Originally scheduled for June 5, the landings were postponed one day for weather—one of the single most difficult decisions of the war—to set back twenty-four hours a timetable involving nearly three million men. After several weeks of intensive aerial interdiction work, the troops finally sallied forth and went ashore, three airborne and then five infantry divisions. All met heavy but not wholly organized opposition, though at one of the American beaches, Omaha, the Germans in good positions threatened to win the day. By nightfall, though, the Allies were securely established.

There followed several weeks of intense fighting as the Germans reacted strongly. The countryside again offered major advantages to the defense, little hedged fields, each of which was a small deathtrap. The British on the left took much of the German pressure, and the Americans slowly worked their way through the hedgerows. Both sides ground away at each other, Allied airpower controlled the skies, and again it was the Germans who broke first. After desperate fighting around the Douve River valley and the town of Saint-Lô, the Americans began to break through. The British finally got the town of Caen, and then, suddenly, at the end of July, the whole front burst wide apart. The British wheeled east, toward the lower Seine, but beyond them, Gen Omar Bradley's Twelfth Army Group, Hodges's First and Patton's Third U.S. Armies, cut the base of the Normandy peninsula, broke into Brittany and out toward the basin of the Loire.

The Germans were exhausted, with nothing at all to put in the way of this. Almost trapped around Falaise, they went reeling back, and in the first weeks of August, the Allies swung into one of those great, exhilarating, destructive pursuits that are the delight of subsequent historians. American armor was making thirty and forty miles a day against dwindling opposition. Allied tactical air forces struck against anything that moved and looked German.

The city of Paris rose against the retreating Germans on the 19th. Hitler ordered that it be destroyed, all its monuments blown up, but the local commanders ignored him. By the 25th, the Allies were across the Seine in several places, Patton's forward elements were as far east as Troyes, ninety miles past Paris. That day the city was liberated by the Second Free French Armored Division, troops under the overall command of Gen Charles de Gaulle, men who had fought all the way from central Africa for this heady, glorious moment of triumph.

The Allies were by no means done yet. They were now faced with huge logistical problems as their supply lines grew ever longer, and more and more of France was liberated, and had to be fed and controlled. In late August another landing was made on the Mediterranean coast of France, and an Allied drive up the Rhône begun. Southwestern France was cleared largely by French forces themselves. The Germans fell back from the Seine toward the Low Countries, the Rhine, and their own frontier, trying to reequip and regroup their units.

Inevitably, an equilibrium set in, as the Allied lines stretched and the German contracted. By mid-September the Germans were along the Moselle River, the Ardennes Forest, and the Dutch frontier. The Allies were closing up to them on a broad front. General Eisenhower as Supreme Allied Commander preferred this approach; he thought the Germans still had fight in them, he had enormous supply problems, and it appeared to him that the best way to proceed was all in step until, at some point, the Allies got another break.

His British field commander, Field Marshal Montgomery, thought he could manufacture that break if given the resources. A difficult subordinate who thought he knew all about war and everything else, he finally got his chance. Eisenhower allocated him resources to try to break across the lower Rhine, with a sixty-mile deep rapier thrust toward the bridge at Arnhem. It did not work. The Allies ended up with a spear fifty miles long and one tank wide, and they just could not carry the day. Eisenhower had been right after all; there was more resilience in the Germans than anyone wanted to admit, and as gloriously successful as the campaign of France had been, the war was not over yet.

♦ ♦ ♦

The Russians had promised a spring offensive to help the Allies with their invasion, and they delivered a massive blow to the Germans on the Eastern Front. By early 1944 they had ten army groups facing the Germans; in February they drove along the Baltic coast, in March they hit the Germans in the Ukraine, in May they cleared the cut-off Crimea. But all these were mere preliminaries. In late June they opened offensives along an entire thousand miles of front, from the Baltic coast all the way south to the Carpathians. In three weeks they drove 250 miles around the Pripet Marshes, and the Germans, vastly outnumbered in men, tanks, and artillery, simply could not stop them. By the first week of August, they were in Poland and approaching Warsaw.

Here the first faint cloud appeared on the Allied horizon for the postwar world. In 1939 Germany and the Soviet Union, then more or less partners, had divided Poland between them. The British, and subsequently the Americans, had recognized a Polish government-in-exile in London. Polish units had fought valiantly in British uniform; after Hitler invaded the Soviet Union, thousands of Poles were released from Russian prison camps and sent to the Mediterranean, where they eventually formed a corps in the British Eighth Army. It was actually Poles who had captured the monastery at Cassino, at a cost of hundreds of dead, and they raised there a poignant monument that says, "We Polish soldiers, for your freedom and ours, have given our bodies to Italy, our hearts to Poland, and our souls to God."

Several thousand Polish officers had disappeared, massacred by the Soviets, who have only just recently admitted doing it. When the Russians approached Warsaw, the Polish government-in-exile called for an uprising in the city; they believed that Poland must liberate itself rather than falling under the Russians. As the citizens of Warsaw took to the streets, fighting desperately, the Russian armies stopped, publicly announcing they needed time to regroup, and thus gave the Germans fair notice that they could suppress Warsaw as they pleased. The tragedy was soon played out; Polish resistance destroyed, which the Germans also publically announced, whereupon the Reds took up their offensive once more. Sometimes there is honor among thieves. The western Allies protested carefully and watched impotently; they needed the Russians, and they could help Poland even less in 1944 than in 1939. Some futures were not going to be bright after the war.

♦ ♦ ♦

While all this was happening, the Allied strategic bombing offensive finally reached its peak as well. For years the Allies, first the British and then they and the Americans, had waged a slowly accelerating campaign against German industry and German cities. They developed new planes, better radar, better bombs, and gradually they perfected their techniques of target selection and target marking. Their objectives slowly evolved as well. At first they believed they could bomb accurately and destroy carefully chosen industrial targets. Gradually the British found that was impossible, and they moved to "area bombing," or "terror bombing," as the Germans called it, and they began to lay waste huge sectors of the German cities. When the Americans arrived they made many of the mistakes the British had already made before them, but eventually both learned what they were about and got the equipment to do it. There was no one single breakthrough, though long-range escort fighter aircraft, especially the North American P-51 Mustang, and radar that would allow bombing through clouds came close. For the most part it was a cumulative process of lessons hard learned and painfully absorbed.

The Germans tried to ignore this at first, but they gradually devoted more and more resources to it: camouflage, fighter defenses, dispersal of factories, air raid services. The Allies hoped German morale would crack under the repeated hammer blows, but it never did; the Germans were too tough, and government control too rigid, for that. In fact, in many areas German production actually increased, the result of Albert Speer's efficiency measures—a fact which both amazed and upset Allied planners, who were unaware of how much surplus capacity there was in the German economy.

But by late 1944 they were finding and hitting the right targets; transportation and petroleum facilities were hard to hide, and slowly the German economy edged ever nearer to collapse. They still produced tanks, guns, and planes, but they had greater and greater difficulty getting them to the front, or finding fuel to fly the planes, or training pilots. In 1940 it had been the Germans who had the experience and the better planes; no more. Now the air belonged to the Allies. On D day in Normandy, the Allies flew more than fourteen hundred sorties over the beaches; the Germans flew fourteen.

By the end of 1944 the Luftwaffe was all but done, its airfields subject to attack, its antiaircraft defenses nearly smothered by Allied bombers, its factories and support elements buckling under the pressure. The Germans produced the world's first operational jet aircraft, and Hitler, in a fit of spite, ordered that it be used for hit-and-run bombing of England, wasting yet another potential resource. The Germans developed the first rockets, hitting England with the V-1, really a self-propelled pilotless bomb, and the V-2, a real rocket. But they could not sustain full production under the pounding, so yet another weapon came too late for them. The cities of western Germany lay in rubble; on Valentine's Day of 1945 the Allies virtually wiped out the city of Dresden. It was the last of the great raids. There were not enough targets left.

Still the Germans fought on.

Wearing Down the Japanese

By late 1944, the Americans were ready to invade the Philippine Islands. As they had penetrated deeper and deeper into the Japanese empire, the strategic questions became ever more pressing. The enemy possessed an eccentric system, with Japan near the northern perimeter, and the resources she had conquered near the southern. The actual geographic center of her empire was somewhere in the East China Sea, around the island of Formosa. There was some divergence of view among American planners: Should they head for Formosa itself, or the China coast, or the Philippines? Either of the first two would effectively disrupt imperial communications and lead to further profitable developments; the latter was the logical culmination, both geographic and emotional, of MacArthur's East Indies-New Guinea campaign and the fulfillment of his pledge, "I shall return." Though the planners initially intended to land on the coast of China, around Hong Kong, and then expand from there, the eventual decision was for the Philippines. The Japanese had been hard hit, but they were far from done. No one thought it was going to be easy.

In Japan, too, it was time for some major decisions. Premier Tojo had been removed after the Battle of the Marianas and the loss of the island of Saipan, but that did not indicate any lessening of Japanese resolve. Their war plans had by now been significantly revised. The initial intention had been to seize a distant perimeter and exploit the resources within it while waiting for the Americans to move against them. When they did so, Japan would fight a great naval battle somewhere in mid-ocean, and the imperial fleet, which had never known defeat, would emerge triumphant. The decadent and pragmatic Americans would accept the situation and go home, back to their ball games and their soft living.

The battles along the perimeter had come, but the Americans had not been defeated, and they had not gone home. They had broken into the empire, either bypassed the perimeter, as at Truk and Rabaul, or smothered it as at Tarawa and New Guinea and the Solomons. They had paid heavily, but they had learned their lessons, and they had the material resources and the manpower to make good on their losses and keep coming while the Japanese had been progressively ground down, their superiority whittled away at the Coral Sea, Midway, and in the naval battles around Guadalcanal. By the time a big naval battle had come, in the Philippine Sea, the Japanese were already far weaker than they wanted to be, and their expected victory had turned into the ashes of defeat. With the navy weakened, they had to rely more on land forces, and they began to reinforce the Philippines to hold the central lifeline of the empire.

But they still hoped and plotted to turn the tide. As American planners got ready for the invasion of the Philippine Islands, the Imperial Japanese Navy mustered its still formidable resources for the last great struggle.

On October 20, 1944, troops of the U.S. Sixth Army under Lt Gen Walter Kreuger landed on the island of Leyte, in the central Philippines. They were landed and supported by the U.S. Seventh Fleet, commanded by Adm Thomas Kincaid, and the whole operation was further covered by the U.S. Third Fleet under Adm William Halsey. Together the two fleets had 32 aircraft carriers, 12 battleships, 26 cruisers, and 144 destroyers plus literally hundreds of amphibious and smaller support vessels.

The Japanese planned to trap the Americans, to decoy their covering forces away, and then to crash in upon and destroy the amphibious and support ships. They still had nine battleships, four carriers, seventeen cruisers, and thirty-one destroyers. They developed a complicated converging attack by four separate forces, and it almost worked. Third Fleet was decoyed away, and one Japanese element got close to the vulnerable American units before turning away under the sacrificial attacks of smaller American ships. Both sides fought with the same courage and ferocity, and even as little American destroyers were launching torpedoes against Japanese battleships, young Japanese pilots were deliberately crashing their aircraft into American targets in suicidal attacks. But when it was all over, the Japanese had lost three of their battleships and all four of their carriers and ten of their cruisers. In numbers of men and vessels involved, it was the greatest naval battle in the history of the world, and it finished Japan as a naval power.

At first undecided where to make their stand, the Japanese finally committed themselves to holding the island of Leyte itself. Fighting there—in wild terrain—went on until the end of the year. When it was done, Japanese air strength in the Philippines was depleted, and seventy thousand troops were lost, against American casualties of some fifteen thousand. The Americans then moved on to other islands, to Mindoro and then to Luzon itself, where, ironically, the Americans landed at the same place the Japanese had back in 1941. On this main island the fighting lasted until the very end of the war. Manila was liberated after vicious battles in February, and the Japanese, ever more isolated, were pushed back and confined in the central highlands of the island, long bypassed but still over again.

For a few days the Germans made impressive gains; some American units rocked back, some fought hard, some were literally massacred. But GIs who had come ashore green at Normandy knew their business now, and the Panzers could not expand their flanks. They could not get past the vital road block at Bastogne. Patton wheeled his army ninety degrees and crashed into their southern flank, while Hodges's First Army struck from the north. Hitler wanted to go all the way to Antwerp; he never even got to the Meuse. After ten days of heavy fighting, the Germans were fought out. Then the sky cleared, and Allied tactical air units covered the front like a blanket. The only real effect of the Battle of the Bulge was to use up the last of the Germans' strategic reserve, and with it their mobility. It was not 1940 after all.

In early February of 1945, Roosevelt, Churchill, and Stalin met for the last time, at Yalta. By the next Allied conference, Roosevelt would be dead, and Churchill going out of office. They knew Germany was all but finished; Churchill made one last try to get the western Allies into the Balkans, and lost. Roosevelt, already dying, wanted a Soviet commitment to enter the final stages of the war against Japan—even he could not know how suddenly and dramatically Japan was going to collapse, or under what conditions—and he was willing to give away part of Manchuria to get it. The leaders also agreed on the postwar division of Germany, plans and discussions that had been long in the making. Critics subsequently charged that Roosevelt at Yalta had given away the whole postwar world to Stalin and communism, but that was not really fair. For the most part, the leaders merely put an official seal on what had already happened, or what was going to whether they liked it or not.

As the sixth spring of the war came on, the climax approached. The Italian front was the first to crack. Here the Germans had managed to throw a line together on the very last barriers before the Po Valley and the Lombard Plain. All winter the weary men of the U.S. Fifth and British Eighth Armies had slugged it out with their equally tired and weakened opponents. By now the Italian campaign was a sideshow, everyone said so; that may not have made life any harder, but it certainly did not make it any easier, either, and both sides just kept grinding away.

Finally the Germans broke. On April 2 the Allies opened a major drive, with the British jumping off on the right, followed by the Americans in the center putting everything they had into a drive for Bologna. It took almost three weeks of steady fighting, but on April 20 the front was broken wide open, and the Allies raced into open country at last, out of the mountains and able to move. For ten days they romped through the Po Valley, reaching the foothills of the Alps, and on May 2, the Germans surrendered—the first major capitulation of the end of the war.

The Allies in western Europe had made equally steady progress. Once the Battle of the Bulge was over, General Eisenhower set to work clearing German pockets of resistance and closing up to the frontier all along its length. He was then ready for a phased advance to the Rhine. He had three army groups, seven armies, under his command; four American, and one each of British, Canadian, and French. His overall concept was reasonably simple. Starting in the north, the Allied armies would attack in succession; the pressure on each German force should help the next attack as it went on, and the whole should gather sufficient momentum to carry the Allies to the Rhine. After that, it would be necessary to see what looked most promising.

The Rhineland campaign was actually one of the great ones of World War II, though overshadowed in the public mind by the excitement of the Bulge that preceded it or the collapse of Germany that followed it. But it was in these six weeks from mid-February to late March that German power in the west was actually destroyed. Adolf Hitler, living in an increasingly unreal world, mishandled the few opportunities available to the Germans, and the Allies took advantage of all his mistakes. By the end of the campaign, the Germans had given up a quarter of a million prisoners, and lost sixty to seventy-five thousand killed or wounded.

No one could afford that, but even worse happened in the east. As the Germans opened their attack in the Bulge, the Soviets unleashed an offensive that carried them through western Poland to the frontier of Germany itself and also overran most of East Prussia. An exodus of horrified Germans began out of the Balkan provinces, fleeing before the hated and rightfully vengeful Russians. By mid-February the Russians were on the Oder River in the north and took Vienna in the south. They then paused to regroup, out of supplies, which had not been able to keep up with them. For almost two months there was a portentous pause, then in mid-April, under a veritable canopy of artillery and rocket fire, they jumped off again in a final drive that carried them to Berlin itself. Within a week, they had reached the German capital, and there was desperate fighting around the suburbs and avenues of the city. Hitler lived out a troglodyte existence, issuing orders from an underground bunker to armies that had long since disappeared. His generals had wanted to put all their resources in the east; far better, they said, for Germany to be conquered by the British and Americans than by the Russians. Hitler did not care about what happened to Germany after him: If Germany fell, it was because the German people had proven unworthy of his leadership, unfit to be the master race, and they therefore deserved whatever fate they got.

While the Russians fought to and in Berlin, the western Allies took up their advance once more. On March 7, through a stroke of good fortune, units of the U.S. Ninth Armored Division had seized a bridge across the Rhine at Remagen. Before the Germans managed to recover, the Americans had a strong bridgehead across this most formidable water barrier in western Europe. On the twenty-second the Allies began the final campaign of the war in Europe, attacking out of the bridgehead, while Patton's Third Army jumped the upper Rhine, and then Montgomery's British troops crossed the lower reaches of the river. Within two weeks German Army Group B was encircled in the Ruhr, Germany's industrial heart, and Allied troops were pounding it from all sides. On April 18 the remnants of in the second, Iwo Jima.

Iwo Jima is a little volcanic island, only eight square miles. It gave radar warning of the American raids, and it was heavily fortified and garrisoned with 21,000 troops, each one of whom was ready to die for Japan. On February 19, 1945, marines of the Fourth and Fifth Marine Divisions landed on the island. They suffered 2,400 casualties in the first day; on the twenty-third, they took the high point of the island, Mount Suribachi, and raised the American flag there. The fighting for the little island lasted until the end of March, costing all 21,000 of the Japanese—only about 200 lived to be taken prisoner—and almost 25,000 American casualties, 6,800 of them killed. Proportionately, Iwo Jima was the bloodiest battle of the Pacific war; if things got much worse than this, they were going to get very bad indeed.

Okinawa is a large and beautiful island. Here the Japanese planned to fight a delaying action with their garrison of 120,000 men; while they did so, suicide planes, kamikazes, would destroy the American fleet. That accomplished, the defenders would sally forth and drive the invading army into the sea. At some point the Americans must be stopped, and these desperate measures ought to do it.

Of course they did not, though the price was high indeed. Landings began on April 1, after the island had been isolated and bombarded. It took nearly three months to secure the whole place—three months that cost 50,000 Americans killed and wounded, and 110,000 Japanese killed. While the soldiers and marines fought ashore, the navy fought to keep them there. For this last effort, the Japanese had formally organized suicide air units, young men who attended their own funerals and flew off in planes loaded with explosives. Most of what they hit were radar picket vessels, though some got through to the bigger ships; the Americans had 36 ships sunk and 368 damaged for a cost of 7,830 Japanese aircraft and their crews. Japan was within the reach of American medium-range bombers, but it was painfully obvious that the closer they got, the worse it was going to be. Planners estimated that overrunning the home islands could well cost a million American lives.

Unknown to almost everyone, American scientists were working on a project that might make a difference. In August of 1939, the great physicist Albert Einstein had written President Roosevelt about the possibility of creating a controlled nuclear reaction, in other words, an atomic bomb that would possess incalculably greater force than weapons then in existence. For two years most of the preliminary work in this direction was done by scientists without a great deal of government interest, but in 1942, with the country at war, the Manhattan Project, as the whole enterprise came to be called, took shape. Plants and test sites were developed, at Oak Ridge, Tennessee; Hanford, Washington; and Los Alamos in New Mexico. The first controlled nuclear chain reaction was produced in a squash court at the University of Chicago in December, 1942; it took another two and a half years, and several billion dollars, to turn that into a workable bomb. On July 16, 1945, the first atomic bomb was exploded near Alamogordo, New Mexico. Though few people knew about it, those who did realized mankind had entered a new era.

As the bomb was being tested, President Harry S. Truman, Roosevelt's sudden successor, was meeting in Potsdam, in the ruins of the Third Reich, with Marshal Stalin and Winston Churchill, who was about to leave office. The leaders were primarily concerned with the occupation of Germany and the terms and conditions to be imposed on the defeated Nazis. They did not get along too well. The Americans still wanted Russian help against Japan, and it was apparent that the Soviets had a different view of what the postwar world ought to be like than their allies did. Truman told Stalin that the United States had a new weapon and that it was going to use it against Japan. In a joint statement, the Allied leaders called upon Japan to surrender or face "utter destruction"; they did not want to be too specific.

Some Japanese were in fact ready to give up, but not unconditionally, and some were determined to fight to the bitter end; they were preparing to arm civilians with spears and pikes. There was a half-hearted attempt to open exploratory negotiations through the Soviet Union, still a neutral, but these led nowhere. Stalin, looking to his country's future in the new world, saw no need for shortcuts or to let anyone off any of several hooks.

President Truman authorized use of the new weapon any time after August 1. Ironically, most of the vast machine that was the American and Allied armed forces kept right on rolling along. Japan was bombarded by naval aircraft and bombed by the B-29s; the army was getting ready to move closer; troops were preparing to move from Europe to the Far East. The British had already sent a Pacific Fleet and were organizing a long-range bomber contribution; the Australians were still fighting to secure the East Indies. The war might well go on to its preordained finish.

♦ ♦ ♦

Of course, even if anyone had known about the atomic bombs, they still would not have known how well they would work. Proof of that came only on August 6, 1945, when the B-29 *Enola Gay* dropped the first bomb on the city of Hiroshima. The one bomb, weighing nine thousand pounds, had the force of twenty-nine thousand tons of conventional TNT. The center of the city, previously untouched, was wiped out. American estimates were of about eighty thousand dead, though some ran as high as a quarter million. Here was Armageddon indeed.

Two days later, the Soviet Union declared war on Japan, and Red Army troops began flooding into Manchuria. The next day, August 9, the Americans dropped a second bomb on the city of Nagasaki. Again the center of a city and thousands of lives disappeared in an instant. Meanwhile the B-29s were still bombing conventionally, and American and British naval forces were bombarding coastal cities.

♦ ♦ ♦

The Japanese had finally had enough. They announced their willingness to surrender; there was still some confusion over terms, especially the position of the emperor, but there was no hope left for them now. A few diehards tried to stage a coup, but it collapsed after some confused fighting in Tokyo. The surrender was announced on the 14th, and the 15th was designated V-J Day. Although there were surrenders in areas such as the Philippines and the East Indies, the formal surrender did not take place until September 2, on board the new battleship USS *Missouri* anchored in Tokyo Bay. Thousands of aircraft flew overhead, and the waters of the bay were covered with the hundreds of Allied ships manned by young men who had come so far and fought so hard for this day. It was a solemn matter; in the midst of rejoicing, all were conscious of the millions who were not there. World War II was over at last.

Conclusion

A half-century after it ended, World War II's effects are still being worked out around the globe. The remaking of eastern Europe, eastern Asia, and the Middle East are all part and parcel of things done, or not done, in and through the great wars of the first half of the twentieth century. Out of any number of developments that might be suggested, several deserve special consideration.

The most startling political change was the readjustment of the world's power structure, for international politics, no matter how much the fact may be deplored, is a matter of power and the projection thereof. Before 1939 the world consisted of a number of great powers, some more local than others, but some of worldwide dimensions. After 1945 there were only two great powers left, the United States and the Soviet Union; they had become, indeed, the superpowers. All the others, winners as well as losers, were so exhausted by their efforts as to become little more than satellites of these two states or systems. This was not immediately obvious for everyone; China, indeed, collapsed into civil war; Britain and France tried to preserve the illusion of great-power status, only to see their empires fall away and their influence wane rapidly. It cost them almost as much to win the war as it had the Axis to lose it.

What really happened was that, with the destruction, both physical and political, of western and central Europe and of the east Asia-western Pacific area, the world suddenly had two enormous power vacuums, and these had to be filled. Politics abhors a vacuum as much as nature does. It happened that both the United States, with its belief in the triumph of democratic values, and the Soviet Union, with its belief in the victory of militant communism, had messianic and expansionist tendencies. This was much more clearly understood in Russia than in America, or at least it was understood by Stalin, the only man who counted in Russia, more than by the whole host of Americans who had to reach some sort of agreed conclusion to make anything happen. So the power vacuums were filled, hastily, rapaciously, and gleefully by the Soviets, who grabbed everything they could get in eastern and central Europe, as far as the Elbe and the Balkans, and who strongly supported their surrogates in China and east Asia. By 1950 they had what appeared to be a monolithic block that ran from Germany to Korea. The process was completed by the Americans flowing in from the opposite direction. In 1939 the United States' strategic or geopolitical frontiers were on the Atlantic seaboard of America and at Hawaii. By 1950 they were in West Berlin and along the islands and peninsulas of the coast of Asia.

These developments flowed logically from the defeat of the Axis powers. In 1945 Germany was totally prostrated, and the Allies, after having fought her twice in very living memory, were not going to let it happen again. Germany was occupied by the four major European Allies, and shortly, given the rapidly appearing split between the western three and the eastern one, split into two hostile states. Though few realized it, the western European clock had been put back to before 1870, that is, to before the unification of Germany by Otto von Bismarck. Unfortunately, western Europe as of 1870 was no balance for the Soviet Union as of 1945, and that was what dragged the Americans, as the strongest of the western occupying powers, back into Europe when all they really wanted to do was go home and forget all about it.

More or less the same thing happened on the western Pacific rim. By 1949 Chiang Kai-shek, America's man in China, was finished, driven off the mainland and onto the island of Formosa, where he survived courtesy of the United States and its money and naval power. The vast bulk of China proper belonged now to the Communists. The United States was virtually the sole occupier of Japan, a task it carried out so effectively, and so generously, that within a generation Japan was among the greatest economic, if not military, forces in the world. Japan, in fact, gained infinitely more by losing the war than it could ever conceivably have gained by winning it. It got full access to America's expanded economic sphere while the United States inherited Japan's strategic and military problems, including Korea—which was not a very good exchange.

If all this were not confusing enough, the colonial powers came back to Southeast Asia too, or tried to. The British found themselves unwelcome in India now, told to get out of Burma, and tolerated in Malaya only because they protected the country from a Communist insurgency. The Dutch fought a low-level war in the East Indies, now Indonesia, before getting out from under American anticolonial pressure. The French returned to Indochina and rapidly got into a war that ultimately saw the United States taking France's place and which dragged on agonizingly into the 1970s. It was no accident that most of the large-scale international crises of the quarter-century after 1945 were along the fault lines where the two superpowers and their respective systems met: the Balkans, the city of Berlin, Korea, the Formosa Strait, Indochina, Malaya.

In retrospect, there was an enormous irony in all of this, for a judicious observer would have noted that the United States and the Soviet Union, however antithetical their political systems, had a far greater common interest in preserving a world political and economic order in which they stood conveniently at the top than they did in jostling each other around the fringes and bankrupting themselves by arms races and surrogate wars. Unfortunately, such retrospection is by definition denied to human beings at any given time.

The new world order was achieved at tremendous cost, in money, material, and human suffering. It cost the world roughly one trillion contemporary dollars, given the decline in money values over the last half-century. That figure means far less now than it did in 1945, and the imagination can hardly encompass such a figure anyway. The United States spent the most, $288 billion, to win it, and Germany second most, $212 billion, to lose it.

Much of this cost consisted of property damage, either private or national. More than five thousand Allied merchant ships were sunk, a total of 21,600,000 tons, with, of course, all their cargoes. Another 6,000,000 tons of Japanese merchant shipping was sunk, as well as virtually all of the Japanese and German navies, and large numbers of everyone else's navies, too. On land, China was in ruins, Japan had been bombed back into pre-industrial times, and there was a swath of destruction laid across Europe from the Pyrenees to Moscow. Bridges were blown up, dams blown out, canals blocked, cities razed; road networks had collapsed, and railroad systems were masses of twisted metal. Cathedrals were gutted, whole square miles of cities were piles of crumbled brick and stone; masses of people were homeless, starving, wandering vaguely through the ruin of their lives and countries.

The number of people actually killed in, during, or by the war is to some extent a matter of conjecture. Some states kept better records than others, some records did not survive the war, some recorders counted different casualties in different categories. Nonetheless, in general terms there were about 15,000,000 battle deaths, and about 25,000,000 wounded. It is estimated that there were at least 35,000,000 civilian deaths, and figures recently released in the Soviet Union suggest that that number should probably be amended upward; there may well have been as many as 50,000,000. The United States had just under a million military casualties, about 300,000 killed and the rest wounded. The Soviet Union, out of 20,000,000 military personnel, had 13,600,000 dead. Stalin once remarked that the United States paid for World War II in money, Britain in time, and the Soviet Union in blood. In Poland, one person in four died; seven out of ten European Jews died. Thus the costs of the Axis dream of a new world order, and the costs of stopping it.

There were all sorts of unanticipated changes as a result of the war. The unsuccessful Republican candidate for president in 1940, Wendell Willkie, subsequently wrote a book that he called *One World.* That was what World War II made of the globe. Modern technology penetrated the farthest reaches of the planet; American airfield builders in New Guinea must have looked as amazing to the natives as did the first Spanish arriving on horses in their New World. Communication facilities shrank times and distances. It was not only new weapons that were developed; there were also new medicines, new methods of transportation. The war gave society a technological shot of adrenalin on whose effects it is still running, a quantum leap that has gained incremental momentum ever since and that, in some areas, threatens to overwhelm its creators. The rhythms of life changed, seemingly "forever," which is the term we egocentrically use when we mean "as far as we can see."

In fact, much did change: the power structure, technology, the lives of millions of individuals; and much remained the same: state rivalries, human ambitions and aspirations. Though the world found new solutions, old problems still remained.

But that was not the fault of the men and women who met the challenges of World War II; a generation can face only its own problems, not its children's. The American men and women of 1941-45 met their country's and their world's needs head on. Indeed, fifty years later, The War looks like a time of political innocence and manly vigor, "When Duty whispered low, Thou must," and "Youth replied, I can." It was, like the Revolution and the Civil War, one of America's heroic ages.

James L. Stokesbury

BIOGRAPHICAL NOTE

James L. Stokesbury is professor of history at Acadia University in Wolfville, Nova Scotia, Canada. Born in Connecticut, he served in the U.S. Navy from 1953 to 1957. He received his B.A. from Acadia, his M.A. from the University of Western Ontario, and his Ph.D. from Duke University, where he was a James B. Duke Fellow. He is the author of more than sixty articles and reviews in the United States, Canada, Great Britain, Greece, and Spain. Of his seven books, two, *Navy and Empire* and *A Short History of Air Power*, were Book-of-the Month Club selections, and two, *A Short History of World War II* and *A Short History of the American Revolution*, were History Book Club selections. He lives in Gaspereau, Nova Scotia, and is married and has three children.

THE EXHIBITION

For those who lived and fought through it, World War II is often considered the most challenging and exciting event in their lives—in spite of the fact that it was usually filled with boredom, occasionally terror, discomfort, loneliness, and indignity.

This exhibition reflects the several facets of the war: that it was terrible, that it was cruel, dislocating, occasionally funny, often tragic. There were many more privates than there were generals, so this exhibition is about real people—some famous, but most unknown—caught in the turmoil of war. Their diaries, documents, letters, photographs, and the things they used show how Americans waged their war; how they went from innocence and defeat to knowledge and victory; and what they saw, thought, and felt about it as they did so. At the same time, you will see how similar was the experience of those from other countries who fought by their side—and indeed on the other side as well.

Many of the letters and diaries in the exhibition are shown in this publication in transcript form only.

Transcripts reflect the original spelling and punctuation.

A World at War

World War II consisted of four great interlocking wars. Nazi Germany, Japan, and Italy began their careers of aggressive expansion in the 1930s and gradually formed a loose alliance, called "the Axis."

Japan openly invaded China in 1937. By then Mussolini's Italy had overrun Ethiopia. But it was Adolf Hitler in Germany who turned these separate episodes into one great war. Coming to power in 1933, he undertook a series of aggressions that culminated in September of 1939, when he invaded Poland. The Poles fought, and Britain and France at last declared war.

In rapid succession, Poland, Denmark, Norway, the Netherlands, Belgium, and finally even France itself, were all invaded and crushed by the seemingly invincible German war machine. Only Britain, supported by its empire and safe behind the Channel, managed to resist through 1940.

In the spring of 1941, Hitler lost interest in the British. Turning east, he invaded Yugoslavia and Greece and then hurled his armies against the Soviet Union. The Russians were swamped, and the mighty German host drove toward Moscow.

Meanwhile, Japan turned covetous eyes to the south, to the riches of southeast Asia. Only the Americans stood in the way of further conquest....

Facing page:
The headlines read, "U.S. and Japan Fail to Reach Pacific Agreements; War or Peace Seen Hinging on Tokyo's Next Move"—*Albuquerque Journal*, November 27, 1941
Life-size figure by Studio EIS, Brooklyn, New York
Photograph by Elliot Schwartz

Confidential

Office of the Chief of Naval Operations

Op16-F-2
(SC)A16-3/EF37
Serial No. 09716

Feb. 1, 1941

CONFIDENTIAL

10465

From: Chief of Naval Operations
To: Commander-in-Chief, Pacific Fleet

Subject: Rumored Japanese attack on Pearl Harbor.

1. The following is forwarded for your information. Under date of 27 January the American Ambassador at Tokyo telegraphed the State Department to the following effect:

> "The Peruvian Minister has informed a member of my staff that he has heard from many sources, including a Japanese source, that in the event of trouble breaking out between the United States and Japan, the Japanese intend to make a surprise attack against Pearl Harbor with all of their strength and employing all of their equipment. The Peruvian Minister considered the rumors fantastic. Nevertheless he considered them of sufficient importance to convey this information to a member of my staff."

2. The Division of Naval Intelligences places no credence in these rumors. Furthermore, based on known data regarding the present disposition and employment of Japanese naval and army forces, no move against Pearl Harbor appears imminent or planned for in the forseeable future.

16-F

Jules James,
By direction

16-F-2

Dictated Jan. 31, 1941
" by Lieut. Comdr. A. H. McCollum
Typed by M. E. Morse

CC - Com 14 10466

Confidential

(SC)A16-3/EF37

War Threatens The United States

The vast majority of Americans wanted no part of the rest of the world's war. As the dictators grew more bellicose, Americans grew more isolationist and passed neutrality acts designed to keep their country from being sucked into war as it had been a generation earlier.

But the greatest industrial power in the world could not avoid a highly industrial war. Slowly opinion began to shift to favor the western Allies. The neutrality laws gave way to cash-and-carry, which was then replaced by lend-lease. The government passed a National Defense Tax Bill, began building ships and planes, and in 1940 introduced the first peacetime draft in American history.

By mid-1941 it was Japan that caused Washington its most pressing worry. Tension mounted through the fall. The Japanese sent a special envoy to Washington, but they had already decided on a sudden attack upon the United States.

The American government knew much but not enough of this plan. In late November, Japanese fleet movements suggested an attack against British Malaya or Singapore. Although they had broken several of the Japanese codes, American intelligence analysts had lost the Japanese carrier striking force. By the afternoon of Saturday, December 6, they knew something was about to happen; they still did not know exactly what, or where, or when....

Facing page:

Memorandum, Chief of Naval Operations to Commander-in-Chief, Pacific Fleet, February 1, 1941

Although indications of Japanese intentions toward U.S. installations in the Pacific were reported, the official attitude was one of disbelief.

National Archives and Records Administration

... When the Jap Prime Minister requested a meeting with you he indicated a fairly basic program in generalities, but left open such questions as getting troops out of China, tripartie pact, non-discrimination in trade in Pacific.

We indicated desire for meeting, but suggested first an agreement in principle on the vital questions left open, so as to insure the success of the Conference.

Soon thereafter, the Japs narrowed their position on these basic questions, and now continue to reje[ct] the meeting at Juneau.

My suggestion is to recite their more liberal attitude when they first sought the meeting with you, with their much narrowed position now, and earnestly ask if they cannot go back to their original liberal attitude so we can start discussions again on agreement in principle before the meeting, and reempahasizing your desire for a meeting—

Memorandum, Secretary of State Cordell Hull to President Franklin D. Roosevelt, September, 1941

Secretary Hull advises the president in regard to deteriorating relations with the Japanese government.

Franklin D. Roosevelt Library, National Archives and Records Administration

THE WHITE HOUSE
WASHINGTON

When the Jap Prime Minister requested a meeting with you he indicated a fairly basic program in generalities, but left open such questions as getting troops out of China, Tripartite pact, non-discrimination in trade in Pacific.

WE indicated desire for meeting, but suggested

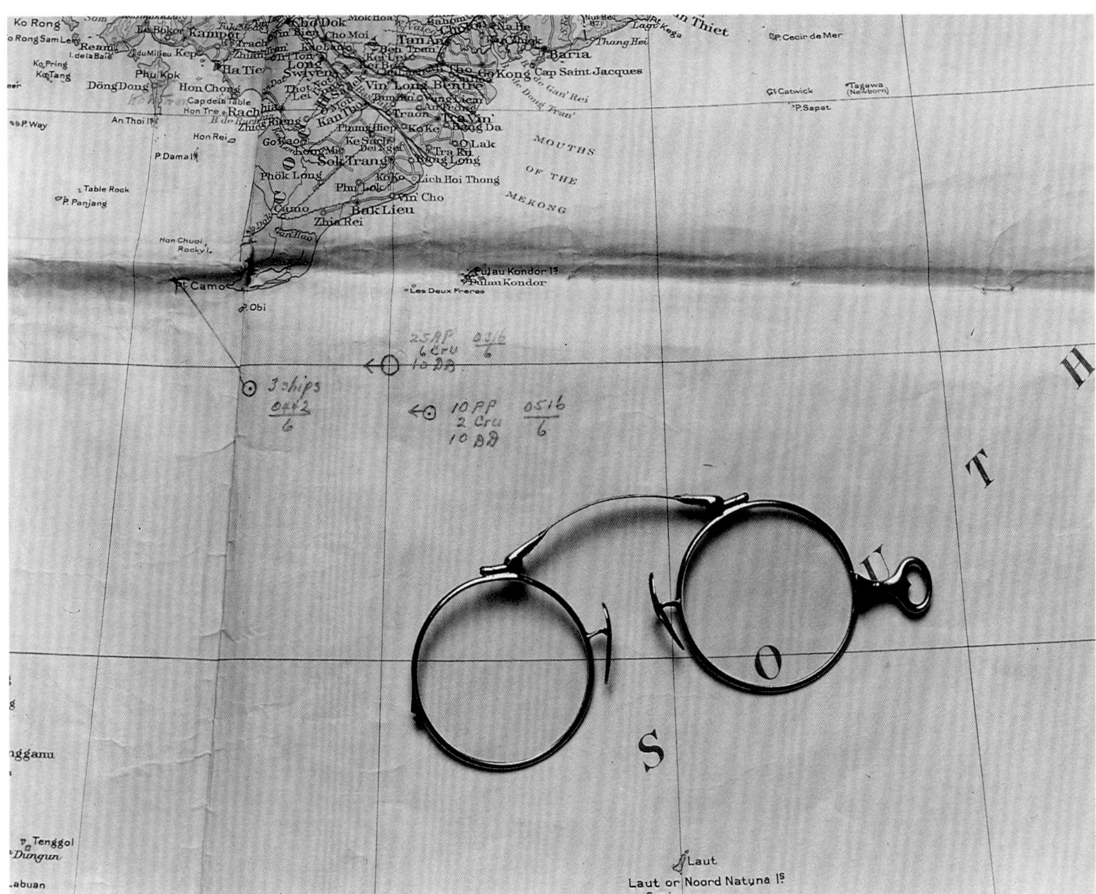

Map, Malay Peninsula and South China Sea

This map with penciled notations showing the location of the Japanese fleet was studied by President Roosevelt in the Oval Office on December 6, 1941. There was a second fleet at sea heading for Pearl Harbor of which the United States was unaware.

Mr. George M. Elsey

Pince-nez worn by President Franklin D. Roosevelt

National Park Service, Home of Franklin D. Roosevelt National Historic Site

Japanese envoys Kichisaburo Nomura and Saburo Kurusu leave the U.S. State Department in Washington after engaging in talks with Secretary of State Cordell Hull.

National Archives and Records Administration

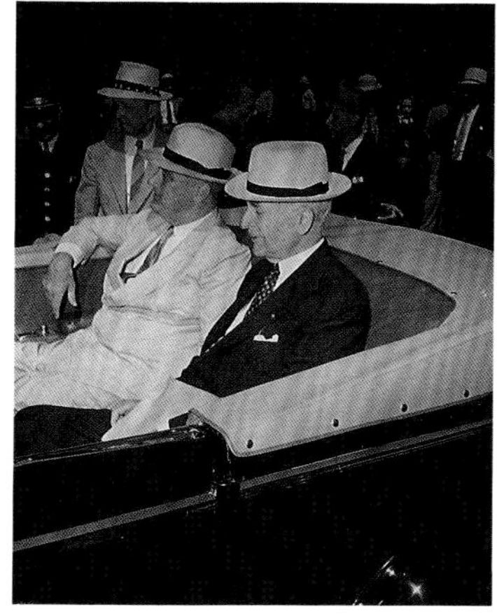

President Roosevelt and Secretary of State Cordell Hull ride together after the Atlantic Conference.

National Archives and Records Administration

Peacetime Pearl Harbor

The last six months of peace were a strange time for Americans. In the western North Atlantic, American naval units were convoying ships bound for Britain. There was, in fact, an undeclared war going on there, but it was in neither side's interest to acknowledge it.

American army troops were working up to war strength, but peacetime attitudes died hard. In the Pacific, the fleet was busily training; in summer of 1941 it remained at Pearl Harbor instead of returning, as usual, to west coast ports.

There was a peculiar ambience to life in the islands. Just as Indian territory had been a century ago, so now the Pacific was America's frontier, and Honolulu and Pearl Harbor were the crossroads of that frontier, the place where America met the East. Servicemen there trained hard, played hard, and grew up fast. Almost the whole world was at war, and America was on the knife edge of it; in December of 1941, Hawaii was an exciting place to be.

Facing page:

Ships of the Pacific Fleet lie at anchor in Pearl Harbor while rowing crews train.

Bernice P. Bishop Museum, photograph by Tao Sing Loo

U. S. S. ARIZONA

April 8, 1941

Dear Mamma and Daddy,

Well, here I am at my destination — the USS ARIZONA —

We left San Francisco on the 28th of March. It was a 7 day trip across on the Wharton and boy did I get _sea sick_.

Hawaii is a wonderful place and the climate is so healthy like. I have been feeling fine.

The Arizona is a swell ship and the officers sure have treated us swell.

I was sorry to hear of Mr. Byram's death and also of Mr. Andrew Sevier's illness. I suppose that he is dead by now — I hope not.

I received your birthday card and also one from Aunt Marion and _Cousin_ Nancy — had

April 8, 1941

Dear Mamma and Daddy,

Well, here I am at my destination—The USS ARIZONA—

We left San Francisco on the 28th of March. It was a 7 day trip across on the Wharton and boy did I get sea sick.

Hawaii is a wonderful place and the climate is so healthy like. I have been feeling fine.

*The Arizona is a swell ship and the officers sure have treated us swell***

I was sorry to hear of Mr. Byram's death and also of Mr. Andrew Sevie's illness. I suppose that he is dead by now—I hope not.

I recieved your birthday card and also one from Aunt Marion and Cousin Nancy ...

I hope Jack buckles down to his studies—oh! how he will regret not having an education—Boy, I really know—

Tell that little Baby Sister that Uncle Ray is going to send her something nice as soon as I get settled down— ...

*Most of the boys are from Annapolis, but they are the finest bunch of boys I have met***

Tell Daddy boy and Grandpa hello for me and write soon to this address—

Love to all,
Ray ...

Ens Thomas Ray Jones, U.S. Navy, Tallulah, Louisiana

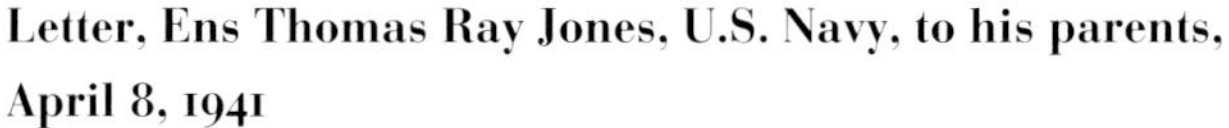

Letter, Ens Thomas Ray Jones, U.S. Navy, to his parents, April 8, 1941

Ensign Jones tells his parents about his first days aboard the USS *Arizona.*

USS Arizona Memorial Museum, National Park Service

The battleship USS *Arizona*

Fireman First Class Wesley John Heidt, U.S. Navy, Los Angeles, California

Nov. 22, 1941

Hello Mom,

This is your bad son again. Boy Have I been catching hell for not writing. I don't know why you worry about us so much, if any thing happenned to us you would hear from the Navy the first thing; so until you hear from them there is no need of worrying. I am safer on this battleboat then I would be driving back and forth to work if I was home. You know Mom there is lots of thimes I start to write but I have to give up because there is nothing to write about except our navy activities and I am not aloud to say anything about them. Tell Louise not to repeat anything her sailor friends say. For instance she wrote and said that some sailor told her that he saw our ship in Honolulu, and mentioned his name. Now if that letter to us happened to be cencored the Navy could find who her sailor friend was and have him court martialed for giving out information. So please be carefull and don't believe anything you hear. The only time to expect us home is whem you see us. I don't think it will be long now. I hope.

Well woppie I must say good bye for now and will write soon.

Your third and favorite Son …

Letter, Fireman First Class Wesley John Heidt, U.S. Navy, to his mother, November 22, 1941

The mother of Wes and Bud Heidt, both stationed on the USS *Arizona*, finally gets a letter from Wes.

USS Arizona Memorial Museum, National Park Service

Dear Julia.
... I guess he getting pretty old ... God! damn, if he doesn't recieved a letter from us kids every week he think that we don't want to write to him. God! he sure is funny.

Well Julia, I don't know any thing new to tell you, but I can add that; you sure are lucky to be home and enjoying all thats there.... God, when I see how some of the sailors aboard ship that have wives and kids home and can't see them suffer its terrible. We even got some that never seem there baby yet and God knows when they will. I know one thing, they can keep this navy, but whem my time it up I am going out. The navy is all right, but not for me.

Tell Norman that I said hello and I will come over to see him if this pig iron son of a _____ every gets back to the states again. Please don't wait as long to write as I did, so now I will send you

All My Love
Bud

Fireman First Class Edward Joseph (Bud) Heidt, U.S. Navy, Los Angeles, California

---

Letter, Fireman First Class Edward Joseph (Bud) Heidt, U.S. Navy, to Julia, November 24, 1941

From his post on the USS *Arizona* Bud Heidt describes the experience of being away from home. His brother Wesley was also aboard the *Arizona*.

USS Arizona Memorial Museum, National Park Service

Overleaf:
American servicemen off duty in Honolulu
Bernice P. Bishop Museum, photograph by R. J. Baker

PLAYLAND
PLAYLAND
Coca-Cola
HO

RECREATION
CENTER
Coca-Cola
Coca-Cola
Coca-Cola
HARRY KAHNE'S
JEWELRY MART
246

Pearl Harbor
December 7, 1941

The Japanese attack on Pearl Harbor on December 7, 1941, not only catapulted the United States into World War II, but it has long been shrouded in controversy: How, Americans asked themselves, could such a surprise have happened?

When American diplomatic pressure left Japan no options between war and giving up her imperial ambitions, it chose war, and began it with a surprise attack upon the vulnerable and still unsuspecting Americans.

American naval, military, and diplomatic intelligence misassessed the possible Japanese targets. Although the Hawaiian area was warned and precautions were taken—against sabotage—the attack was still a complete surprise. In the space of an hour, American air and naval power in the Pacific was crippled. Fortunately, Admiral Nagumo's carrier pilots neglected crucial basing, repair, and fuel storage facilities.

The Japanese made strategic misjudgments as well as tactical ones; they thought the Pearl Harbor strike would alter the balance of the Pacific in their favor over the long term. Instead, it brought an enraged United States unanimously into the war. Pearl Harbor guaranteed Japan a few months of victory, and eventual defeat.

Facing page:

This captured Japanese photograph was taken before the attack on Pearl Harbor.

The crew waves to the pilot as the plane leaves the deck of the carrier.

National Archives and Records Administration

Pvt Earl M. Schaeffer, Jr., U.S. Army Air Corps, Salina, Kansas

... Towards 0800 I heard explosions and aircraft, not too loud as I was in the Communications Shack which was between two hangers, numbers 5 & 6. The noises became louder and when things started shaking and rattling and parts of the ceiling coming down, I ran out in the hanger, over to the end where the large doors were to see what was the matter. Well, I saw many fires, aircraft burning, buildings afire, much smoke coming from the Pearl Harbor area. It was too much! I just could'nt comprehend just what was going on. I did'nt have to wait long to learn the awful truth. Three aircraft came flying very low across the field firing their wing guns at our B-18's, B-17's and others. As they passed by, I saw the big red balls on the sides of their aircraft! The awful truth came home with a jolt and nausia in my gut I knew from the aircraft identification classes we had that I was looking at three Japanese Zero Fighter Planes....

Memoir, Pvt Earl M. Schaeffer, Jr., U.S. Army Air Corps, December 7, 1941

On switchboard duty at Hickam Field near Pearl Harbor when the attack began, Private Schaeffer describes his reaction.

Mr. Earl M. Schaeffer

Jumper, U.S. Navy, worn by Pharmacist's Mate First Class Path, Ford Island Clinic, who helped to rescue survivors from the *Arizona*

USS Arizona Memorial Museum, National Park Service

Captured photograph taken from a Japanese fighter plane during the attack on Pearl Harbor

National Archives and Records Administration

Japanese aerial photograph

National Archives and Records Administration

Extra Priority

All
Army & Corps Area Commanders

Japan opened hostilities in Hawaii at eight oclock Hawaiian time by air attack apparently from carrier involving approximately fifty Japanese planes stop attack still in progress stop Hangars at Nichols Field and Wheeler Field are in flames and Japanese planes reported as machine gunning over Hickam Field stop Rumored one U.S. battleship struck in Pearl Harbor but no confirmation this report stop. Our army and navy planes are in the air stop Manila has also been attacked but no details yet stop In cooperation with F.B.I. round up all the suspicious characters on your lists stop Corps Area Commanders will notify manufacturers to take all special measures for protection against sabotage

Adams

Draft of telegram, Maj Gen Emery S. Adams, Adjutant General of the Army, to all army commanders, December 7, 1941

An official report of the attack on Pearl Harbor is transmitted to commanders in the Pacific region.

National Archives and Records Administration

A B-17C at Hickam Field sits on the ground with the tail section blown away.

National Archives and Records Administration

Long Beach California
Dec. 7-8-41-

My own Dear son.

I heard all, and am almost-
beside myself. however I am sure
our U.S.S. fleet. can handle it,
God bless our men- and officers
of the fleet- help. them to keep up,
and going. Francis I am alright.
only worried about- my dear boys.
have you seen Norman. I am only
writing a line, as I am feeling very
sad of course, and am afraid to
write any news I had your Nice letter
written on your birthday it is very-
sweet-. and am going to try to get- in touch
with Dotty. Now dear son. I repeat
that you have always been the best son
a mother ever had. God. bless both
you and Norman and all men and
officers of our Big fleet, so I will say
good bye now. and, may God bless you
and keep you. Lovingly your mother.

Box 803- address 21- South Daisy ave.

Long Beach California
Dec. 7-8-41-

My own Dear son,

I heard all, and am almost beside myself. however I am sure our U.SS. fleet. can handle it, God bless our men- and officers of the fleet- help. them to keep up, and going. Francis I am alright. only worried about my dear boys.

have you seen Norman. I am only writing a line, as I am feeling very sad of course, and am afraid to write any news I had your nice letter written on your birthday it is very-sweet. and am going to try to get in touch with Dorthy. Now dear son. I repeat that you have always been the best son a mother ever had. God. bless both you and Norman and all men and officers of our Big fleet. so I will say good bye now. and, may God bless you and keep you. Lovingly your mother.

Box 803—address 21-South Daisy ave.

Mrs. Clara May Morse,
Long Beach, California

Letter, Mrs. Clara May Morse to her son Francis Jerome, December 7, 1941

Unaware that the ship on which her two sons are stationed has been sunk in the attack on Pearl Harbor, Mrs. Morse tries to reassure herself by writing a letter to one of them.

Colorado Historical Society, Books and Manuscripts Department

Overleaf:

(from left to right) The U.S. warships *Arizona*, *Tennessee*, and *West Virginia* send huge clouds of black smoke into the air. The *Arizona* was lost, but the *Tennessee* and *West Virginia* were repaired and later participated in the war.

National Archives and Records Administration

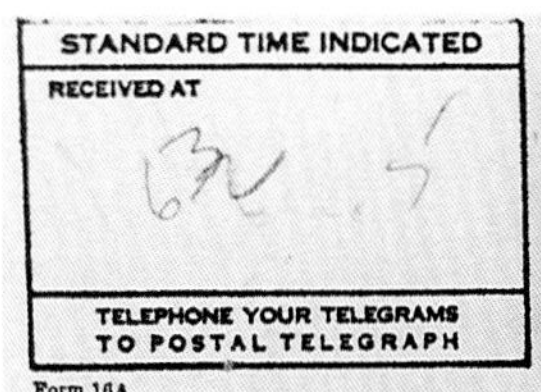

STANDARD TIME INDICATED

RECEIVED AT

632

TELEPHONE YOUR TELEGRAMS TO POSTAL TELEGRAPH

Form 16A

Postal Telegraph
Mackay Radio
All America Cables
Commercial Cables
Canadian Pacific Telegraphs

THIS IS A FULL RATE TELEGRAM, CABLEGRAM OR RADIOGRAM UNLESS OTHERWISE INDICATED BY SYMBOL IN THE PREAMBLE OR IN THE ADDRESS OF THE MESSAGE. SYMBOLS DESIGNATING SERVICE SELECTED ARE OUTLINED IN THE COMPANY'S TARIFFS ON HAND AT EACH OFFICE AND ON FILE WITH REGULATORY AUTHORITIES.

FB616 69 GOVT 6 EX CK US DELY OR OL CHGS

1942 JAN 24 PM 6 31

DX WASHINGTON DC 24 719P

MRS GENEVIEVE DUNLAP 1005

3545 LINDA VISTA TERRACE LOSA

AFTER EXHAUSTIVE SEARCH IT HAS BEEN FOUND IMPOSSIBLE TO LOCATE YOUR SONS, WESLEY JOHN HEIDT FIREMAN FIRST CLASS US NAVY AND EDWARD JOSEPH HEIDT FIREMAN FIRST CLASS US NAVY AND THEY HAVE THEREFORE BEEN OFFICIALLY DECLARED TO HAVE LOST THEIR LIFE IN THE SERVICE OF THEIR COUNTRY AS OF DECEMBER SEVENTH NINETEEN FORTY ONE X THE DEPARTMENT EXPRESSES TO YOU ITS SINCEREST SYMPATHY

REAR ADMIRAL RANDALL JACOBS CHIEF OF BUREAU OF NAVIGATION.

STANDARD TIME INDICATED

THIS IS A FULL RATE TELEGRAM, CABLE-

Telegram, Rear Adm Randall Jacobs, U.S. Navy, to Mrs. Genevieve Dunlap, January 24, 1942

Mrs. Dunlap receives the news that her sons Wes and Bud Heidt are considered to have been killed in the attack on Pearl Harbor.

USS Arizona Memorial Museum, National Park Service

Wes and Bud Heidt, U.S. Navy, Los Angeles, California

Dec. 7, 1941
3:50 p.m.

MEMORANDUM FOR THE PRESIDENT

The Japs attacked Honolulu time about eight o'clock this morning. The first warning was from a submarine that was outside the harbor which was attacked by a destroyer with depth bombs. Result unknown. Another submarine was sunk by aircraft. They attacked with aircraft, with bombs and torpedoes. At least two aircraft were known to have a swastika sign on them. The attacks were in two divisions; first on the air fields and then on the navy yard. Severe damage. The Oklahoma has capsized in Pearl Harbor. The Tennessee is on fire with a bad list., and the Navy Yard is attempting to drydock her.... The air fields at Ford Island, Hickam, Wheeler and Kanoehe were attacked.

Hangers on fire and Hickam field fire is buring badly. The PBY's outside of hangars are burning. Probably heavy personnel casualties but no figures. So far as Block knows Honolulu was not hit.... This came over the telephone and we are getting nothing out here whatever. Mr. Vincent called but I have given out nothing, pending further word from you. The Japanese have no details of the damage which they have wrought.

Memorandum to President Franklin D. Roosevelt, December 7, 1941

Details of the surprise attack on Honolulu are outlined in this document. Most information was relayed to the White House by the Department of the Navy.

Franklin D. Roosevelt Library, National Archives and Records Administration

The USS *Arizona* burns out of control.

National Archives and Records Administration

Japanese Type A two-man submarine was captured during the attack on Pearl Harbor. These subs could be launched from seaplane tenders or warships and traveled at speeds of nineteen knots underwater.

National Archives and Records Administration

The USS *Shaw* sends flames and metal shooting into the air as it explodes.

National Archives and Records Administration

To a Commanding Officer:

From Japanese Naval Officer
KAZUO SAKAMAKI…

2. *RECORD OF BATTLE*
Your honorable "have" country instituted an economic blockade of Japan, a "have not" country, refusing to sell us oil, cotton and the like, until we had no choice but natural collapse. Because of this we began diplomatic negotiations with your country, but these ended in failure. Therefore, with a friend, I set out for Pearl Harbor with the purpose of sinking a battleship, but … since the _____ accident was fatal to the submarine, we determined to proceed without hesitation on the surface of the water, and dashing into the harbor, and climbing the gang-way ladder, hoped to leap onto the deck and die simultaneously with blowing up the enemy warship just as in olden times, during the Mongol invasion … Later, finally being unable to do anything with the submarine, I swam through the ocean and reached an enemy airport. Due to my exhaustion, I was captured without having time to even fight. And thus my sad fate began.

Due entirely to my inexpert navigation and strategy, my honor as a soldier has fallen to the ground. Thus I betrayed the expectations of our 100,000,000 [people] and became a sad prisoner of war disloyal to my country…. I will commit suicide upon my return to my native land. Even though we are unarmed, to bite with teeth and fight to the last is the Japanese spirit….
Showa 16th year [1941], 14th day [Month omitted]

Kazuo Sakamaki
Naval Sub-lieutenant

Translation of statement, Ens Kazuo Sakamaki, Japanese navy, December 14, 1941

Although he survived the stranding of his midget submarine on a coral reef, Sakamaki became the first Japanese prisoner of war.

National Archives and Records Administration

DRAFT No. 1 December 7, 1941.

PROPOSED MESSAGE TO THE CONGRESS

Yesterday, December 7, 1941, a date which will live in world history, the United States of America was simultaneously and deliberately attacked by naval and air forces of the Empire of Japan.

The United States was at the moment at peace with that nation and was continuing the conversations with its Government and its Emperor looking toward the maintenance of peace in the Pacific. Indeed, one hour after Japanese air squadrons had commenced bombing in Hawaii and the Philippines the Japanese Ambassador to the United States and his colleague delivered to the Secretary of State a formal reply to a former message from the Secretary. This reply contained a statement that diplomatic negotiations must be considered at an end, but contained no threat and no hint of an armed attack.

It will be recorded that the distance of Manila, and especially of Hawaii, from Japan makes it obvious that the attack was deliberately planned many days ago. During the intervening time the Japanese Government has deliberately sought to deceive the United States by false statements and expressions of hope for continued peace.

Annotated draft of speech delivered to the Congress by President Franklin D. Roosevelt on December 8, 1941

President Roosevelt adds the famous *Day of Infamy* reference to the original dictated version of this speech asking for a declaration of war against Japan.

Franklin D. Roosevelt Library, National Archives and Records Administration

President Roosevelt signs the Declaration of War against Japan on December 8, 1941.

Franklin D. Roosevelt Library, National Archives and Records Administration

Radioman First Class Raymond M. Tufteland, U.S. Navy, Lemon Grove, California

Dec. 7, 1941.

The Chicago was out from Pearl Harbor three days when the war broke loose. I was on watch on the circuit that broadcast the news of outbreak. At about Ø83Ø first message came:—From Cincpac—To—All Ships Hawaiian Area—"Air Raid on Pearl Harbor x This is not *a drill"! A fewer minutes later—"Hostilities with Japan commenced with air raid on Pearl." At Ø9ØØ—"Execute war plan '46' against Japan."—from Secnor....*

Dec. 12.

Our force entered Pearl to witness a ghastly sight of sunken ships—oil covered water—wreckage and ruins.

We first passed the Nevada which had been beached to prevent sinking. Next one was California—badly damaged and on bottom. The hull of the Oklahoma then came in sight after having capsized. The Tennessee and West Virginia behind her were both damaged. However the Tenn. got underway and left the W. Va. still on bottom. The Arizona was completely blown up and a twisted mass of iron.

Bodies were still being taken from ships and out of water a week after attack. It was a sight none of us like to remember but must avenge! ...

Diary, Radioman First Class Raymond M. Tufteland, U.S. Navy, December 7 and 12, 1941

Aboard the USS *Chicago*, Radioman Tufteland receives the news of the attack on Pearl Harbor and later witnesses the destruction.

Mr. Raymond M. Tufteland

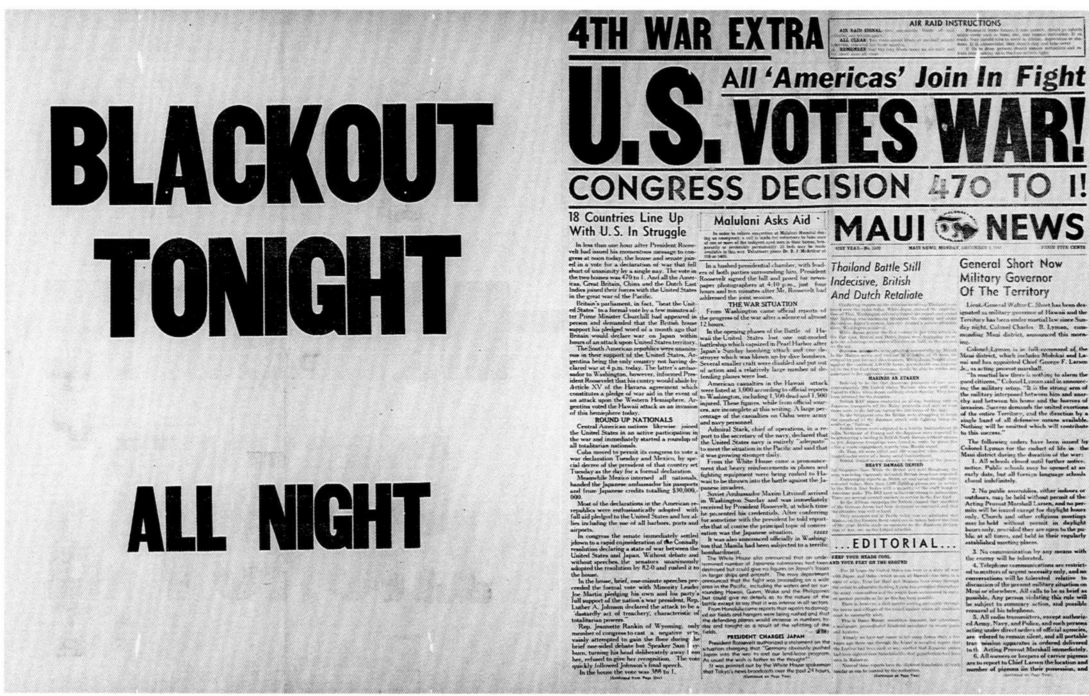

BLACKOUT TONIGHT

ALL NIGHT

4TH WAR EXTRA

AIR RAID INSTRUCTIONS

All 'Americas' Join In Fight

U.S. VOTES WAR!

CONGRESS DECISION 470 TO 1!

MAUI NEWS

18 Countries Line Up With U.S. In Struggle

In less than one hour after President Roosevelt had issued his momentous message to congress at noon today, the house and senate joined in a vote for a declaration of war that fell short of unanimity by a single nay. The vote in the two houses was 470 to 1. And all the Americas, Great Britain, China and the Dutch East Indies joined their forces with the United States in the great war of the Pacific.

Britain's parliament, in fact, "beat the United States" to a formal vote by a few minutes after Prime Minister Churchill had appeared in person and demanded that the British house support his pledged word of a month ago that Britain would declare war on Japan within hours of an attack upon United States territory.

The South American republics were unanimous in their support of the United States, Argentina being the only country not having declared war at 4 p.m. today. The latter's ambassador to Washington, however, informed President Roosevelt that his cuntry would abide by Article XV of the Havana agreement which constitutes a pledge of war aid in the event of an attack upon the Western Hemisphere. Argentina voted the Hawaii attack as an invasion of this hemisphere today.

ROUND UP NATIONALS

Central American nations likewise joined the United States in an active participation in the war and immediately started a roundup of all totalitarian nationals.

Cuba moved to permit its congress to vote a war declaration Tuesday and Mexico, by special decree of the president of that country set Tuesday as the day for a formal declaration.

Meanwhile Mexico interned all nationals, handed the Japanese ambassador his passports and froze Japanese credits totalling $30,000,000.

Most of the declarations in the American republics were enthusiastically adopted with full aid pledged to the United States and her allies including the use of all harbors, ports and airports.

In congress the senate immediately settled jdown to a rapid cojnsideration of the Connally resolution declaring a state of war between the United States and Japan. Without debate and without speeches, the senators unanimously adopted the resolution by 82-0 and rushed it to the house.

In the house, brief, one-minute speeches preceded the formal vote with Minority Leader Joe Martin pledging his own and his party's full support of the nation's war president. Rep. Luther A. Johnson declared the attack to be a 'dastardly act of treachery', characteristic of totalitarian powers."

Rep. Jeannette Rankin of Wyoming, only member of congress to cast a negative vote, vainly attempted to gain the floor during the brief one-sided debate but Speaker Sam Rayburn, turning his head deliberately away from her, refused to give her recognition. The vote quickly followed Johnson's final speech.

In the house the vote was 388 to 1.

Malulani Asks Aid

In a hushed presidential chamber, with leaders of both parties surrounding him, President Roosevelt signed the bill and posed for newspaper photographers at 4:10 p.m., just four hours and ten minutes after Mr. Roosevelt had addressed the joint session.

THE WAR SITUATION

From Washington came official reports of the progress of the war after a silence of almost 12 hours.

In the opening phases of the Battle of Hawaii the United States lost one out-moded battleship which capsized in Pearl Harbor after Japan's Sunday bombing attack and one destroyer which was blown up by dive bombers. Several smaller craft were disabled and put out of action and a relatively large number of defending planes were lost.

American casualties in the Hawaii attack were listed at 3,000 according to official reports to Washington, including 1,500 dead and 1,500 injured. These figures, while from official sources, are incomplete at this writing. A large percentage of the casualties on Oahu were army and navy personnel.

Admiral Stark, chief of operations, in a report to the secretary of the navy, declared that the United States navy is entirely "adequate" to meet the situation in the Pacific and said that it was growing stronger daily.

From the White House came a pronouncement that heavy reinforcements in planes and fighting equipment were being rushed to Hawaii to be thrown into the battle against the Japanese invaders.

Soviet Ambassador Maxim Litvinoff arrived in Washington Sunday and was immediately received by President Roosevelt, at which time he presented his credentials. After conferring for sometime with the president he told reporters that of course the principal topic of conversation was the Japanese situation.

It was also announced officially in Washington that Manila had been subjected to a terrific bombardment.

The White House also announced that an undetermined number of Japanese submarines had been destroyed but could give no figures on Japan's losses in larger ships and aircraft. The navy department announced that the fight was proceeding on a wide area in the Pacific, including the waters and air surrounding Hawaii, Guam, Wake and the Philippines but could give no details as to the nature of the battle except to say that it was intense in all sectors.

From Honolulu came reports that repairs to damaged air fields and hangers were being rushed and that the defending planes would increase in numbers today and tonight as a result of the refitting of the fields.

PRESIDENT CHARGES JAPAN

President Roosevelt authorized a statement on the situation charging that "Germany obviously pushed Japan into the war to end our lend-lease program. As usual the wish is father to the thought."

It was pointed out by the White House spokesman that Tokyo's news broadcasts over the past 24 hours,

Thailand Battle Still Indecisive, British And Dutch Retaliate

MARINES AS STAKES

HEAVY DAMAGE DENIED

...EDITORIAL...

KEEP YOUR HEADS COOL AND YOUR FEET ON THE GROUND

General Short Now Military Governor Of The Territory

Lieut.-General Walter C. Short has been designated as military governor of Hawaii and the Territory has been under martial law since Sunday night, Colonel Charles R. Lyman, commanding Maui district, announced this morning.

Colonel Lyman is in full command of the Maui district, which includes Molokai and Lanai and has appointed Chief George F. Larsen Jr., as acting provost marshall.

"In martial law there is nothing to alarm the good citizens," Colonel Lyman said in announcing the military setup. "It is the strong arm of the military interposed between him and anarchy and between his home and the horrors of invasion. Success demands the united exertions of the entire Territory, and the direction by a single hand of all defensive means available. Nothing will be omitted which will contribute to this success."

The following orders have been issued by Colonel Lyman for the conduct of life in the Maui district during the duration of the war:

1. All schools closed until further notice. notice. Public schools may be opened at an early date, but all foreign language schools closed indefinitely.

2. No public assemblies, either indoors or outdoors, may be held without permit of the Acting Provost Marshall Larsen, and no permits will be issued except for daylight hours only. Church and other religious meetings may be held without permit in daylight hours only, provided they are open to the public at all times, and held in their regularly established meeting places.

3. No communication by any means with the enemy will be tolerated.

4. Telephone communications are restricted to matters of urgent necessity only, and no conversations will be tolerated relative to discussion of the present military situation on Maui or elsewhere. All calls to be as brief as possible. Any person violating this rule will be subject to summary action, and possible removal of his telephone.

5. All radio transmitters, except authorized Army, Navy, and Police, and such persons acting under direct orders of official agencies, are ordered to remain silent, and all portable transmission apparatus is ordered delivered to the Acting Provost Marshall immediately.

6. All owners or keepers of carrier pigeons are to report to Chief Larsen the location and number of pigeons in their possession, and

Maui News, December 8, 1941

Mr. John T. Moir

Bataan, Corregidor

The United States never expected to hold all of the Philippine Islands. Prewar plans called for the defense of the Bataan Peninsula and finally the island of Corregidor in the mouth of Manila Bay until eventual relief should arrive. The islands were attacked a few hours after Pearl Harbor, and most American aircraft were destroyed on the ground. After the Japanese landing on Luzon, Gen Douglas MacArthur conducted a skillful but belated withdrawal into Bataan. This left him with large numbers of troops, many of them untrained, but short of supplies.

Nonetheless, the Americans conducted a tenacious holding action, although there was no real chance of relief. The final Japanese assault was opened on April 3, 1942, and a week later twelve thousand Americans and sixty-four thousand Filipinos, all of them starving and disease-ridden, surrendered. In the notorious "Bataan Death March," as many as ten thousand may have died on their way to prison camps.

Corregidor lasted another month under constant artillery and air bombardment. Japanese landings were made on May 5, and within two days the island was overrun. Gen Jonathan Wainwright, MacArthur's successor, was forced to surrender both his own troops and the remaining isolated garrisons in the other islands. Numerically, the heroic defense of Bataan and Corregidor was the worst defeat of the war for the United States.

Facing page:

A prisoner of war

Life-size figures by Studio EIS, Brooklyn, New York

Photograph by Elliot Schwartz

Maj George Fisher, U.S. Army, Plumville, Pennsylvania

Sept 19, 1941

Dear Jean,
So the little "whooping cough" bug caught up with you. Do be a brave girl and take your medicine. It is just another kind of bug and gets in your throat instead of outside. Why not have mummie get you innoculated against diphtheria? perhaps that would help.

By the time this gets to you you will be up and back to school. You will have to study hard now to catch up. But do not forget that everything you get out of life is paid for either in regrets or leisure time. It is worth just what you put out for it.

Did you have a cake for your birthday? How many of the candles did you blow out the first time? How blows did it take? Did you find any money in the cake?

I miss you very much. Let's pretend tonight that I'm there to get a good night hug & kiss from you. Remember me in your prayers.

Daddy

Letter, Maj George Fisher, U.S. Army, to his daughter Jean, September 19, 1941

Just four months after writing this letter to his young daughter, Major Fisher was killed at the village of Abucay in the Philippine Islands.

Mrs. Jean Fisher Hall

Telegram, Adjutant General to Mrs. George Fisher, March 25, 1942

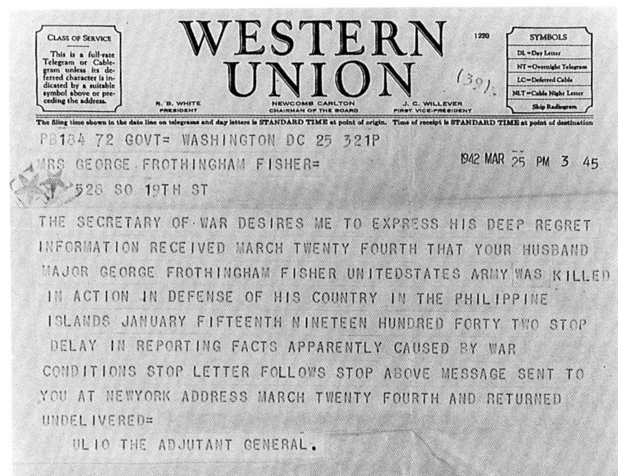

CLASS OF SERVICE
This is a full-rate Telegram or Cablegram unless its deferred character is indicated by a suitable symbol above or preceding the address.

WESTERN UNION

1220

SYMBOLS
DL = Day Letter
NT = Overnight Telegram
LC = Deferred Cable
NLT = Cable Night Letter
Ship Radiogram

R. B. WHITE, PRESIDENT — NEWCOMB CARLTON, CHAIRMAN OF THE BOARD — J. C. WILLEVER, FIRST VICE-PRESIDENT

The filing time shown in the date line on telegrams and day letters is STANDARD TIME at point of origin. Time of receipt is STANDARD TIME at point of destination

(39).

PB184 72 GOVT= WASHINGTON DC 25 321P

MRS GEORGE FROTHINGHAM FISHER= 1942 MAR 25 PM 3 45

528 SO 19TH ST

THE SECRETARY OF WAR DESIRES ME TO EXPRESS HIS DEEP REGRET INFORMATION RECEIVED MARCH TWENTY FOURTH THAT YOUR HUSBAND MAJOR GEORGE FROTHINGHAM FISHER UNITEDSTATES ARMY WAS KILLED IN ACTION IN DEFENSE OF HIS COUNTRY IN THE PHILIPPINE ISLANDS JANUARY FIFTEENTH NINETEEN HUNDRED FORTY TWO STOP DELAY IN REPORTING FACTS APPARENTLY CAUSED BY WAR CONDITIONS STOP LETTER FOLLOWS STOP ABOVE MESSAGE SENT TO YOU AT NEWYORK ADDRESS MARCH TWENTY FOURTH AND RETURNED UNDELIVERED=

ULIO THE ADJUTANT GENERAL.

Sept 1.9.1941

Dear Jean,

So the little "whooping cough" bug caught up with you. Do be a brave girl and take your medicine. It is just another kind of bug and get in your throat instead of outside. Why not have mummie get you innoculated against diphtheria? perhaps that would help.

By the time this gets to you you will be up and back to school. You will have to study hard now to catch up. But do not forget that everything you get out of life is paid for either in regrets or leisure time. It is worth just what you put out for it.

Did you have a cake for your birthday? How many of the candles did you blow out the first time? How blows did it take? Did you find any money in the cake?

I miss you very much. Let's pretend tonight that I'm there to get a good night hug & kiss from you. Remember me in your prayers.

Daddy

Transcript selection made from diary entries for December 8, 10, 11, 21, 24, 25, 26, 30, 31

[Dec. 8, 1941] *Message from Far East Hq. at 4:25 A.M. this date that Japan had started hostilities by bombing U.S. Fleet in Pearl Harbor - Notified by radio that state of War with Japan exists. Heavy air raid on Clark Field. T.O. 12:36 to 12:50 Pm. Casualties: - 13 - B17's. 22 P40's. Military - 53 killed (incl 6 off.) 93 wounded. Civil. 29 killed 18 wounded Total 193 k&w.*

[Dec. 10] ... *Enemy landed at Apparri and Vigan Para-troops landed near Arrayatt. & Mabalacat. 26 cav sent out to destroy them. Manila & Iba heavily bombed.*

[Dec. 11] ... *I destroyed the docks at Masinlock* ...

[Dec. 21] *A very dark day - Enemy landed in force south of San Fernando* ... *Pilipine Army troops did not hold. Moved 26" Cav. forward.*

[Dec. 24] *26" Cav again held when Philippine army Infantry ran away. A devoted little band of about 200 cavalrymen held Binaloan against heavy attacks by Inf -, tanks and air from day light till 3: 30 PM. I was in this fight with them -*

[Dec. 25] *A bleak Christmas. I am more proud of the Cavalry today than ever in my life. By battle casualties (No stragglers) they are now cut down to 127 men and about ten officers. They have 9 officers killed. Many wounded. I withdrew tonight behind the Agno Riv.*

[Dec. 26] *Went to Pampanga Dugar central at Bamban - Divisions withdrew as per schedule....*

[Dec. 30] *Gen. Stephens Div, 91st Heavily attacked at 7:00 am and 5:30 Pm. by Cav. anty & Inf. His men did not behave well. Retreated about 15 miles east of Pampanga river....*

[Dec. 31] *Gen. Jones with some troops of South Luzon Force arrived at Pibardiel in A.m.... ordered him to withdraw when all S.L.F. had cleared. To have the bridge at Calumpit blown and to have Stevens hold the Right bank of the River till further orders. I intend to start a general withdrawal to Bataan tomorrow night. Jan 1, 1942 -*

Diary, Lt Gen Jonathan Wainwright, U.S. Army, December, 1941

Through General Wainwright's diary the story of the deteriorating American position on the island of Luzon is told.

U.S. Army Military History Institute

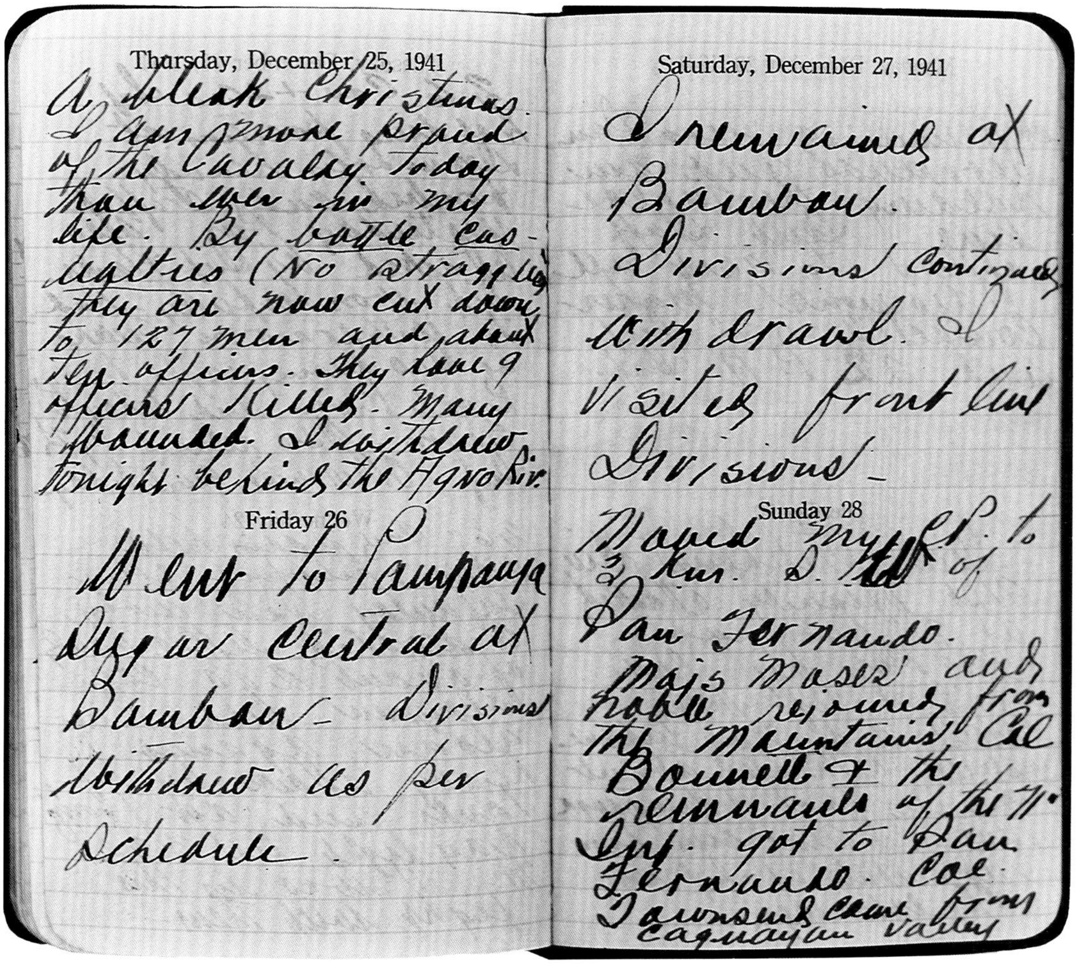

Thursday, December 25, 1941

A bleak Christmas. I am more proud of the Cavalry today than ever in my life. By battle casualties (No stragglers) they are now cut down to 127 men and about ten officers. They lost 9 officers killed. Many wounded. I withdrew tonight behind the Agno Riv.

Friday 26

Went to Pampanga Sugar Central at Bamban. Divisions withdrew as per schedule.

Saturday, December 27, 1941

I remained at Bamban. Divisions continued withdrawal. I visited front line Divisions.

Sunday 28

Moved my CP to 3 km. N of San Fernando. Majs Moses and Noble rejoined from the Mountains. Col Bonnett & the remnants of the 71st Inf. got to San Fernando. Col. Townsend came from Cagayan Valley

Col Clifford Bluemel, U.S. Army, Trenton, New Jersey

My dear Elsie,
... We were waiting in reserve at this place, called Guitol, expecting to go in the line to relieve the Phil Div. The next day we organized an all around defense with fox holes. After dark the Japs attacked. They have peculiar proceedures. They signal their movements on a drum. A drum was heard close to our lines, an american officer threw a hand grenade in that direction, no more drum. They shot fire crackers from mortars so as to land in rear of our lines. All our men had been cautioned about the fire crackers. One package lit on a soldiers head. They harrased us all night. Some of there machine guns got close so I put 2 75's in action. They fired muzzel bursts and that finished the MA's. At daylight I attempted an attack with a Bn of the 21st Div attached to me but it was too slow getting started so I got no results. The Japs carry away their dead and wounded....

Letter, Col Clifford Bluemel, U.S. Army, to Mrs. Bluemel, February 7, 1942

Colonel Bluemel, the commander of the Thirty-first Division of the Philippine Army, describes being attacked by the Japanese during the night. Bluemel was later taken prisoner.

Special Collections, United States Military Academy Library

When we were not actually operating, we were patching rubber gloves and putting up supplies and sterilizing them. We would see the firing in the distance and figure about how many hours—usually one to four—before we would be receiving more patients.

From *Warrior in White* by Lucy Wilson Jopling, 2d Lt. U.S. Army

2d Lt Lucy Wilson, U.S. Army, Tyler, Texas

Mrs. Lucy Wilson Jopling

... A one thousand pounder struck along the walls and curved the overhanging roof into rolls like the curvature of a China pagoda. Strips of corrugated tin roof scattered around crazily like bits of waste paper. Telephone lines went down as though by command. The steel rail and ties of the local street car line were torn upward and twisted like a hairpin. A five hundred burst took off the roof of my quarters. The lawn became a gaping, smoking crater. The sky began to turn from blue to mottled gray.

Then came strafing and again the bombing. Always they followed the same pattern. Their own orders could not have enlightened me more. What I learned I used to advantage later. They kept it up for three hours. There was a constant screaming and throbbing of dive bombers, the hailstone rattle of machine gun bullets, the sharp crack of anti-aircraft guns. Then they left in the artificial gloom of the pulverized dust that rose from the tortured earth like a fog. I left, too, very promptly, and established headquarters in the Malinta tunnel. There were three cottages nearby. One had been assigned the High Commissioner, the second to the Quezons, and I now took the third.

The so called tunnel was, in fact, a wide driveway, with street car tracks, cut at an incline through the rocks. Lateral shafts radiated from this central artery, some used as hospital wards, others as storerooms and ammunition magazines....

Autograph manuscript, page from *Reminiscences* by Gen Douglas MacArthur, U.S. Army, 1964

Under constant attack by the Japanese, MacArthur moved his headquarters to Malinta Tunnel, the terminal point of a streetcar line deep within the rocks of Corregidor.

The General Douglas MacArthur Memorial

blue to mottled gray.
Then came strafing and again the bombing.
Always they followed the same pattern. Their own
orders could not have enlightened me more. What I
learned I used to advantage later. They kept it up
for three hours. There was a constant screaming
and throbbing of dive bombers, the hailstone
rattle of machine gun bullets, the sharp crack of
anti-aircraft guns. Then they left in the
artificial gloom of the pulverized dust that
rose from the tortured earth like a fog. I left, too,
very promptly, and established headquarters in
the Malinta tunnel. There were three cottages
nearby. One had been assigned the High Commissioner,
the second to the Quezons, and I now took the third

... A second endlessly recurring charge centered on the fact that the Cantonese nurse, AhChen, was taken out in preference to some American. Ever since Arthur was born this amah had been an intimate member of the family. If and when Corregidor finally succumbed, it was certain that this Chinese woman would be singled out for special torture and slow death.

I had decided to try and pierce the blockade with PT boats rather than go under with a submarine. We still had four of these craft left comprising Motor Torpedo Boat Squadron No. 3, under the command of Lieutenant John D. Bulkely. They were numbered 32, 34, 35 and the flagship 41. I called in Bulkely and we worked out the plan of operation. If discovered there was no intention of running but to attack.

The PTs, seventy feet of light plywood from stem to stern, were powered by Packard motors which after long and arduous service were clogged with carbon and rust, but still capable of outrunning a Japanese cruiser or destroyer. Each boat had torpedoes fore and aft, making sixteen in all. There is nothing that a cruiser fears more than a torpedo. Bulkely planned the formation of the four boats, a lozenge figuration predicated on their fire power. If a Japanese cruiser spotted us, the plan was to launch an immediate attack, spreading a torpedo pattern in simultaneous salvos and depend on superior high speed maneuverability.

I sent for General Wainwright who was to be left in command, to tell him goodbye. He had been a plebe at West Point when I was a first class man and I had had much to do with his early military development. He became the First Captain of the class of 1900. A fine soldierly figure, he had already done wonders in the campaign, and was popular with both officers and men "Jim," I told him, "hold on till I come back for you." I was to come back, but it would be too late—too late for those battling men in the foxholes of Bataan, too late for the valiant gunners at the batteries of Corregidor, too late for Jim Wainwright.

Autograph manuscript, page from *Reminiscences* by Gen Douglas MacArthur, U.S. Army, 1964

General MacArthur was urged by President Roosevelt to turn over his command in the Philippines and leave the island. Lt Gen Jonathan Wainwright was left in command of the encircled armies on Bataan and Corregidor.

The General Douglas MacArthur Memorial

... Apr 18 - More corpses along road from Lamao to ______, Jap artillery moving south Capt. Steigler & two men pulled out of ranks just north of Orion for having Jap money & souvenirs in possession - He heard later they were killed - ran most of the way to Pilar as our heavy guns firing fr Corregidor Guards using horse whips & clubs especially on Sr. officers. Moved on to Balanga (129) for night's stop. Water allowed at Pilar only.

Apr 19 - Remained at Balanga - Jap detail takes most of canteens away. Given moldy rice at dusk - first food - buried five Filipinos.

Apr 20 - ... F's shot along road - Filipino [c]ivilians giving away food regardless o[f Jap thr]eats.... In compound there merciless b[eatin]gs.

Apr 21 - Left at daylight for Lubao. Saw bombers bound for Corregidor. More F shot ... Long halts in sun usual [pro]cedure....

[Ap]r 22 - Set out to Lubao - Straggling F's a menace, [caus]ing beatings, double timing, stop & go & prevented [gettin]g water....

Diary written on cigarette paper during Death March, by Col Albert Svihra, U.S. Army, April 12 to April 31, 1942

Defeated by starvation and disease as well as by the Japanese forces, American and Filipino troops on the Bataan peninsula were forced to march to Camp O'Donnell, where they were held as prisoners. Colonel Svihra's notes convey some of the horrors of that time.

Special Collections, United States Military Academy Library

Apr 13-25 Maj. M. J. Dunmyer
– noticed a few bodies on road proceeding
from 166.5 to Lamao 152. Corpses at Cabcaben

Apr 18 – More corpses along road
from Lamao to ———; Jap artillery moving
south. Capt Stiegler + two men pulled out
of ranks just north of Orani for having Jap
money + souvenirs in possession – He heard later
they were killed – ran most of way to Pilar
as our heavy guns firing fm Corregidor.
Guards using horsewhips + clubs especially
on Sr officers. Moved on to Balanga (129)
for night's stop; water allowed at Pilar only

Apr 19 – Remained at Balanga – Japs took [illegible]
most of canteens away. Given moldy rice at
dusk – [illegible] buried live Filipinos

Apr 20 – More F's buried – frisking [illegible]
left about noon – F's shot along road – [illegible]
civilians giving away food regardless [illegible]
[illegible]ats. (Had no canteen) Arrived [illegible]
[illegible]k. In compound where merciless [illegible]

Apr 21 – Left [illegible] for
Lubao [illegible] bound for
Corregidor. Most of the Jap
supply compound [illegible] with [illegible]
food [illegible] in sun [illegible]
[illegible] Reached Lacienda (100) NE of Lipa
[illegible] at 2.00 P.M. Stayed there the night

[illegible] 22 – Set out to Lubao. Straggling F's a menace,
[illegible]ing beatings, double timing, stop + go + prevented
[illegible]g water. Herded in to house at Lubao (86)
[illegible] on outside. All F's and A's crowded in w'house
[illegible] night/w all doors closed. Amer in corner which
[illegible] been used as latrine. Over score dead next AM

[illegible]r 23 – Resumed march 7:00 AM. w/o sufficient
[illegible]ne to eat b'fast (rice) – F's running + crawling to
water sources. "Heat" treatment. Arrived SF (70)
+ put in school yard – best so far

Prisoners with their hands tied behind their backs during the Bataan Death March

National Archives and Records Administration

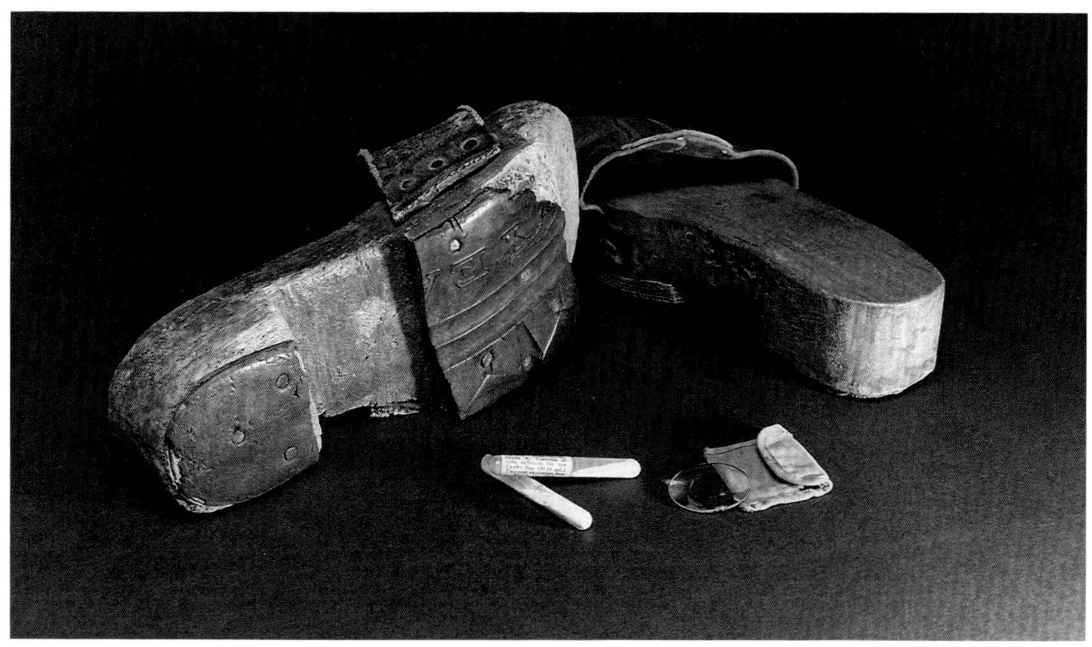

Ampules of chlorine water purifer for canvas water bags used by prisoners at Bilibid Prison
Burning glass, a lens from a vision-testing set, used by prisoners at Bilibid Prison to start small cooking fires
Wooden "go-ahead" shoes, made from mahogany and the backs of old shoes, with rubber cut from old tires for the soles, worn by Capt Paul Ashton, Medical Corps, as a prisoner

Dr. Paul L. Ashton, M.D.

Capt Paul Ashton, Medical Corps, San Francisco, California

URGENT

From: *Fort Mills*
To: *Chief of Staff*

No Number May 6, 1942

For the President of the United States. With broken heart and head bowed in sadness but not in shame I report to your Excellency that today I must arrange terms for the surrender of the fortified islands of Manila Bay (Corregidor) (Fort Hughes) (Fort Drum) and—

Radiogram, Lt Gen Jonathan Wainwright, U.S. Army, to the War Department, May 6, 1942

General Wainwright sent this final radiogram before surrendering. Communications were broken before clarification of the last section could be received.

U.S. Army Military History Institute

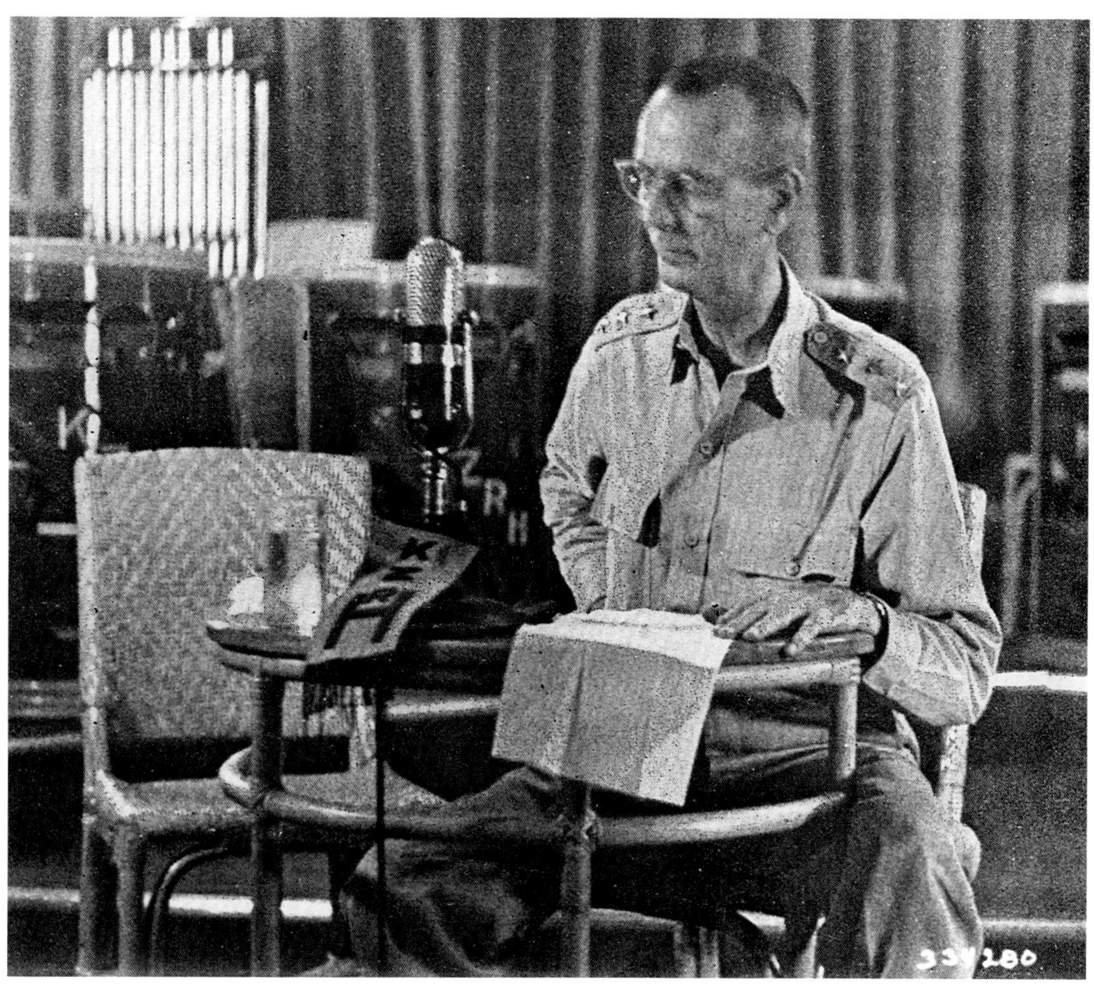

General Wainwright announces the surrender of Corregidor.

National Archives and Records Administration

11:15 am
The flag of truce was carried out by a Marine officer of the East Sector

Meanwhile all records of value to the enemy, secret maps, papers, diaries, etc were destroyed.

A detail under Maj SM Mellnik placed a barricade of trucks and other vehicles across the road at east entrance to Malinta Tunnel.

Disregarding the flag of truce, artillery fire, dive bombing and MG fire continued unabated.

1:30 P
The Marine officer returned to Malinta Tunnel with the word that Gen Wainwright should come out to him to discuss terms.

2:00 P
Gen Wainwright and Gen Moore accompanied by their aides and under a white flag proceeded by car to the foot of Kindley Field water tank hill where they left car and walked up the hill to meet the Nipponese commander.

Dead and dying were on every hand, the proportion being about 3 Nipponese for one American. Arrangements were made for Gen Wainwright and party to be taken to Bataan to meet Gen Homma....

***Log of Events on Day of Surrender* at Corregidor,**
Col Theodore Mosher Chase, U.S. Army, May 6, 1942
As duty station officer, Colonel Chase kept a record of the surrender.

Special Collections, United States Military Academy Library

Holding up a white flag, American troops surrender to the Japanese at Corregidor, May 1942.

National Archives and Records Administration

Flight jacket worn by 2d Lt Henry A. Potter, navigator on the lead bomber

Col Henry A. Potter, USAF (Ret.)

Replica of "Mark Twain" bombsight used by Doolittle Raiders
Originally developed by Captain Ross Greening, this simple bombsight was designed for use under four thousand feet. Its nickname refers to the "led line" depthfinder used on old Mississippi riverboats. None of the original bombsights survived the raid. This replica has been approved—and inscribed—by the surviving raiders.

Reproduced by Lt Col Horace E. Crouch, USAF (Ret.)

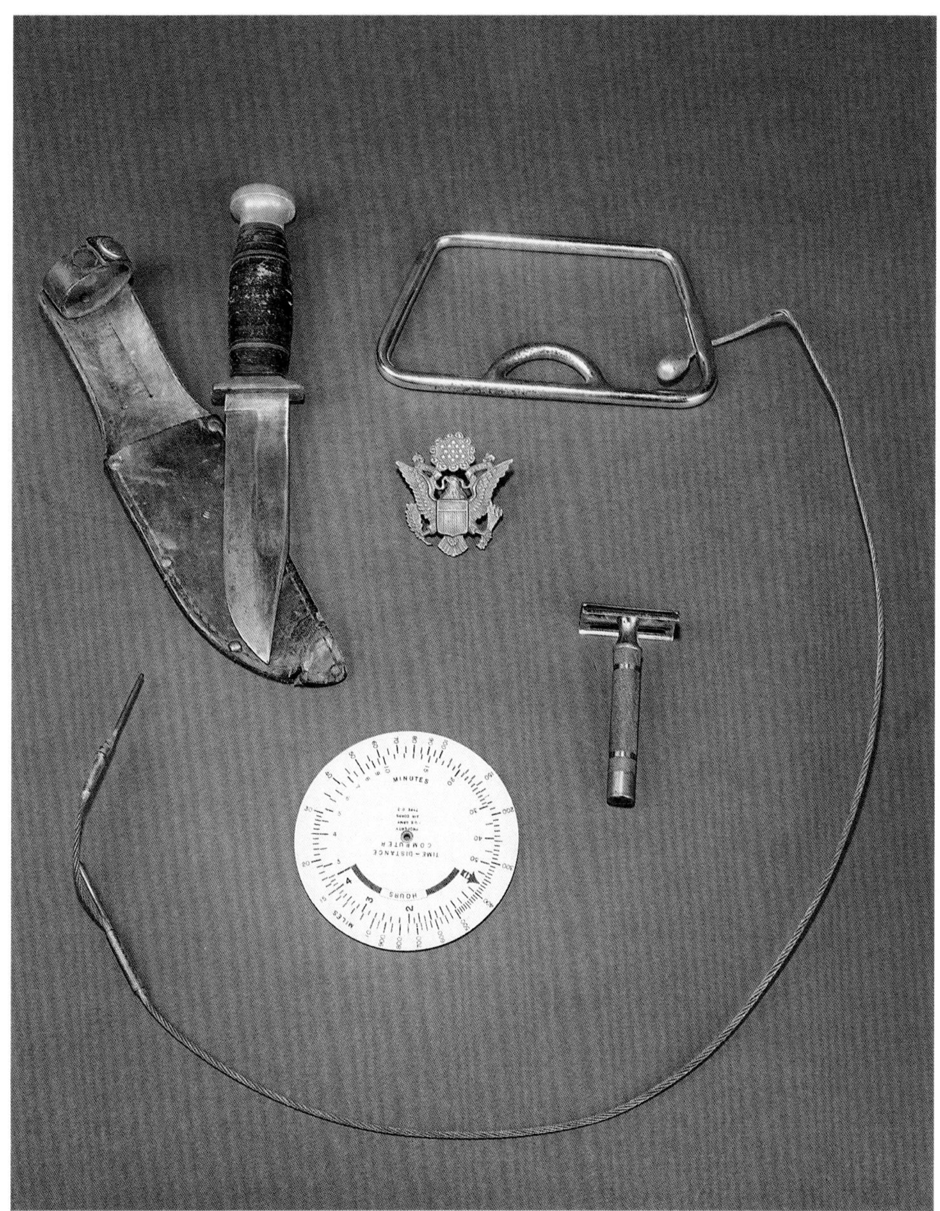

Ripcord and handle from parachute, survival knife, and time-distance computer used by 1st Lt Richard E. Cole

Mr. Richard E. Cole

Safety razor and officer's insignia recovered from one of the B-25 bombers that crashed in China after the crew had bailed out

Mr. Bryan Moon, Expedition Leader, 1990 Doolittle Raiders China Expedition

May 4, 1942.

Dear Folks:

I haven't the slightest idea when you will get this letter, but hope it will be soon. I realize you are probably both worried an wondering as to my whereabouts and saftey. The long silence on my part was imparative and someday you will know why. I cannot say where we are, but can tell you that I am and have been well and happy and hope you are the same.

It is pretty hard to write a letter without writing about your activities, but I guess it's O.K. to tell you that I have had my first taste of combat and find it not too bad. "Lady Luck" is still riding on my shoulder an I hope she stays there in the future.

I have no present address so you cannot write me and will have to be content with my letters when I get a chance to send them. Remember, I think about you as much as you think about me and silence on my part does not mean otherwise. Are there a lot of strawberries this year? Boy! Would I like to have some. I suppose the "Reds are beating the Cards" as usual this year — Hey Pop!. The last four weeks have vindicated my life-long opinion — that there is no place as good as the United States — No Place —

My regards to everyone and all my love to you

Dick

Letter, 1st Lt Richard E. Cole, U.S. Army Air Corps, to his parents, Mr. and Mrs. Fred Cole, May 4, 1942

Now that the raid on Tokyo has taken place, Dick Cole is able to share with his parents a little of the exhilaration which he feels.

Mr. Richard E. Cole

WAR DEPARTMENT
WASHINGTON

May 20, 1942

Mrs. Fred Cole
747 Faulkner Avenue
Dayton, Ohio

Dear Mrs. Cole:

I am pleased to report that Dick is well and happy although a bit homesick. I left him in Chungking, in China, a couple of weeks ago. He had recently completed a very hazardous, extremely important and most interesting flight — the air raid on Japan. He comported himself with conspicuous bravery and distinction. He was awarded the Distinguished Flying Cross for gallantry in action, and also was decorated by the Chinese Government.

Transportation and communication facilities are extremely bad in the Far East and so it may be sometime before you hear again from Dick directly. I assure you, however, that everything is going smoothly with him and although plans for the future are uncertain he will probably be returning home sometime in the not too distant future.

I am proud to have served with Dick, who was my co-pilot on the flight, and hope that I may have an opportunity to serve with him again.

Very sincerely yours,

J. H. Doolittle

J. H. Doolittle
Brigadier General, U.S.A.

Letter, Brig Gen J. H. Doolittle, U.S. Army Air Corps, to Mrs. Fred Cole, May 20, 1942
Out of concern for the relatives of his men, General Doolittle takes time to write to the family of each man who took part in the raid.

Mr. Richard E. Cole

Coral Sea, Midway

The Battles of the Coral Sea and Midway, in May and June of 1942, marked the end of an era in naval warfare and signaled the turn of the tide in the Pacific war. In the Coral Sea, the Americans and Japanese traded aircraft carriers; at Midway, the Americans sank four Japanese carriers in return for one of their own. Henceforth, with a few notable exceptions, the aircraft carrier instead of the battleship was to be the arbiter of naval warfare. From this time on, American production of ships and aircraft, and training of pilots, so rapidly outpaced the Japanese that they never regained their superiority of early 1942.

At the Coral Sea the Japanese were attempting to attack Port Moresby, on the south coast of New Guinea, and were turned back by a successful American ambush. At Midway, they attempted to take that little island, westernmost of the Hawaiian chain, and were again ambushed, beaten far more severely, and turned back. In both battles the Americans enjoyed the advantage of having broken Japanese codes, a breakthrough that contributed a major factor to the victory. But they also utilized inferior resources more cleverly and more carefully than their opponents. In war, where few things are clear, seldom has victory been better deserved or more distinctly perceived than in these two battles.

Facing page:

Douglas Dauntless A24 dive-bombers in flight during the Battle of Midway, June 4th to 6th, 1942. The Japanese cruiser *Mikuma* is shown burning at the center of the photograph.

National Archives and Records Administration

Fire Controlman Clifford M. Dunn, Jr., U.S. Navy, Cisco, Texas

[May 8, 1942] … *1700—Lex. signals that she she is standing by to abandon ship. Fire completely out of control and several small explosions occur -*
1741—Officers & men of Lex. abandon ship and are picked up by destroyers and cruisers standing close by—She is now burning furiously in the twilight and sinking by the bow—A fighting ship but now beyond hope of recovery or repair …

It's getting quite dark now and the flames finally reach the planes on her stern that couldn't get off … Ammunition left in the guns along flight deck explodes and the tracers shoot up in the sky as if someone was still firing them—She is now completely covered by flames and her hull is white hot, lighting up the sky & water for miles around—Colors were dipped for her as she lay there burning so brightly in the night.

More violent explosions and she starts to sink slowly—As the cold water hits the white hot steel is flares up … 1950—She is almost down when a great explosion shakes her and she settles into the ocean—More explosions occur as she goes on down under the surface and can be felt aboard here …

The USS Lexington sank in the Coral Sea, May 8, 1942 in Latitude 15° 18' 00" S—Longitude 155° 33' 30" E—Her crew, officers, and men totaled approximately 2600 and out of that number 2300 were saved …

Diary, Fire Controlman Clifford M. Dunn, Jr., U.S. Navy, May 8, 1942

Mr. Clifford M. Dunn, Jr.

DUNN, C.M. FC3/c (FRIDAY MAY 8, 1942)

U.S.S. PORTLAND

JAPANESE AIR ATTACK ON TASK FORCE 17 DURING THE BATTLE OF THE CORAL SEA –
"SINKING OF U.S.S. LEXINGTON"

1114 – Enemy torpedo planes sighted –

1117 – Enemy torpedo planes attacked carriers.

1118 – First at…

1119 – Increase… maneuver… enemy a…

1120 – Destroyer… down plan… into flam… into sea…

1121 – Enemy t… launched… Lexington… port side…

1122 – Heavy… pouring a… Now listin… Another t… on stbd… turns he… Enemy di…

-4-

1145 – Violent explosions forward on Lex. and fire breaks out again. She reverses course so as to move downwind.

1155 – Lex. burning badly and now stopped, lying to. Destroyers + Cruisers stand by. Crew fighting fire gallantly but it seems hopeless. All ships circle her + wait.

1200 – 1600. Crew still fighting fire but it is out of control.

1700 – Lex. signals that she she is standing by to abandon ship. Fire completely out of control and several small explosions occur.

1741 – Officers + men of Lex. abandon ship and are picked up by destroyers and cruisers standing close by. She is now burning furiously in the twilight and sink-

Following the Battle of the Coral Sea, a severely crippled USS *Lexington* burns while members of her crew leap from the deck into the Pacific.

National Archives and Records Administration

Navy torpedo planes swarm around the burning and disabled Japanese aircraft carrier *Shoho* during the Battle of the Coral Sea. The *Shoho* was the only Japanese carrier lost in the battle.

National Archives and Records Administration

A Japanese torpedo plane plummets toward the Pacific as smoke pours from under the fuselage.

National Archives and Records Administration

This frame from a captured newsreel shows a Japanese torpedo plane taking off from the flight deck of a carrier as crew members wave from the bridge.

National Archives and Records Administration

NORTH IOWA'S DAILY PAPER EDITED FOR THE HOME

Mason City Globe-Gazette

"THE NEWSPAPER THAT MAKES ALL NORTH IOWANS NEIGHBORS"

HOME EDITION

VOL. XLVIII — MASON CITY, IOWA, FRIDAY, JUNE 5, 1942 — THIS PAPER CONSISTS OF TWO SECTIONS SECTION ONE — NO. 203

MIDWAY BATTERS ENEMY

Jap Battleship, Aircraft Carrier Damaged by Defenders

1,000 or More RAF Planes Raid France

UNCHALLENGED BY LUFTWAFFE IN DAY SWEEPS

Targets Along Nazi-Held Coast, North France Hit

Six Months Ahead of Schedule

Wheeled into the open during the noon lunch period, this four-engined Boeing B-17 "Flying Fortress" bomber is inspected by hundreds of Vega Aircraft corporation employes who helped build her at Burbank, Cal. The young Vega factory, newest of southern California's major aircraft plants, is six months ahead of schedule with the B-17's being manufactured under a pooled facilities agreement with Boeing and Douglas companies.

Japs Warned Against Use of Poison Gas

WASHINGTON, (AP) — President Roosevelt told Friday of official information that Japan was using poison gas against China and grimly declared that if the Japanese persisted in this form of warfare, the United States would mete out "retaliation in kind and in full measure."

The reports that Japan on several occasions had resorted to gas warfare were described by the chief executive to his press conference as authoritative. He read a brief formal statement, which he said the state department had prepared, making it unequivocally clear that the United States would consider the use of gas against China or any other united nation as an action against the United States.

The text of the statement follows:

"Authoritative reports are reaching this government of the use by Japanese armed forces in various localities of China of poisonous or noxious gases. I desire to make it unmistakably clear that, if Japan persists in this inhuman form of warfare against China or against any other of the united nations, such action will be regarded by this government as though taken against the United States, and retaliation in kind and in full measure will be meted

Jap Attacks Indicate Axis General Drive

By DeWITT MACKENZIE
Wide World War Analyst

Expansion of the Japanese raid on Dutch Harbor into an attack on our Midway island, with heavy naval and air forces, compels us to take a wider view of these operations and note they are further indications that we are on the verge of a general axis onslaught which will try to force a decision in the world war this year.

* * *

While the precise purpose of the Japanese raids is still in doubt, they fit in perfectly with the signs that the axis volcano is about to erupt. Certainly the fact that the Japs struck at little Midway in strength, even employing a battleship, would seem to indicate that they are bent on something more than hit-and-run raids. They are building towards a climax.

Also a part of this broad picture is the thus far unsuccessful but determined offensive of wily nazi Marshal Rommel in an effort to get set for a drive against Egypt and the Suez canal across the Libyan sands. That is an integral item in the Hitlerian strategy for conquering the middle east and thus reaching the supplies which Germany must have.

* * *

In short, the nazi fuehrer is about to strike, and his allies and henchmen are coming into action.

Any day now we may expect him to launch against the Muscovites that much advertised "spring" offensive which has been so long delayed that summer already is edging on to the southern Russian steppes. We are on the verge of the conflict which bids to be the greatest and bloodiest of history, for upon its course depends in major degree the outcome of the entire world war, both in Europe and the Pacific.

* * *

Private advices state that the nazi chief has ready for action some 200 divisions of fresh troops —say in the neighborhood of two and three-quarter million men. There are in addition to the millions and a half who have been holding the long Russian line during the past fierce winter of Napoleonic tragedy. They are resting on new arms which have been pouring from the hard pushed factories of Germany and the occupied countries.

* * *

Then we have that vast nazi air fleet which has been largely idle for months. Hitler apparently has been husbanding and adding to his aerial striking power for coming events. The strength of this armada is, of course, problematical but military experts are agreed that it is a mighty force.

All this sounds formidable— and indeed it is. Any allied complacency because of recent successes certainly would be badly misplaced, and it should be emphasized that the allied high command is in no way underrating Hitler's strength.

What we can note with satisfaction is that drawn up against him is a Russian force which numerically is superior. Whether the reds are equipped to withstand the mechanized German onslaught cannot be answered in advance of the event.

We can say, though, that if the Russians can hold the Germans— keep them from breaking through to the resources of the Caucasus and middle east—then the allies will have Herr Hitler neatly speared on the toasting fork. In other words the reds don't have to roll the Hitlerites back and invade Germany at this juncture in order to achieve ultimate victory.

Furious Fight for Possession of Tiny Island in Progress

HONOLULU, (AP) — American defenders, spurred by initial successes, closed battle Friday with a strong Japanese sea-air task force in what may be a finish fight for possession of Midway island.

Already the island garrison had scored hits on an enemy battleship, an aircraft carrier and possibly other war vessels. Raiding planes were brought down in great number.

And, said Admiral Chester W. Nimitz, commander-in-chief of the Pacific fleet, "our attacks on the enemy are continuing."

* * *

This latest assault on the tiny island outpost, last line of defense before Hawaii itself, began shortly after dawn Thursday.

It found the American forces keyed to fighting pitch by long preparation and patently strengthened in the months since they first repulsed such an attack Dec. 7.

It found them alert and forewarned by the preceding day's raid upon Dutch Harbor, 2,000 miles to the north. It seemed the enemy may have stepped unwittingly into a spot too hot to handle.

* * *

But it also appeared strongly possible the Japanese did not intend this as a hit-and-run affair, like their five preceding forays against Midway.

Presence of capital ships in the attacking force and the heavy toll the defenders were able to exact in the first few hours of the operation suggested the enemy was at hand with the sole purpose of taking over the island, completely and finally.

And Midway, with the tradition of Wake island as its guide, was obviously in no mind to let the issue go by default.

* * *

Admiral Nimitz' communique indicated the Americans' first success was achieved at little cost to themselves. He reported that damage to materiel and installations on the island, 1,149 miles northwest of Hawaii, was minor.

* * *

"No reports of personnel casualties were received," the communique added.

Nor did the admiral clarify which units of the United States defenders delivered the telling blows against the Jap battleship and carrier.

"The attack was repulsed by local defenders in which all armed services are represented," he said, indicating that marine, sea and air forces were in action.

The admiral's communique told this terse story:

"At 6:35 a. m. today, (Thursday,) Midway time, that island was heavily raided by Japanese carrier-based planes. The attack was repulsed by local defenders

Low Temperature of 64 at Decorah; 98 Reported at Iowa City

DES MOINES, (AP)—Iowa cannot seem to shake off this Turkish bath spell of weather.

Temperatures again pointed to torrid heights Friday after touching a searing 98, the state high, Thursday at Iowa City.

Thursday night's low was 64 at Decorah. There was no rain reported.

The 9 a. m. temperature here Friday was 82.

WANT FARM LABOR

ALBANY, N. Y., (AP)—New York state, pressing for a 5 to 32 per cent expansion of its first war-year crops, will ask every available man from 16 to 50 years old to help harvest them.

21 Killed in Arsenal Blast in Illinois

NAZI WARSHIPS HIT BY BRITISH

Score Hurt in Explosion at Joliet

One-Time Star of Silent Screen Dies

Weather Report

A Japanese naval squadron which attacked Midway island (arrow) was reported by the navy department to have been handed a stinging defeat. Dutch Harbor, Alaska, (circled) had previously been raided by enemy planes. This map locates Dutch Harbor and Midway and shows distances from Japan to various Pacific points.

Mason City Globe-Gazette, June 5, 1942

Lyndon Baines Johnson Library and Museum, National Archives and Records Administration

After being attacked by a task force of U.S. aircraft, this Japanese heavy cruiser of the *Magame* class sits ravaged and burning during the Battle of Midway.

National Archives and Records Administration

Radio compass from a Japanese plane brought down in the Battle of Midway
The compass was made in Waterbury, Connecticut.

Franklin D. Roosevelt Library, National Archives and Records Administration

Seaman's cap

Dwight D. Eisenhower Library,
National Archives and Records Administration

Japanese planes bomb the USS *Yorktown* during the Battle of Midway Island.

National Archives and Records Administration

[June 4, 1942] ... *Received word that enemy was sighted about 120 miles away—Steaming to intercept them—Yorktown launched planes for attack—Planes return about 1330, all except one—Enemy planes contacted & our planes return to intercept them—Dog fights observed on stb'd beam & quarter ... Planes falling like flies to stb'd—Our fighters accounted for about 14 in this dogfight ... Yorktown is hit on stb'd. side of flight deck aft of stack—She turns sharply to port—Heavy smoke & flames pour from her stack—Her guns downed plane that dropped bomb—Another near miss on stern—She's burning pretty badly now and slowing down—Engine rooms evidently hit hard ... Attack repeled—Twenty-four known planes go down & probably more, their attack complete failure except for 1 bomb hit on Yorktown—She is at fire quarters now and is gradually putting out fire ... All inflamibable material thrown over side—Fire is out now & the hole in flight deck has been patched already—Receive signal to standby to take her in tow ... Then to our surprise she signals that her speed is 5 kts, then 10, 12, 15, and finally 17 kts. What a ship!!*

Diary, Fire Controlman Clifford M. Dunn, Jr., U.S. Navy, June 4, 1942
The USS *Yorktown*, already badly damaged and hastily repaired after the Battle of the Coral Sea, stayed afloat after being hit several times at the Battle of Midway.

Mr. Clifford M. Dunn, Jr.

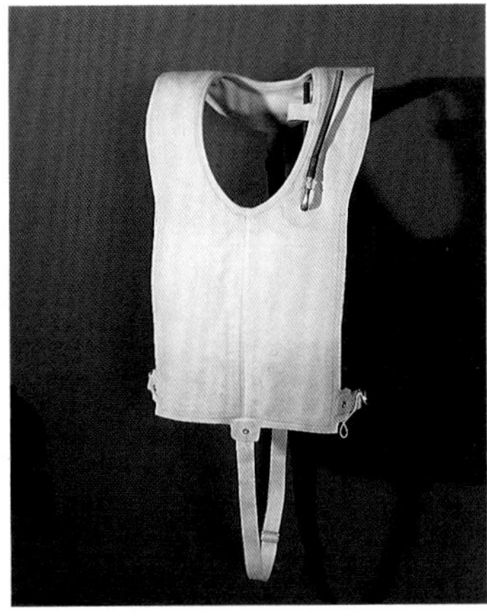

Life vest, Type B-4, popularly known as a "Mae West"

American Airpower Heritage Museum, Inc.

Sinking of U.S.S. Yorktown

Japanese Air attack on Task Force 17 on 4 June -

1403 - Sighted dogfight bearing 0??0

1406 - Cha[...] dodg[...]

1409 - Pla[...] Cam[...]

1413 - Dir[...] nea[...] bur[...] hea[...] off s[...]

1414 - Both[...] pulle[...]

1420 - Attac[...] Jap p[...]

1435 - Frien[...] crash[...] when[...] Pilots[...] by de[...]

1525 - M[...] for t[...] in J[...]

1545 - Yo[...] Sme[...]

5

stack - Her guns downed plane that dropped bomb - Another near miss on stern - She's burning pretty badly now and slowing down - Engine rooms evidently hit hard - Plane goes down on stbd bow + pilot takes to parachute - Attack repeled - Twenty-four known planes go down + probably more, their attack complete failure except for 1 bomb hit on Yorktown - She is at fire quarters now and is gradually putting out fire - She does not have any way on at all - All inflamibable material thrown over side - Fire is out now + the hole in flight deck has been patched already - Receive signal to stand by to take her in tow - Towing gear is broken out - Fire in engine rooms starts to

Electricians Mate Second Class
A. J. Ehlert, U.S. Navy,
Bay City, Texas

[June 4, 1942] ... They put a rope buoy around me and I swam out about 30 yards to help the survivors get aboard. I stayed out there about 30 minets. I them came in next to the ship and tied ropes aroung the survivors so they could be pulled a board. We picked up survivors for about 1 hour. On the last life raft there was a sight I will remember as long as I live. There were about 25 people on the raft to start with and after they all had left it there was one man left in the bottom of it Dead. He had his leg broke in so many places that it was limber like a rag. We left the dead man in the life raft and as we shoved it off our captain Hollered down. "Are you shure that there is no chance for that man to be alive." We told him that there was not. and he went off to his waterie grave. We picked up over 400 survivores.... I gave most all my clothes away to the survivors. It is clamed that 90 perset of the crew was saved—The Yorktown was still afloat and they are going to try to toe it back to Pearl Harbor....

Diary, Electricians Mate Second Class A. J. Ehlert, U.S. Navy, June 4, 1942

Ehlert describes his participation in the rescue of the crew of the USS *Yorktown* at the Battle of Midway. For security reasons, the keeping of diaries was not allowed during the war. Like many others, Ehlert wrote his in the cramped and darkened conditions of his bunk. The *Yorktown* was sunk by a Japanese submarine the next day.

Mrs. A. J. Ehlert

Aboard a listing USS *Yorktown*, crew members and fliers examine the extensive damage inflicted on the ship in the Battle of Midway.

National Archives and Records Administration

North Africa

The war in North Africa began when Mussolini's Italian troops from Libya invaded British-held Egypt in September of 1940. Though the outnumbered British nearly overran Libya in response, they were then distracted into Greece while the Germans sent Erwin Rommel and the Afrika Korps to aid the Italians. The campaign went back and forth several times, first one and then the other side in the ascendant, depending largely upon the availability of supplies. Much of the North African campaign was determined by how well the Allies were keeping the sea lanes open in the Battle of the Atlantic, illustrating the interdependence of the theaters of war.

The climax of this campaign came in October of 1942, when British forces under Lt Gen Sir Bernard Montgomery crushingly defeated the Axis at the Battle of El Alamein and began the final advance westward. Two weeks later, on November 8, Anglo-American forces under Gen Dwight D. Eisenhower landed in French North Africa. The Allied intention was to advance rapidly into Tunisia and pinch out the Axis between Eisenhower and the British from Egypt.

The plan was accomplished eventually, though not before the Germans reinforced Tunisia and delivered some nasty blows, especially at Kasserine Pass to the Americans going into combat for the first time in the war against Germany. It was in Tunisia that George S. Patton emerged as a combat commander, and it was May of 1943 before the campaign was finally, triumphantly completed, with the Axis losing a quarter of a million men and vast amounts of supplies as well. Essentially a campaign of attrition fought on the periphery, North Africa contributed substantially to wearing down the Axis but may have delayed the actual invasion of Europe.

Facing page:

An English soldier equipped for North Africa

Life-size figure by Studio EIS, Brooklyn, New York

Photograph by Elliot Schwartz

German Field Marshal Erwin Rommel with his Fifteenth Panzer Division near Tobruk, Libya. Tobruk's harbor was an extremely valuable supply point that both sides coveted during the fighting in Africa.

National Archives and Records Administration

Compass owned and used by Field Marshal Erwin Rommel in North Africa

Herr Manfred Rommel

Panzergruppe Africa *1-17-42*
Commander-in-chief *rec'd 1-24-42*

Dearest Lu!

The mail is working. Thanks for your dear letters of 1-2 and 12-18. The situation is developing well and my head is full of plans, that I don't dare to share with anybody around me. They would consider me crazy. But I certainly am not. I just see a little further than they do. Well—you know me: our plans are matured early each morning. And how often have they been put into effect in a matter of hours during the last year and in France. It will and should stay that way in the future.

I am thinking of you and Manfred, and I am sending best wishes and a heartfelt kiss

Your Erwin

Letter, Field Marshal Erwin Rommel, Commander, German Afrika Korps, to his wife, January 17, 1942

Herr Manfred Rommel

In the center of a tank battle at Miteiriya Ridge, El Alamein, Egypt, a British tank is ablaze. The smoke on the left is coming from burning German armor.

Imperial War Museum

8-2-42
rec'd: 8-13-42

Dearest Lu!
Still quiet. It seems like the English still have enough from their last attack. Our situation is stabilizing. Tanks and reinforcements are arriving continuously. Holding out in the position of the taken Alemein was the hardest part of all the battles in Africa. Now it looks like we did that too. I am doing fine. We all have the heat diarrhea now, alone it is bearable. A year ago I had jaundice and that was much worse.

It is very reasonable if you all go to Simmering for a few days. It will especially do you good again.

Many heartfelt wishes for both of you and dear kiss
Your Erwin.

The pictures of Obersalzburg are wonderful. I would like to be there some day.

Letter, Field Marshal Erwin Rommel, Commander, German Afrika Korps, to his wife, August 2, 1942

Although the Afrika Korps had fought steadily during the previous months and both officers and men were suffering from disease and exhaustion, Marshal Rommel is still able to lighten the mood of his daily letter home.

Herr Manfred Rommel

2. 8. 42

an: 13.8.42

From: London
To: The President of the United States

No. 142, August 31, 1942

Former Naval person to President personal and secret number one four one.

Rommel has begun the attack for which we have been preparing. An important battle may now be fought.

Prime.

Cable, Prime Minister Winston Churchill to President Franklin D. Roosevelt, August 31, 1942

The British, expecting that Rommel will attempt to break out of the stalemate on the Alamein line, have prepared to meet the attack.

Franklin D. Roosevelt Library, National Archives and Records Administration

English soldiers in mortar positions under attack

Imperial War Museum

Lt Gen Sir Bernard Montgomery stands in the turret of a Grant tank at Tripoli. His army took Tripoli from the Italians in January of 1943.

National Archives and Records Administration

H.Q. Eighth Army
M.E.F.
1-11-42

My dear Tom

I attach a cheque for £300. This should keep you in funds for David and his expenses for about a year, when added on to what you already have. I will always keep you round about the £500 mark.

I am fighting a terrific battle with Rommel. It began on 23 October and he is resisting desperately. I hold the initiative. But it has become a real solid and bloody killing match. I do not think he can go on much longer. I am dealing him a terrific blow in the very early hours of tomorrow 2nd Nov and it may well be that that will knock him off his perch. I hope so. You will follow in the papers the events and if you keep 2nd Nov in your mind, and study events from that date, it may help you.

I have received all your letters sent via the War Office. The last one was dated 5 October. It is a very much quicker way than air mail.

My letters probably get to you quicker than yours get to me.

I have heard from David since he has been back at school, and also from Robertson. He seems in very good form and is obviously very happy at being in the charge of you and Phyllis. He had me on the wireless and Robertson's description of the

H.Q. Eighth Army
M.E.F.
1-11-42

My dear Tom
... I am fighting a terrific battle with Rommel. It began on 23 October and he is resisting desperately. I hold the initiative. But it has become a real solid and bloody killing match. I do not think he can go on much longer. I am dealing him a terrific blow in the very early hours of tomorrow 2nd Nov and it may well be that that will knock him off his perch. I hope so. You will follow in the papers the events and if you keep 2nd Nov in your mind, and study events from that date, it may help you.

I have received all your letters sent via the War Office. The last one was dated 5 October. It is a very much quicker way than air mail. My letters probably get to you quicker than yours get to me....

Letter, Lt Gen Sir Bernard Montgomery, Commander, British Eighth Army, to Tom Reynolds, November 1, 1942
Montgomery is days away from final victory in the decisive battle of North Africa at El Alamein.

Imperial War Museum

28 May 43

My dearest Margery,

... Nobody knew what was happening & all thought it was a retreat, & expected Jerry to pounce any moment. Morning came & we were still moving, trying to get as much warmth as possible with the vehicle sheeting over us, & we found ourselves back at the Wire. The skeleton of an Italian plane lay a little distance from us, with the grave of its occupants....

Then the period of water shortage arrived. For tea we poured one mug of water each into the tin so that none would be left over. A wash & shave was extended to every other day & then only once on that day. What is more a proper wash was out of the question. The amount of water I used filled, almost, my mug which was between 1/2 & 3/4 of a pint, & the same water had to be used for teeth, a shave & a wash in that order. After a while I found I could get quite a good wash in spite of such a small amount, by making a lather in the normal way & then pouring a small amount of water into one hand & swilling over my face & neck till it was all gone. A further idea which was tried to conserve water, was to empty the used water through sand in a tin with a perforated bottom, into an empty tin underneath, & so filter it after a fashion....

Letter, L/Sgt H. J. Griffin, British Eighth Army, to his wife, May 28, 1943

The Allies in North Africa having achieved complete victory, Sergeant Griffin describes some of the techniques used by the troops to conserve water and otherwise maintain themselves in the desert environment.

Imperial War Museum

German canteen

Harry S. Truman Library, National Archives and Records Administration

Two German soldiers carrying canteens of precious water.

National Archives and Records Administration

Dr. Josef Goebbels (seated on the aisle, first row) with Adolf Hitler (center) and Field Marshal Herman Göring

National Archives and Records Administration

The British are extremely enraged with Rommel and are personally mad at him for not accepting battle with them. They can't help but admit that he turned around on his own free will and not under their pressure. Now they are complaining heavily that they are more than a thousand kilometers away from Cairo and half of their transportation equipment has to be made available alone to supply water. Montgomery is talking about how it is a battle of the minds now. But, of course, that is only a lame excuse for why Rommel tricked him. The Field Marshal is still very much feared by the British because of his earlier attacks, so that in London the question comes up continuously what he may have in mind now.

Diary, Dr. Josef Goebbels, German Minister for Public Enlightenment and Propaganda, December 16, 1942

Although the Axis will never again be able to maintain the upper hand in North Africa, Rommel has temporarily slipped away, to the frustration of the British and to the delight of Dr. Goebbels.

Josef Goebbels Papers, Hoover Institution Archives

- 4-

er sich ihnen nicht zum Kampfe gestellt hat. Sie können nicht umhin einzugestehen, daß er freiwillig und nicht unter ihrem Druck zurückgegangen ist. Sie klagen jetzt sehr beweglich darüber, daß sie über tausend Kilometer von Kairo entfernt ständen und daß die Hälfte ihrer Transportmittel allein für den Wassernachschub zur Verfügung gestellt werden müsse. Montgomery quatscht, es handel sich jetzt um eine Schlacht der Geister. Aber das ist natürlich nur eine faule Ausrede und eine Entschuldigung dafür, daß er sich von Rommel hat übertölpeln lassen. Der Feldmarschall ist bei den Engländern durch seine früheren Schläge noch so gefürchtet, daß man sich in London unentwegt die

8147

As part of Operation Torch, a two-thousand-vessel Allied convoy approaches the coast of French Morocco and Algeria in preparation for an invasion to strike Rommel's Afrika Korps from the rear.

National Archives and Records Administration

11-3-42

Every once in a while the tremendous responsibility of this job lands on me like a ton of brick. But mostly I am not in the least worried. I can't decide logically if I am a man of destiny or a lucky fool. But I think I am destined—five more days will show. I really do very little and have done very little about this show. Perhaps I am happy. I feel that my claim to greatness hangs on an ability to lead and inspire. Perhaps when Napoleon said, "Je m 'engage et puis je vois" [I start the fight and then I see], *he was right. It is the only thing I can do in this case as I see it. I have no personal fear of death or failure. This may sound like ... junk or prophecy in a week.*

We had a C.P.X. [Command Post Exercise] *this morning which was very dull. I can't see how people can be so dull and lacking in imagination. Compared to them I am a genius—I think I am.*

Diary, Maj Gen George S. Patton, Jr., Commander, Allied Western Task Force, November 3, 1942

General Patton is making final preparations for Operation Torch, the landing of the Allied Western Task Force, which on November 8 began the yearlong finale to the war in North Africa.

Library of Congress

German tanks form up prior to battle.

National Archives and Records Administration

An American tank goes into action in Tunisia.

National Archives and Records Administration

A U.S. cargo ship burns furiously after being hit amidships by a five-hundred-pound bomb during a Japanese air raid at Lunga Beach, Guadalcanal.

National Archives and Records Administration

A B-17 flies over Gizo Island on a bombing sortie in the Solomon Islands.

National Archives and Records Administration

A Navy Grumman F4F Wildcat at Henderson Field, Guadalcanal

National Archives and Records Administration

S1c Richard Thomas Mariner, U.S. Navy, Toledo, Ohio

... Now get this- this is out third major battle in twenty four hours. The one on Buka, Treasury, now the one on the Jap Task Force. Mother or Dad, whom ever I am reading this too, I was scared to death, that means I could hardly get my breath twice. we were chasing two Jap cans we fired torpedoes, and got them both.... The captain yelled, "Stand by for a ram." It was coming at us at thirty-two knots and we were doing thirtyfive and that is doing some on the sea. It seems like eighty to ninety miles per hour. The captain yelled, "Stand by for a Ram", the captain quick witted shot out on the port side, the left otherwise, to avoid a head on collision, God was with him. It side swiped us (Spence) and scared the livin hell out of us.... I was over the scare in a hurry when I soon found out we sunk a P.T. boat and two cans ... I was scared to death at first of the Jap Torpedo planes over head. Soon, "Stand by!!" "Stand by!!" "Two planes coming in for us on the port bow".... the only casualty the fan tail was blown off. 36 men sacrificed, but as the planes were coming in we blacked them out like lights. The more came overhead. I yelled "God Spare us please," and fourty eight P-38's fighter planes, ours of course saved us and were knocking them down left and right....

Diary, S1c Richard Thomas Mariner, U.S. Navy, October 31, 1943

Aboard the USS *Thatcher*, Richard Mariner describes action against the Japanese elsewhere in the Solomon Islands.

Mrs. Jeanann Mariner Olds

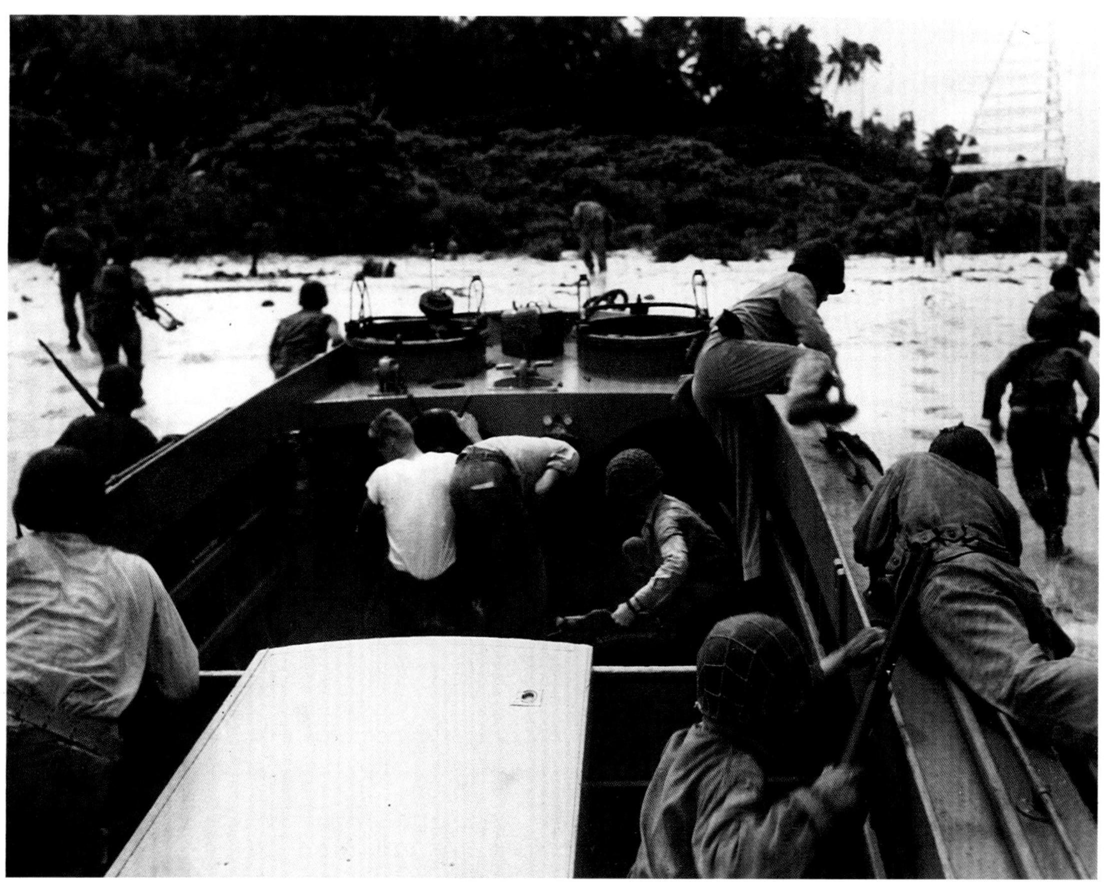

Marines leap out of their landing boat and race across the beach and toward the jungle during the initial American landing on Guadalcanal.

National Archives and Records Administration

Electrician's Mate First Class George W. Beaver, U.S. Navy, Austin, Texas

GEORGE W. BEAVER E.M.I.C.
46TH C.B. COMPANY–C.
C/o FLEET POST OFFICE,
SAN FRANCISCO CALIF.
July 16TH 1943

Dear Frances:

Well its high time you was hearing from me dont you think? There is nothing to tell you about this place that you don't already know, but am going to drop you a line or two. In your letters you sound as if you thought you had been a little busy this Summer. I wonder just what in the bald headed hell you think we have been doing the last six months. Playing games I guess? I get a good kick out of your good letters anyhow. You are bound to have a rough go of it back there in the States. How would you like to trade places with me for a while? I am going to join the Circus when I get out of here and take the job of assorting Wild Cats. It wont be a damn bit rougher after what we have gone through. This outfit is a going Jessie I am telling you, and wont quit.

We have been doing alright working like hell every day seven days a week and are getting the job done. Thats what we joined this Navy for. We have made a big showing let me tell you. Every man in here has done his best and we are a proud bunch of Seabees....

Must sign off for this time

Always your devoted brother
George Beaver

Letter, Electrician's Mate First Class George W. Beaver, U.S. Navy, to Frances, July 16, 1943

The Seabees, the construction arm of the navy, saw their first action on Guadalcanal. George Beaver tells his sister how hard he has been working.

Mrs. Patricia Partridge

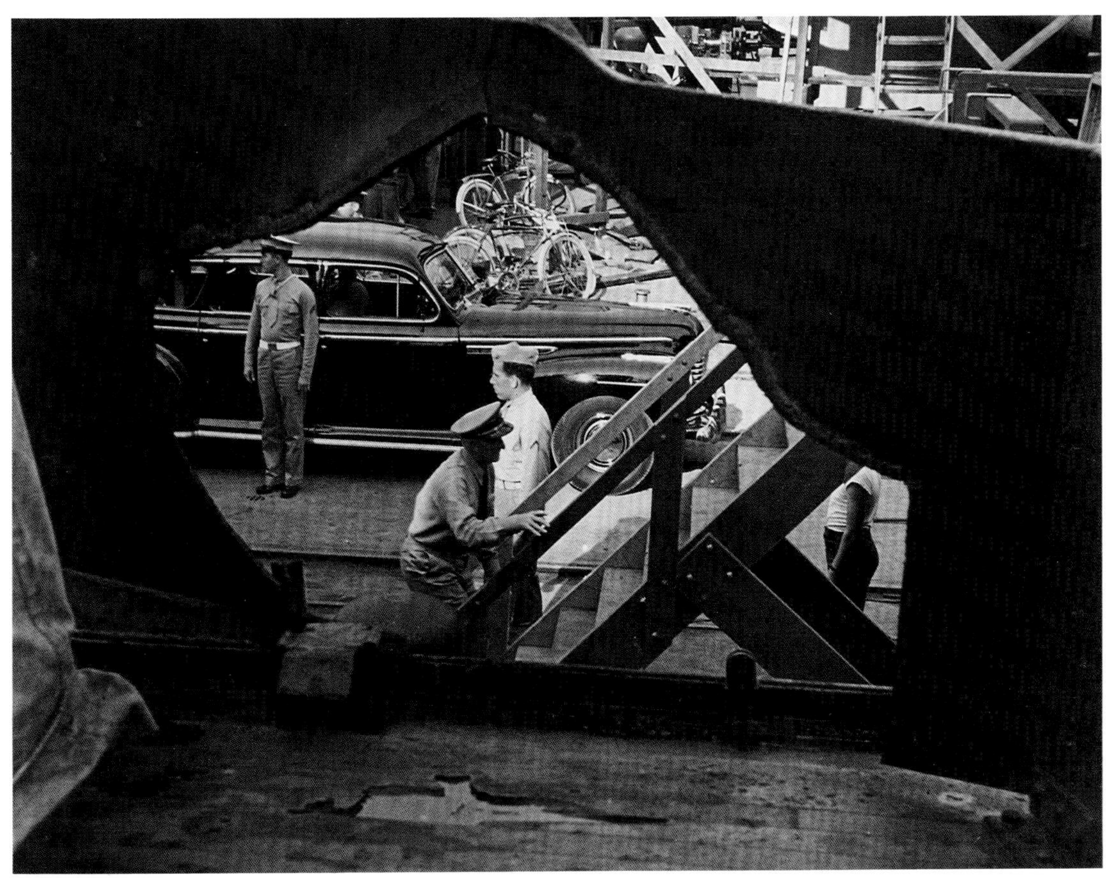

Adm Chester W. Nimitz boards the USS *San Francisco* in Pearl Harbor. The cruiser had participated in night-fighting off Savo Island, near Guadalcanal. The hole was caused by enemy fire.

National Archives and Records Administration

Henry Mason Geselbracht, Jr., American Volunteer Group, Glendale, California

[January 4, 1942]
... We climbed to 20,000 feet ... Then we let down in a long dive ... When we got to about 12000 feet I saw a bunch of Jap fighters just below us and presumed that Christman saw them also. He continued down though until we were about 1000 feet below them. Before I though he was getting into position for an underneath attack but then I figured he didn't see them. I pulled my section away, we scattered, and I zoomed at one of the I-96's. I gave him a burst from an aft beam shot and saw his plane begin to smoke. Planes were all over the sky and whenever one would get close to my tail I dove strait down & corkscrewed. Then I would zoom up and get in a few shots & enter a dive. The combat lasted about 4 minutes and coming up from my last dive I couldn't see a plane in sight. I circled for about 5 minutes then headed for the bay thinking the Japs were on their way home. I encountered nothing but a P-40 which wouldn't join on me so I went back to the field and landed. There were no holes in my ship. Merritt and Paxton had landed just previous to me. The former was OK but Paxton's ship was wrecked at the end of the runway. I examined it and it looked like a sieve.... The cock-pit was a mess of broken glass, oil and blood. Paxton had a 30 caliber in his right side, one in his right shoulder and slight wounds on his leg. He got out of the ship alright and they carted him to the hospital. He will pull through alright....

Diary, Henry Mason Geselbracht, Jr., American Volunteer Group supporting the Chinese Air Force, January 4, 1942

Henry Geselbracht describes an encounter with Japanese fighters during his tour of duty with the Flying Tigers in Burma. Recruited for the Tigers by then Col Claire Chennault before the United States entered the war, Geselbracht had been a lieutenant in the U.S. Navy.

Mr. Raymond H. Geselbracht

Mon. Feb. 9. Missed the time change. Shots. usual rush. Shoving off Wed. Maybe Tues. P.M. First five of us - maybe 7 - now 14. Etc. Etc. - Saw the Pres. at noon for 20 minutes. Not too impressive. Just talk. 28,000 mi. front, etc. Over in 1943. One year from now to turn. 2000 planes to go to Australia. All in same boat. Tell Chiang bunch that Hitler is the one enemy. All are equally enemies. Independence is also bunk. Only way is fight. We are in to see it through. And till China gets back ALL her lost territory. (Mme. Chiang not to come.) Back at 12:40 - more papers & rush.... Surprise about Chennault.... At 4:30 to White House. Harry Hopkins. Queer gnome. Wants to help. "Great Adventure" - "You're going to command Troops." "C.K.S. may offer you the command of the whole Ch. army."...

Diary, Maj Gen Joseph Stilwell, U.S. Army, February 9, 1942

General Stilwell, preparing to leave for China, gives his version of his meetings at the White House with President Roosevelt and his adviser Harry Hopkins.

Stilwell Papers, Hoover Institution Archives

Joseph Stilwell visits with Maj Gen Claire L. Chennault. Chennault, who commanded the Flying Tigers, strongly disagreed with Stilwell on the allocation of supplies and strategy.

UPI/Bettmann

A squad of "Merrill's Marauders," jungle fighters under the command of U.S. Maj Frank D. Merrill, move through the Burmese jungle.

National Archives and Records Administration

The Tripura Rifles, a collection of guerrilla units fighting in the Kaladan Valley campaign, prepare an ambush near Arakan, Burma.

National Archives and Records Administration

To complete this leg of the long and arduous retreat out of Burma, Gen Joseph Stilwell's party built these rafts and poled down the Uyu River for two days toward the Indian border.

National Archives and Records Administration

After several days of intense house-to-house fighting, British troops move in and take Meiktila, Burma. Meiktila was an important rail and road center for the Japanese.

National Archives and Records Administration

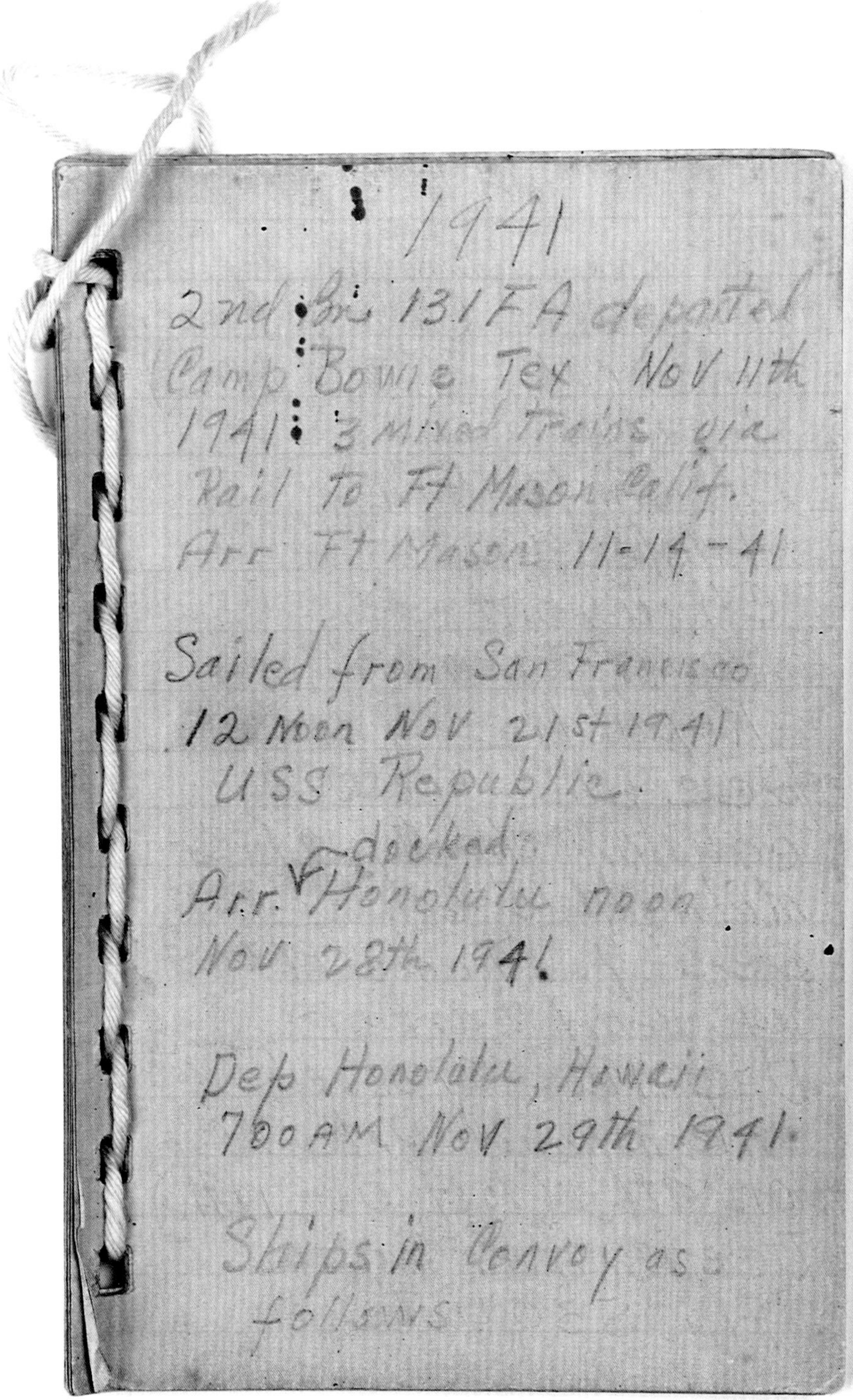

1941

2nd Bn 131 F A departed
Camp Bowie Tex Nov 11th
1941 3 mixed trains via
Rail to Ft Mason Calif.
Arr Ft Mason 11-14-41

Sailed from San Francisco
12 Noon Nov 21st 1941
USS Republic

docked
Arr. Honolulu noon
Nov 28th 1941.

Dep Honolulu, Hawaii
700 AM Nov 29th 1941.

Ships in Convoy as
follows

1941

2nd Bn 131 FA departed Camp Bowie Tex Nov 11th 1941
3 mixed trains via Rail to Ft Mason Calif.
Arr Ft Mason 11-14-41

Sailed from San Francisco 12 Noon Nov 21st 1941 USS Republic

Arr. docked Honolulu noon Nov 28th 1941

Dep Honolulu, Hawaii 700 AM Nov 29th 1941

Ships in Convoy as follows ...

Dec 6th - crossed equator shortly after midnight 5-6th
Dec-7-Radio report of Pearl Harbor.
Dec 11th- crossed International Date Line on 9th
(lost Dec 10th)
Dec 13. Arr Suva. Fiji 530 date

Diary, Lt Col Blucher S. Tharp, Texas National Guard, November 11 to December 13, 1941

The Thirty-sixth Division of the Texas National Guard was activated for service in 1941. Colonel Tharp's first diary gives details of the journey from Texas to their eventual destination, Java, in the Dutch East Indies.

Col Blucher S. Tharp, Jr.

Sicily, Italy, Anzio

The Italian campaign was a logical progression of Allied efforts in North Africa and the Mediterranean and also a stopgap measure until the Allies were ready to invade France from Britain. Unfortunately, it was also an effort in which Allied hopes exceeded capabilities.

Sicily was invaded on July 9-10, 1943, by American, British, and Canadian forces, the largest amphibious operation of the war. The German garrison of the island fought only delaying actions, some of them fierce, and the island was cleared in five weeks. Meanwhile, in Italy, Mussolini was overthrown, the new government opened secret negotiations, and Allied momentum carried them on to invade the mainland in early September. They hoped to get southern Italy, and even Rome, without much of a fight.

Here, however, the Germans held hard, especially around Cassino south of Rome. To break this block, the Allies tried a landing up the coast at Anzio in December 1943, but that too was contained by the quick response of the Germans. Not until May of 1944 did the U.S. Fifth and British Eighth Armies break through Cassino in a massive, World War I-style attack; the Anzio forces broke out at the same time. Rome was liberated on June 4, and the Germans did not stop retreating until they reached northern Italy, where they held until the very end of the war.

Facing page:

A German soldier

Life-size figure by Studio EIS, Brooklyn, New York

Photograph by Elliot Schwartz

American infantrymen advance carefully along a street through ravaged Messina, Sicily.

National Archives and Records Administration

American soldiers go over the side and down landing nets to waiting landing craft at Salerno, Italy.

National Archives and Records Administration

War correspondent Ernie Pyle (wearing goggles) sits down to talk with a group of soldiers. Concentrating on the experiences of the ordinary soldier at war, Pyle's writing won numerous awards including the Pulitzer Prize.

Ernie Pyle State Historic Site, Indiana State Museum

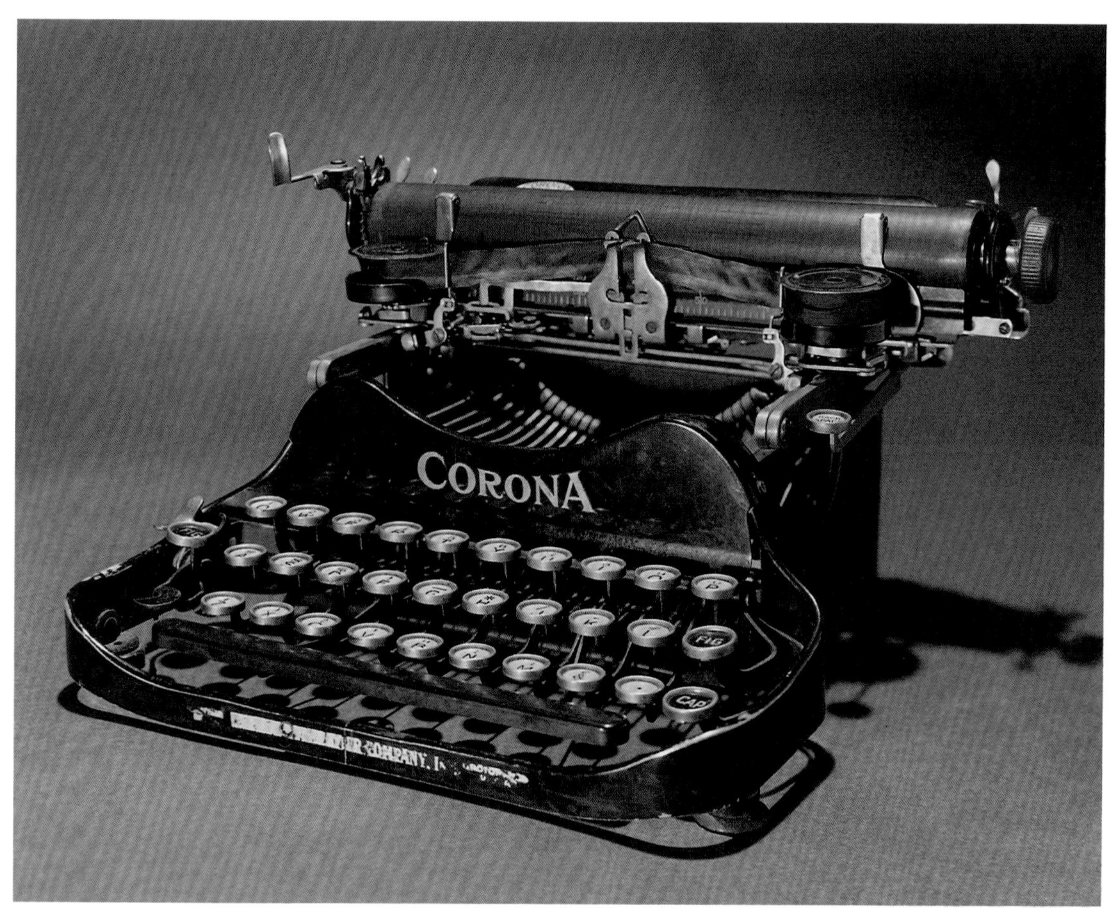

Typewriter used by Ernie Pyle

The Albuquerque Museum, Gift of Don Bell

Hoosier Vagabond *By Ernie Pyle*

AT THE FRONT LINES IN ITALY, JAN. 10 (By Wireless).—In this war I have known a lot of officers who were loved and respected by the soldiers under them. But never have I crossed the trail of any man as beloved as Capt. Henry T. Waskow of Belton, Tex. Capt. Waskow was a company commander in the 36th division. He had been in this company since long before he left the states. He was very young, only in his middle twenties, but he carried in him a sincerity and gentleness that made people want to be guided by him.

"After my own father, he comes next," a sergeant told me.

"He always looked after us," a soldier said. "He'd go to bat for us every time."

"I've never known him to do anything unkind," another one said.

I was at the foot of the mule trail the night they brought Capt. Waskow down. The moon was nearly full, and you could see far up the trail, and even part way across the valley. Soldiers made shadows as they walked.

Dead men had been coming down the mountain all evening, lashed onto the back of mules.

They came lying belly down across the wooden packsaddle, their heads hanging down on the left side of the mule, their stiffened legs sticking awkwardly from the other side, bobbing up and down as the mule walked.

The Italian mule skinners were afraid to walk beside dead men, so Americans had to lead the mules down that night. Even the Americans were reluctant to unlash and lift off the bodies, when they got to the bottom, so an officer had to do it himself and ask others to help him.

The first one came early in the morning. They slid him down from the mule, and stood him on his feet for a moment. In the half light he might have been merely a sick man standing there leaning on the other. Then they laid him on the ground in the shadow of the stone wall alongside the road.

I don't know who that first one was. You feel small in the presence of dead men, and you don't ask silly questions.

We left him there beside the road, that first one, and we all went back into the cowshed and sat on watercans or lay on the straw, waiting for the next batch of new ones.

Somebody said the dead soldier had been dead for four days, and then nobody said anything more about him. We talked for an hour or more; the dead man lay all alone, outside in the shadow of the wall. Then a soldier came into the cowshed and said there were some more bodies outside. We went out into the road. Four mules stood there in the moonlight, in the road where the trail came down off the mountain. The soldiers who led them stood there waiting.

"This one is Capt. Waskow," one of them said quickly.

Five Lying in a Long Row

Two men unlashed his body from the mule and lifted it off and laid it in the shadow beside the stone wall. Other men took the other bodies off. Finally there were five lying end to end in a long row. You don't cover up dead men in the combat zones. They just lie there in the shadows until somebody else comes after them.

The uncertain mules moved off to their olive groves. The men in the road seemed reluctant to leave. They stood around, and gradually I could sense them moving, one by one, close to Capt. Waskow's body. Not so much to look, I think, as to say something in finality to him and to themselves. I stood close by and I could hear.

One solder came and looked down, and he said out loud:

"God Damn it!"

That's all he said, and then he walked away.

Another one came, and he said, "God damn it to hell anyway!" He looked down for a few last moments and left.

Another man came. I think he was an officer. It was hard to tell officers from men in the dim light, for everybody was grimy and dirty. The man looked down into the dead captain's face and then spoke directly to him, as though he were alive:

"I'm sorry, old man."

'Gently He Straightened His Collar'

Then a soldier came and stood beside the officer and bent over and he too spoke to his dead captain, not in a whisper but awfully tenderly, and he said:

"I sure am sorry, sir."

Then the first man squatted down, and he reached down and took the captain's hand, and he sat there for a full five minutes holding the dead hand in his own and looking intently into the dead face. And he never uttered a sound all the time he sat there.

Finally he put the hand down. He reached up and gently straightened the points of the captain's shirt collar, and then he sort of rearranged the tattered edges of his uniform around the wound, and then he got up and walked away down the road in the moonlight, all alone.

The rest of us went back into the cowshed, leaving the five dead men lying in a line end to end in the shadow of the low stone wall. We lay down on the straw in the cowshed, and pretty soon we were all asleep.

***Hoosier Vagabond* by Ernie Pyle**, reprint of his most famous and popular column dated January 10, 1944

Ernie Pyle State Historic Site, Indiana State Museum

... I put two sticks of chewing gum in my mouth to quell my nervousness and excitement before climbing into the cockpit. I hooked up my equipment, oxygen mask last.... A target was cited ... We peeled off and rolled in on a moving German troop train.... The P-51 "Mustang" had three 50-caliber machine guns in each wing. Every fifth bullet in each wing was a tracer bullet.... I could see my tracer bullets converging in a pattern in front of me. I thought I was flying faster than my bullets because they were going past me on both sides. THEN IT OCCURRED TO ME. <u>THEY WERE SHOOTING AT ME!!</u> ... When we returned to our home Field ... I noticed that I had a mouthful of little B Bs. I had chewed the gum so forcefully that ... The gum no longer stuck together.

From an account by 1st Lt Hiram E. Mann, Tuskegee Airman, U.S. Army Air Corps

1st Lt Hiram E. Mann, a member of the Tuskegee Airmen, next to his P-51 Mustang

Mr. Hiram E. Mann

Two German soldiers surrender to U.S. infantrymen as they emerge from their underground hideout.

National Archives and Records Administration

Overleaf:

American pilots of a P-51 Mustang fighter group listen intently during a briefing for a mission over Italy. This group, known as the "Tuskegee Airmen," was named after the army air corps training center in Tuskegee, Alabama.

National Archives and Records Administration

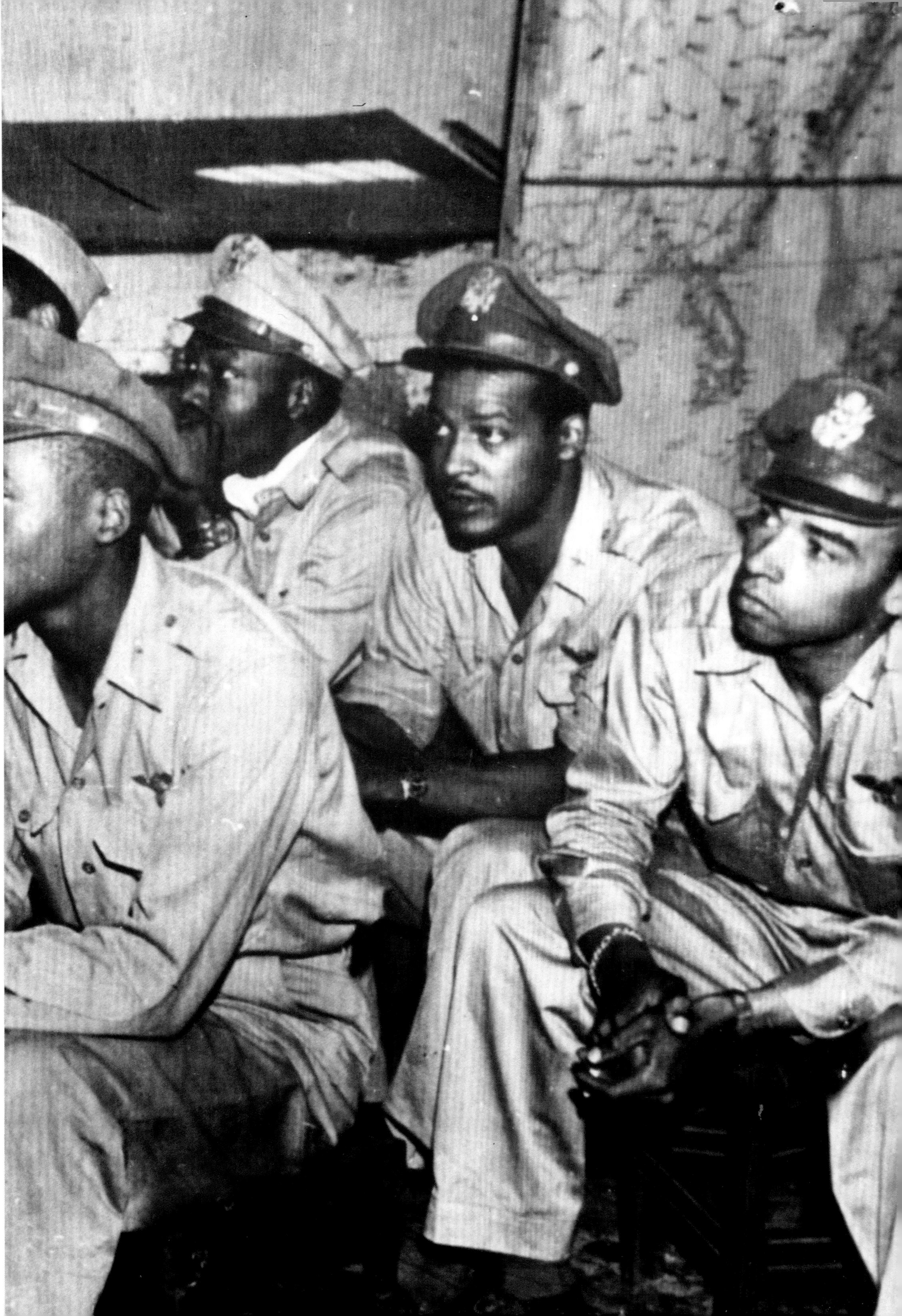

Aug 11, 44

Dear Parents:

I thought, I'd drop you's a few lines and keep you's from worrying. I'll probably will be too busy to write for a while, but don't worry God is taking care of me along with His Blessed Mother. I have been awarded the the Bronze Star for a deed the boy's and I did on the push from Anzio to Rome. My only regret is that the boy's who assisted can't receive something for their gallentry and bravery under fire they sure deserve it. Well, I guess I'll close for now so keep your chin up.

Your Loving Son
Charles F. Logue

A Gentlemen A Soldier & A Good Catholic
Lt. John A. Dascy. [The lieutenant who censored Sgt Logue's letter added this postscript.]

Letter, S Sgt Charles F. Logue, U.S. Army, to his parents, August 11, 1944

Mr. Charles F. Logue

Bronze Star awarded to S Sgt Charles F. Logue

Members of the famed "Go for broke" troops are reviewed by U.S. Gen Mark W. Clark, commander of the Allied Fifth Army. These troops, nearly all Americans of Japanese descent, were cited by General Clark for gallantry in some of the hardest fighting of the Italian Campaign.

National Archives and Records Administration

Italian citizens in St. John's Square cheer the arrival of American soldiers as they enter Rome.

National Archives and Records Administration

Men of the 370th Infantry Regiment move through the town of Prato, Italy.

National Archives and Records Administration

The Eastern Front

The Russo-German war dwarfed all the other parts of World War II for sheer immensity. In December of 1941 the Germans were stopped at the very gates of Moscow, but in 1942 they opened huge new drives in southern Russia. By late summer they had gone all the way to the Caucasus Mountains, but they had stretched themselves very thin, leaving a long vulnerable flank. On the flank, the Russians grimly defended the city of Stalingrad, and it became a magnet that gradually sucked in the major forces of both sides.

Hitler became obsessed with the city and sent more and more troops there. Then, in November, the Russians launched overwhelming counteroffensives on both sides of the city, broke the German lines, and surrounded the German Sixth Army. Hitler tried to hold on too long; his trapped garrison could not break out, relief could not get through, and attempted aerial resupply failed. After three months, resistance finally collapsed. A quarter of a million Germans were lost there, and there were more Russian casualties than the Americans lost in the entire war.

The epic of Stalingrad was the turning point to the war in the East. The Soviets now began a drive to the West that seldom halted, and ended only in the ruins of Berlin.

Facing page:

A Russian soldier in heavy winter uniform

Life-size figure by Studio EIS, Brooklyn, New York

Photograph by Elliot Schwartz

German soldiers advancing on the Eastern Front.

National Archives and Records Administration

German infantry advance into Russia.

National Archives and Records Administration

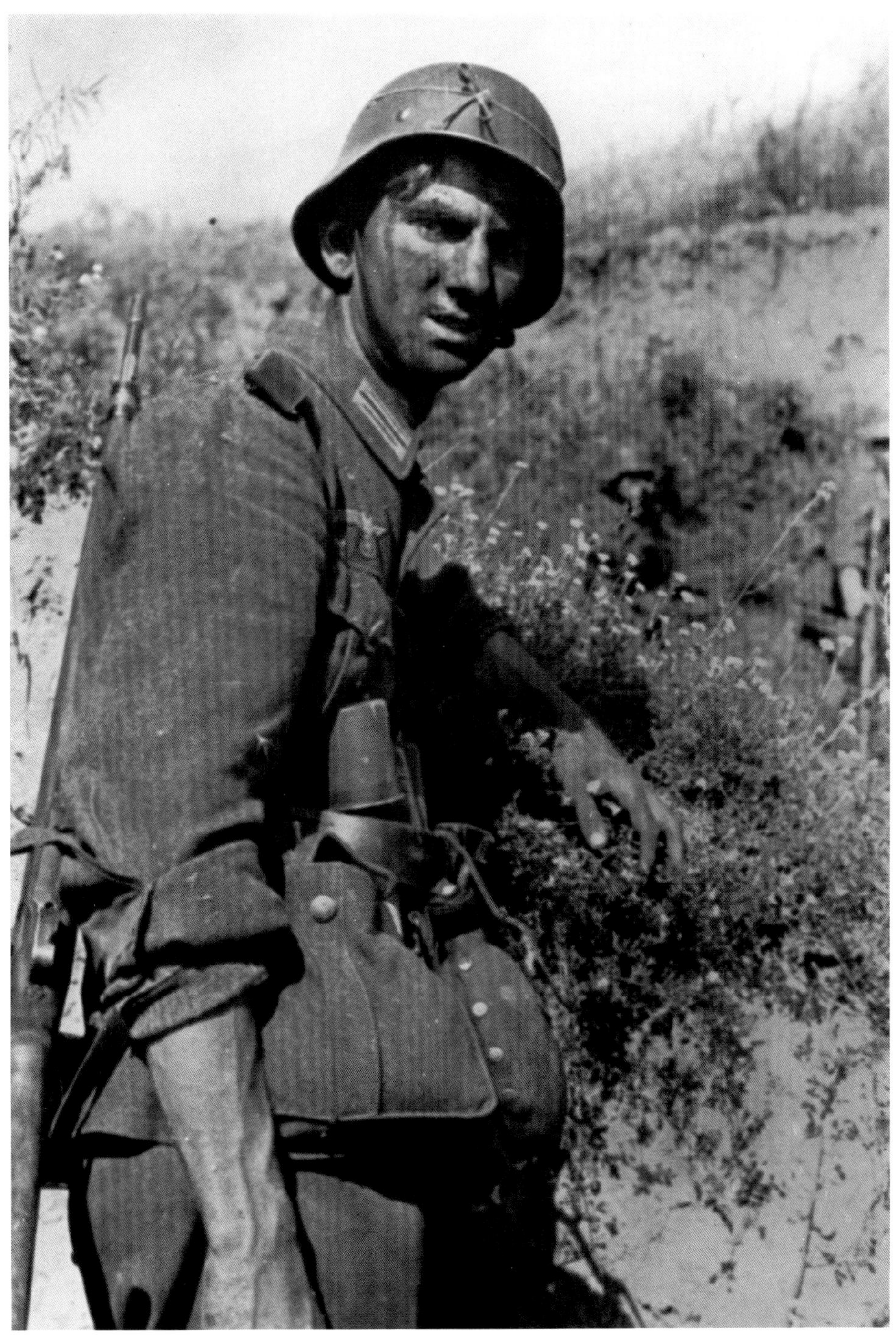

A tired German soldier shows the effects of constant combat.

National Archives and Records Administration

Normandy, France

The invasion of Normandy on June 6, 1944, and the subsequent campaign of France marked one of the most brilliant efforts in the history of warfare. Since Dunkirk, the British had been planning their return to the Continent, and the Americans began pushing for such a move as soon as they entered the war. It was nonetheless two and a half years after Pearl Harbor before all these hopes reached fruition.

Carefully and cleverly deceiving the Germans as to where the blow would be launched, the Allies landed on the Normandy peninsula, west of the Seine basin. Though hard-pressed at one American beach, Omaha, the landing was successfully accomplished. The Germans then chose to give battle in the forward area, and there were several weeks of heavy fighting before the Allies finally broke out of Normandy, the British wheeling east for the lower Seine, the Americans racing south and east for central France, the Loire, and Paris. The depleted and exhausted Germans could not stand against the Allied advance. Further landings were made in southern France, the French Resistance rose up, Paris was liberated on August 25, and the Allies hardly stopped for breath until they had reached virtually the eastern frontiers of France.

Facing page:

American soldiers crouch low in their landing craft en route to the Normandy beachhead.

National Archives and Records Administration

Convoys brought supplies to the United Kingdom prior to the Normandy invasion.

Imperial War Museum

Top Secret

Some Army problems

1. We must get ashore.
Fire support from the sea and air will all be concentrated on the problem of getting the army ashore. In some places we may get ashore easily; in other places with difficulty. These who do get ashore must work outwards and help those who are in trouble. Once ashore we must stop the counter-attack while we get sorted out, and generally build up. Best way to stop counter-attacks is to be offensive ourselves; must not let initiative pass to the enemy; we must crack about and force the battle to swing our way.

2. German is good at the small local counter-attack. We want little firm bases from which infantry and tanks can be offensive without difficulty and can therefore take great risks. Best firm base is A/Tk guns and tanks; vital to get these ashore early. The A/Tk gun is a better A/Tk weapon than the tank....

Memorandum, General Sir Bernard Montgomery, Commander, Allied Ground Forces, to army commanders, spring 1944

As the invasion of Normandy nears, Montgomery puts together some notes for the leaders of the Allied assault troops.

Imperial War Museum

General Sir Bernard Montgomery

Imperial War Museum

Kay Summersby,
General Eisenhower's driver

Dwight D. Eisenhower Library, National Archives and Records Administration

Monday June 5 1944
We leave the C/P early morning and drive to the docks. E. wishes to see the troops embarking. All the forces that E. sees are British, the American troops are not leaving from Portsmouth. Everywhere E. goes he is greeted with shouts of "Good old Ike" In the afternoon there is a press conference at the C/P. The correspondents are inforned of D. Day. 6.30. p.m. E. leaves Portsmouth to visit troops in the Newbury area. 101 Div.... E. drives to three airfields to watch the men getting ready to board the ships.... When he was recognized, the shouts that went up were tremendous.... Bt this time it was getting quite dark, we returned to 101. HQ.... and then proceeded to climb on the roof of the building to watch the aircraft circling over the field getting into formation. It was one of the most impressive sights that anyone could wish to see, visibility was perfect, all the stars were gleaming....

Tuesday June 6 1944
... The next few hours are very trying for E., he has done everything in his powere to ensure success and all he can do now is to wait fro reports to come in.... 8 a.am a report came in to the effect that the airborne landings were very successful, only 21nlost. The landings on thr beaches are going according to schedule, except on gen. Gerows's beach, very heavy artillery fire making landings inpossible. The rest of the day is spent in waiting for reports to come in....

From the diary of Kay Summersby, June 1944

Gen Dwight D. Eisenhower, commander in chief of the Allied Expeditionary Force, gives the order of the day to U.S. paratroopers before the first assault of the invasion of Nazi-held Europe.

Imperial War Museum

Sgt Charles Easter, U.S. Army, Cincinnati, Ohio

I then realized that I had made the same mistake, as had most members or the battalion, of taking too much equipment. I venture to say, with all of my equipment including my chutes, I weighed three hundred and fifty pounds.

We boarded the planes about ten thirty in the evening. Each man had to be pulled or pushed into the plane....

As the planes were warming up I reached back to feel if my 'chute was all right. I discovered that the lacing on the back cover had broken and the silk was spilling out.... No other 'chute was available so the lieutenant stuffed the silk back in and tied up the pack with a piece of cord he obtained from someone in the plane....

Just after the red light came on the anti aircraft batteries opened fire. They must have had every gun in France turned on us that night. The explosive shells and machine gun bullets were red orange and yellow and were as thick as rain, only going up instead of down. There was no hesitation on anyone's part in going out of the door although none of us expected to reach the ground alive.

When I cleared the door the plane was bucking like a crazy horse and the tracers were so thick it looked like a wall of flame....

Letter, Sgt Charles Easter, U.S. Army, to Marion Page Bunge, July 7, 1944

The U.S. 82d and 101st Airborne Divisions had landed during the night in the vicinity of Utah Beach before the seaborne invasion commenced. Sergeant Easter describes his participation in that event. He was killed in action on October 8.

Special Collections, United States Military Academy Library

... The glider flight was bloody! It was of course longer than most I've done before because of the business of getting into formation, collecting fighter escort, & so on. After about 1/4 hr I began to be sick & continued until we were over the channel where the air was much calmer. The channel was a wonderful sight - especially the traffic at this end - Piccadilly Circus was'nt in it.... The landing was ghastly. Mine was the first glider down, though we were not quite in the right place, & the damn thing bucketed along a very upsy-downsy field for a bit & then broke across the middle - we just chopped through those anti-landing poles ... as we went along. However, the two halves of the glider fetched up very close together, & we quickly got out ourselves & our equipment & lay down under the thing, because other gliders were coming in all round, & Jerries were shooting things at them and at us. so it was'nt very healthy to wander about....

Somebody once said that war was composed of intense boredom relieved by periods of acute fear. That is it, in a nutshell. The boys used to hate digging themselves trenches on Salisbury plain, but you should just see how fast they do it now! ...

Letter, Capt C. T. Cross, British Sixth Airborne Division Gliders, to his family, June 23, 1944

Captain Cross gives an account of his D day landing by glider on Sword Beach.

Imperial War Museum

Lt Col Alfred F. Birra, U.S. Army, Alexandria, Virginia

... There weren't many men who got much sleep that night of June 5th. For the most part we sat around, talked, played cards, drank coffee and did the usual things a man does when he is worried and a little scared and doesn't want to show it. At 0230 in the morning breakfast was served of which most of us partook heartily since we knew it would be, if not our last meal, at least the last for quite a few hours or perhaps days.... The small landing craft were loosened from the davits ... As the boat goes down the rail, the ship disappears and with a slap that jars everyone aboard, the craft hits the water. The cables are cast off and now you're entirely on your own and alone....

Now it's our turn. Men scrambled to their feet, equipment is adjusted, lifebelts made more secure, for all around us artillery shells are falling and already several boats have been hit. Rifles are loaded and the safety taken off.... The coxswain signals me that we're about to touch down, the ramp is lowered and the Sgt and I stepped off into four feet of water. I look behind and the men are already off the boat and scattered for protection against the bullets which are singing around us but for the most part hitting the water.... We had about 500 yards of water to cross, we couldn't run cause the water was too deep, we couldn't crouch, we couldn't do anything except just what we did. Wade on into shore....

Letter, Lt Col Alfred F. Birra, U.S. Army, to his wife, July 12, 1944

Mrs. Barbara A. Birra (Mrs. Alfred F.)

Aug. 25, 1944
France

My Darling Wife,

... I was relieved from front line fighting last night for a few days. It sure was a great feeling to have four letters from you waiting for me.

I hardly know how to start this letter, so much has happened to me....

I'll start off with somthing that is always on my mind. You. I love you so very much my darling. I wish I could see how beautiful you are & hold you very close to me. I miss you very much Ruthie. I want you more than anything else in this world. You can't realize darling what you mean to me....

Two hours before H hour we scrambled over the sides of the ship on nets into the small invasion boats.... I rechecked my tommy gun, hand grenades & automatic for the millionth time. (right now darling, while writing this I feel the same way I did then—my stomach is very hollow) We hit the beach & I could here all kinds of machine guns going. I kept wondering when & where will I be hit.... We hadn't gone far when a German anti aircraft gun opened up on us ... The platoon I was with managed to take it & right away 200 yds from us 8 pill boxes fired away at us, a sgt. killed the Germans on the ack ack gun & turned the gun around & used it on the pill boxes & I directed heavy Navy gun fire & levelled the pill boxes.... bedded down for the night I slept on the sidewalk of the town ... I noticed two people lying beside me & one was moaning & half crying. It got on my nerves & I told him to shut up & he answered in German. (he was under the same blanket as I was & tight up against my side) ... They were escaped prisoner & decided to sleep with me. I kicked them - out of my blankets & I went back to sleep....

1st Lt Ernest L. Sheldon, U.S. Army, Johnston, Pennsylvania

Letter, 1st Lt Ernest L. Sheldon, U.S. Army, to his wife, August 25, 1944

Mrs. Ernest L. Sheldon (Ruth)

Allied troops under the command of Gen "Lightnin' Joe" Collins land at Utah Beach.

National Archives and Records Administration

British troops gather on Sword Beach.

Imperial War Museum

2d Lt Audie L. Murphy,
U.S. Army, Farmersville, Texas

<u>*CHAPTER ONE*</u>

... When the squad has completely gathered, we get down to business. If we wait for the tanks, the Germans will have more time to prepare their defense up the road. I decide to take two men, SLIP UP THE STREAM BED, and try knocking out the gun with grenades. The remainder of the men will remain in the ditch to distract the krauts with rifle fire. TACTICALLY THE IDEA IS NOT BRILLIANT; BUT IT IS THE BEST WE HAVE UNDER THE CIRCUMSTANCES....

We crawl in a wide arc to reach the winding stream WITHOUT MISHAP. The banks are lined with bushes; so we can advance UP THE BED in a crouching walk.

I SLIP FORWARD while Brandon covers me; then Steiner passes me while I cover him; Brandon jumps us both; and I go again. It is like a grim game of checkers, because if there ARE BULLETS flying ahead, the man in the lead will be most likely to get THEM.

We are nearing the bridge when Steiner reaches an open space in the bushes. The Germans have anticipated such a maneuver as ours and cut the brush away. For a moment, Steiner hesitates on the edge of the clearing, then HE runs for the bridge. The machine gun blurts. Steiner pitches forward and lies with his body quivering....

Manuscript for *To Hell and Back*, by Audie L. Murphy, no date
The most decorated soldier in World War II, Audie Murphy was serving with the Fifteenth Infantry in France as a second lieutenant when he was awarded the Medal of Honor. Murphy killed or wounded at least fifty Germans as he single-handedly held his company's position. After the war Murphy became a movie actor; he was killed in a plane crash in 1971.

Watch owned and worn by 2d Lt Audie L. Murphy
This army-issue Hamilton watch has Murphy's own Texas-style watchband.

Audie L. Murphy Memorial Veterans Hospital

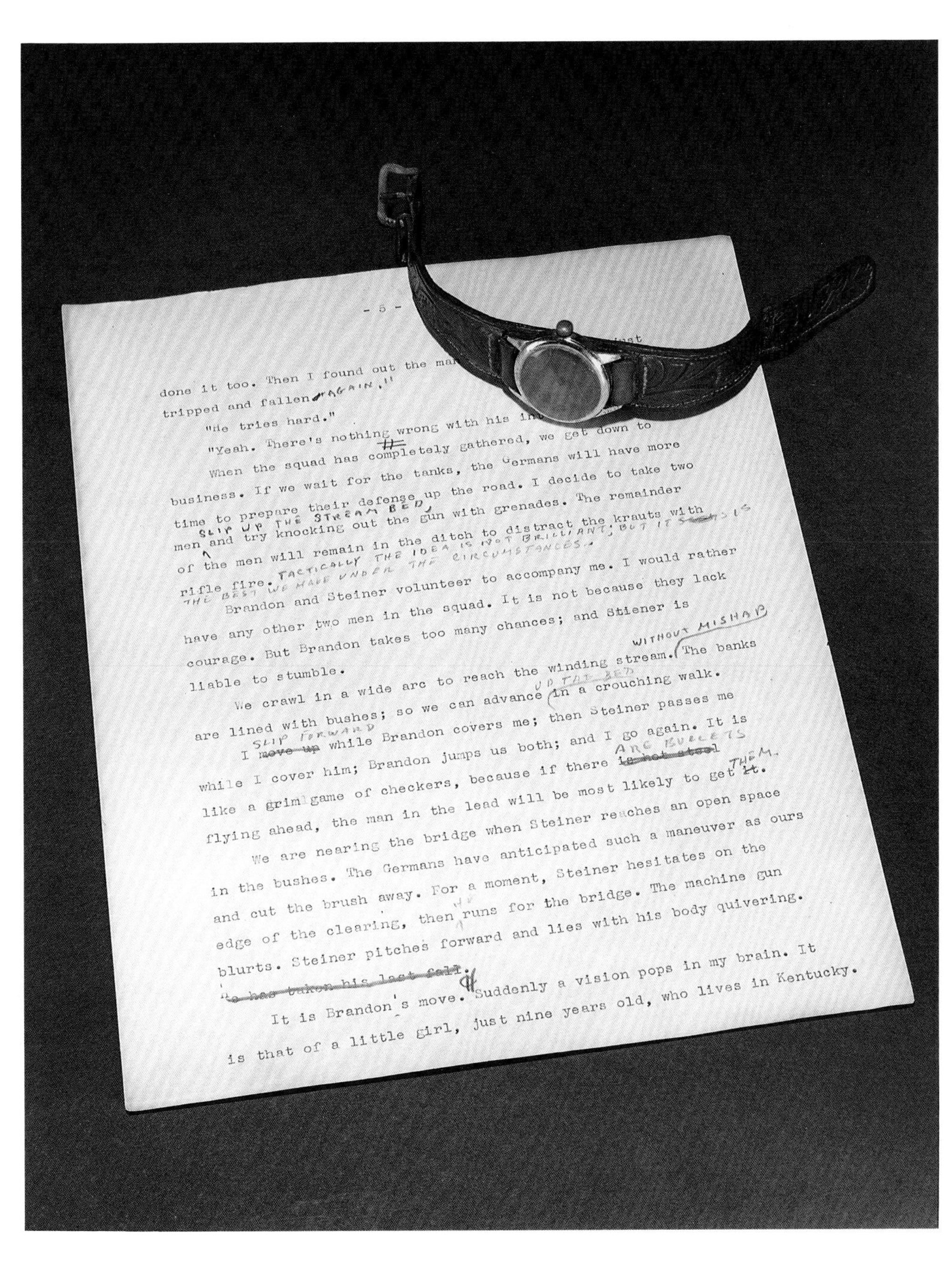

\- 5 -

...ust
done it too. Then I found out the ma...
tripped and fallen AGAIN."
"He tries hard."
"Yeah. There's nothing wrong with his in...
When the squad has completely gathered, we get down to
business. If we wait for the tanks, the Germans will have more
time to prepare their defense up the road. I decide to take two
SLIP UP THE STREAM BED,
men and try knocking out the gun with grenades. The remainder
of the men will remain in the ditch to distract the krauts with
TACTICALLY THE IDEA IS NOT BRILLIANT; BUT IT IS
THE BEST WE HAVE UNDER THE CIRCUMSTANCES.
rifle fire.
Brandon and Steiner volunteer to accompany me. I would rather
have any other two men in the squad. It is not because they lack
courage. But Brandon takes too many chances; and Stiener is
liable to stumble.
WITHOUT MISHAP
We crawl in a wide arc to reach the winding stream. The banks
UP THE BED
are lined with bushes; so we can advance in a crouching walk.
SLIP FORWARD
I ~~move up~~ while Brandon covers me; then Steiner passes me
while I cover him; Brandon jumps us both; and I go again. It is
ARE BULLETS
like a grim game of checkers, because if there ~~is hot steel~~
THEM.
flying ahead, the man in the lead will be most likely to get ~~it~~.
We are nearing the bridge when Steiner reaches an open space
in the bushes. The Germans have anticipated such a maneuver as ours
and cut the brush away. For a moment, Steiner hesitates on the
edge of the clearing, then runs for the bridge. The machine gun
blurts. Steiner pitches forward and lies with his body quivering.
~~He has taken his last fall.~~
It is Brandon's move. Suddenly a vision pops in my brain. It
is that of a little girl, just nine years old, who lives in Kentucky.

Jacket owned and worn by Gen Dwight D. Eisenhower
This style became known as the Ike jacket.

Dwight D. Eisenhower Library, National Archives and Records Administration

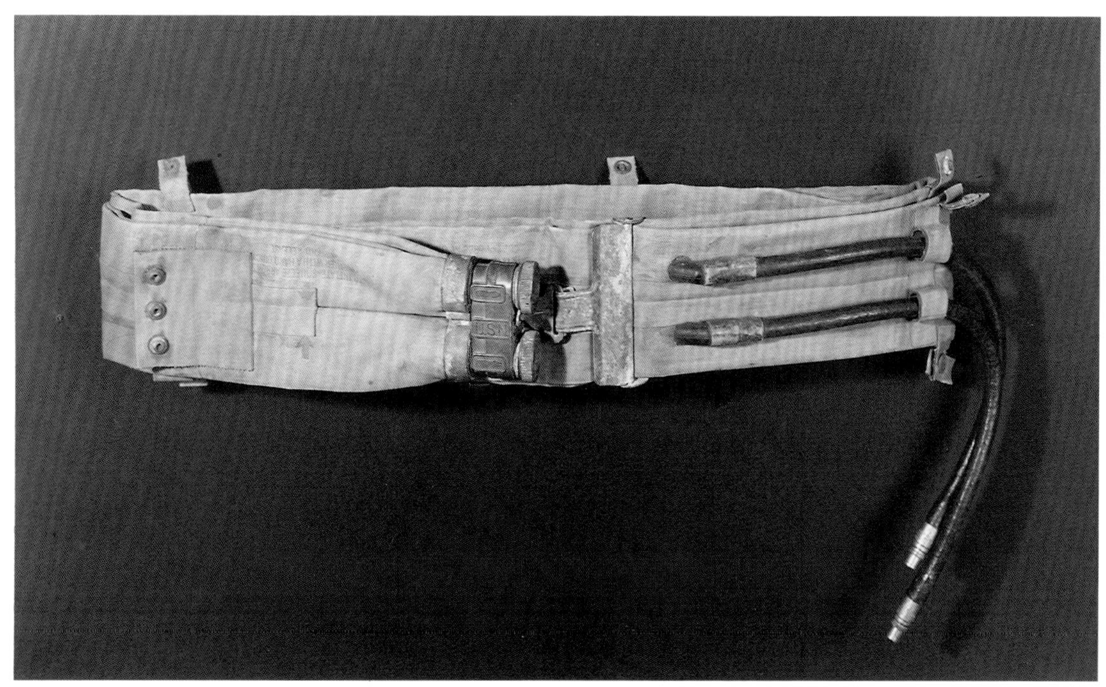

U.S. waist-type life belt

Dwight D. Eisenhower Library, National Archives and Records Administration

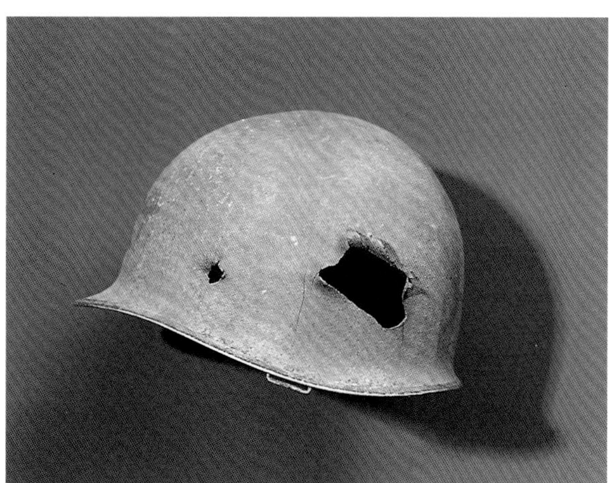

U.S. Army helmet found on the beach at Normandy

Dwight D. Eisenhower Library,
National Archives and Records Administration

From the Bulge to the Elbe

By late 1944, as the Allies were nearing German territory, they thought the enemy was exhausted. Hitler, however, secretly scraped together twenty divisions and launched a surprise offensive against American forces in the Ardennes Forest on December 16.

He hoped to replay the 1940 campaign but lacked the force to do so. Instead, he created a "bulge" in the Allied line; the Americans sealed this off, then in fierce fighting, destroyed it by January of 1945. The result of this was effectively to use up the Germans' last strategic reserve.

The Allies, by contrast, were soon ready to resume their offensive, and in the early spring of 1945 they drove vigorously into the Rhineland. At Remagen, American forces seized an intact bridge across the last great water barrier of western Europe; soon after, the British crossed the lower Rhine. From there, German resistance progressively deteriorated, and though there was still hard fighting, the Third Reich was obviously collapsing. Russian units were already forcing their way to Berlin, and the first meeting between eastern and western Allies came at Torgau on the Elbe River, where Russian and American patrols met on April 25.

Facing page:

American GI in winter uniform

Life-size figure by Studio EIS, Brooklyn, New York

Photograph by Elliot Schwartz

... The next thing I knew the Germans were charging in with bayonets.... I jammed my helmet back on my head, grabbed my rifle, and began a powerful wiggle on my back to and THROUGH the hedgerow barrier.... My steel helmet shielded my head and eyes ... when I reached the other side, my gloves were torn to shreds, every brass button on my great coat was gone, and parts of the great coat were also shreaded.

The enemy did not even try to pierce the hedgerow, but began a frantic race to run around it. Since they had about 75 to 100 yards to go to reach a break, I had a head start.... I continued down the slope, hearing their heavy boots getting closer.... I knew they could pick me off with rifle fire even if the could not catch me, so ... I dived into a small depression partially filled with mountain sage, and quickly covered my self up with all the leaves and pine needles I could find.... The first line in the advance quickly caught up to me, and passed me, uneventfully, except that one German stepped on a finger as he passed. The pain was minimal considering what might have happened....

From the memoirs of Sgt Murray Shapiro, U.S. Army

The Germans met with early success in the Battle of the Bulge, capturing nine thousand American prisoners on the Schnee Eifel during the initial breakthrough.

National Archives and Records Administration

Dec. 19 - "C" ration meat for breakfast. Then marched again - but were surrounded, with heavy firing all around us.... During the battle I was sent with a message ...

I was returning to my platoon over open fields.... Once on falling down, just before I hit the ground, a bullet tore into the ground ... But I got up and ran again and finally got to where my platoon had been.... They were "digging in" in the woods.

Soon word came down that we were going to surrender.... "We haven't fought yet!" But we finally dug holes and disassembled our rifles and buried them and other equipment. Then we marched out onto a road with our hands up....

From the diary of Pfc Arthur A. Kleppinger, U.S. Army

Captured American soldiers who were executed by the Germans lie dead in the snow.

National Archives and Records Administration

LOPEZ, JOSE M.

... Sergeant, U.S. Army, 23d Infantry, 2d Infantry Division. Place and date: *Near Krinkelt, Belgium, 17 December 1944.... Citation: On his own initiative, he carried his heavy machinegun from Company K's right flank to its left ... Occupying a shallow hole offering no protection above his waist, he cut down a group of 10 Germans. Ignoring enemy fire from an advancing tank, he held his position and cut down 25 more enemy infantry attempting to turn his flank.... Although dazed and shaken from enemy artillery fire which had crashed into the ground only a few yards away, he realized that his position soon would be outflanked. Again, alone, he carried his machinegun to a position to the right rear of the sector; enemy tanks and infantry were forcing a withdrawal. Blown over backward by the concussion of enemy fire, he immediately reset his gun and continued his fire. Singlehanded he held off the German horde until he was satisfied his company had effected its retirement.... He fired from this position until his ammunition was exhausted. Still carrying his gun, he fell back with his small group to Krinkelt. Sgt. Lopez's gallantry and intrepidity, on seemingly suicidal missions in which he killed at least 100 of the enemy, were almost solely responsible for allowing Company K to avoid being enveloped, to withdraw successfully and to give other forces coming up in support time to build a line which repelled the enemy drive.*

From Medal of Honor citation

Sgt Jose M. Lopez, U.S. Army,
San Antonio, Texas

Mr. Jose M. Lopez

Medal of Honor

Lyndon Baines Johnson Library and Museum, National Archives and Records Administration

Dog tags worn by infantry 2d Lt Howard M. Randall, U.S. Army
The tags were taped together so they would not make a sound.

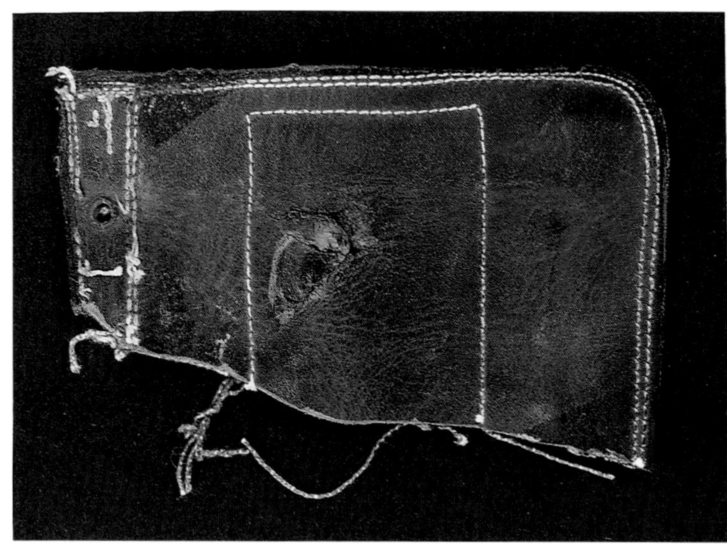

Army boot top with a hole from the metal fragment that wounded 2d Lt Howard M. Randall

2d Lt Howard M. Randall, U.S. Army, Champaign, Illinois

March 3, '45
Luxenburg

Dear Mom & Dad,

... I've never seen anything like that attack even in the movies. We ran down that barren 1000 yd. slope in a skirmish line of two platoons ... All the way down we were constantly under observed mortar, 88, and m.g. fire & snipers. We couldn't see anything to fire at but threw lead all over the place. I took 2 shots at a jackrabbit on the way down. When we were almost at the bottom, 2 mortar shells landed within 20 yds of me. One small hunk of metal went through the top of my combat boot and stuck in my ankle. I jumped in a shell hole and my radio operator jumped in on top of me. We got the piece of metal out and then I caught up with the platoon by shuffling along to beat hell and then we went into the town which was clear of Krauts....

All during the nite enemy patrols bumped into us and gave up. Our two companies took 70 prisoners. At daybreak my ankle was so stiff that I couldn't walk too well ... They thought the small hole a little more serious than I, so am now in a hospital for how long I don't know. However, I do know that I am not quite as anxious to pull off a "Charge of the Light Brigade" stunt as I once was....

Mother, I'm sure it must be God & yourself in partnership who are guiding me.

I walked within 10 feet of a sniper the other night without seeing him and he didn't shoot. The 3rd man behind me dug him out....

Lots of love,
Howard

Letter, 2d Lt Howard M. Randall, U.S. Army, to his parents, March 3, 1945

An infantry rifle platoon leader who participated in attacks on the Siegfried Line from Luxenbourg, Lieutenant Randall gives an account of the action that resulted in his being awarded the Silver Star and that also sent him to the hospital.

Mr. Howard M. Randall

Sunday, Dec. 17, 1944

Dear Marshall:

... Mon. Dec. 18, 1944

Here it is Mon. I had to stop & go to bed, so I'll try to finish this afternoon if I can hold my pen straight. LaVerne has just received a wire from the War Dept. that Pete has been <u>killed</u> in action Nov. 30 in Germany. This is more than we can all take for he was on furlough this time last year. I now have a baby to raise again for LaVerne.

You take good care of yourself for I want you to come back alive I have began to realize how dear you are to me, so I want you to do all things right, both in spirit & body for you are my <u>only</u> son.

I just can't write much more for I am too nervous, but I want you to know, I & all of us love you dearly & send oceans of love to you. I have only one request to ask of you & it is this try & go to church as often as you can & put your trust in God. Lay off the drinks as much as you can & leave the gals alone.

Oceans of love & a Merry Xmas.
Mother

Letter, Mrs. Nichols to her son Seaman Marshall Nichols, U.S. Navy, December 17 and 18, 1944

Mrs. Nichols has just learned of the death of Marshall's brother-in-law, T Sgt J. O. (Pete) Perry, in France. More aware than ever that her son is also at risk, she does all she can do—she tells him to be careful.

The Marshall Nichols family

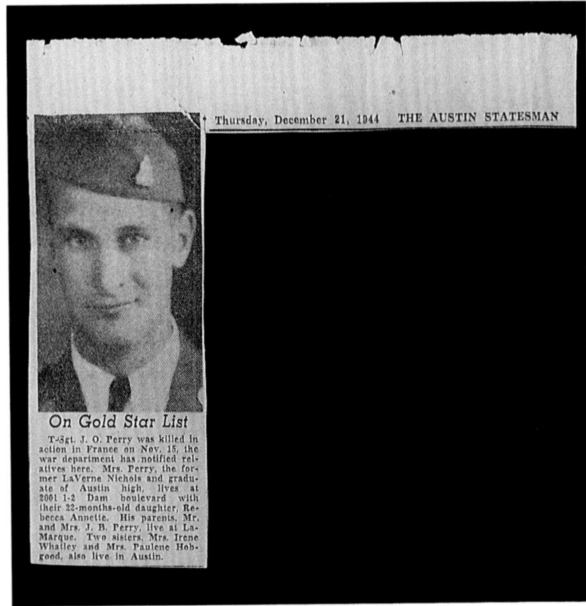

Thursday, December 21, 1944 THE AUSTIN STATESMAN

On Gold Star List

T-Sgt. J. O. Perry was killed in action in France on Nov. 15, the war department has notified relatives here. Mrs. Perry, the former LaVerne Nichols and graduate of Austin high, lives at 2001 1-2 Dam boulevard with their 22-months-old daughter, Rebecca Annette. His parents, Mr. and Mrs. J. B. Perry, live at LaMarque. Two sisters, Mrs. Irene Whatley and Mrs. Paulene Hobgood, also live in Austin.

120 mm Voigtlander Bessa camera used to take secret POW pictures by Sgt Angelo M. Spinelli

When he arrived at Stalag III B in Fuerstenberg-Oder, Germany, Spinelli, a Signal Corps photographer captured by the Germans in North Africa, found a sympathetic guard who would exchange a camera and film for cigarettes. The camera was hidden under Spinelli's clothing when in use and stored under the barracks.

Mr. Angelo M. Spinelli

Sgt Angelo M. Spinelli,
U.S. Army Signal Corps,
New York City, New York

Roll call at Stalag III B, photograph by Sgt Angelo M. Spinelli
In order to confuse the twice-daily head count, an American POW squats down.

Red Cross parcels arrive at Stalag III B, photograph by Sgt Angelo M. Spinelli
While one man carries a parcel into the compound, another discusses the shipment with a guard.

B-17s b

Trading for food at Stalag III B, photograph by Sgt Angelo M. Spinelli
This American prisoner of war is trading a can of margarine from a Red Cross parcel for a kilo of rationed civilian bread.

Two an

… At 6:10 p.m. the Vice President called the Cabinet to order and said: "It is my sad duty to report that the president died 5:48. Mrs. Roosevelt gave me this news, and in saying so she remarked that 'he died like a soldier.' I shall only say that I will try to carry on as I know he would have wanted me and all of us to do. I should like all of you to remain in your Cabinet posts, and I shall count on you for all the help I can get…."

… At 6:45 the Chief Justice administered the oath of office to the Vice President and he became the President of the United States.

From the diary of Undersecretary of the Navy James Forrestal, April 12, 1945

President Harry S. Truman takes the oath of office following the death of Franklin D. Roosevelt on April 12, 1945.

Harry S. Truman Library, National Archives and Records Administration

April 13, 1945

... PERSONAL TO THE PRIME MINISTER FROM PRESIDENT TRUMAN

I am grateful for your message of sympathy to me and to this nation.

In the presence of the great irreparable loss which we have suffered which I know you feel as deeply as I do, I wish to send you this personal message of assurance that with God's help I will do everything in my power to move forward the great work to which President Roosevelt gave his life. At no time in our respective histories has it been more important that the intimate, solid, relations which you and the late President had forged between our countries be preserved and developed....

You can count on me to continue the loyal and close collaboration which to the benefit of the entire world existed between you and our great President.

Approved for transmission
Harry S Truman

Message, President Harry S. Truman to Prime Minister Winston Churchill, April 13, 1945

Shortly after President Roosevelt's death, Truman assures Churchill of his desire to continue the close cooperation between the United States and Great Britain.

Harry S. Truman Library, National Archives and Records Administration

... Suddenly, without warning, we were up on one wing tip, then the other, and then almost upside down.... I was thrown against the top of the plane, and then flat on my back on the floor. My oxygen line was disconnected and I was too numb to fasten it. By this time our plane was back under control and out of the flak area. Shumpert, at the right waist gun directly across the fuselage from me, was right on the ball. He slipped my connections back together and turned on the emergency oxygen supply.... and held me for a minute or two until I was once again functional.... "

From a description of a bombing run over Germany by S Sgt Henry Bethke, U.S. Army Air Force

Oxygen mask

U.S. Air Force Museum Program

The "Dragon's Teeth" of the Siegfried Line, tank obstacles, wind their way along the German border.

National Archives and Records Administration

PRAYER

ALMIGHTY and most merciful Father, we humbly beseech Thee, of Thy great goodness, to restrain these immoderate rains with which we have had to contend. Grant us fair weather for Battle. Graciously hearken to us as soldiers who call upon Thee that armed with Thy power, we may advance from victory to victory, and crush the oppression and wickedness of our enemies, and establish Thy justice among men and nations. Amen.

G. S. Patton, Jr., Lieutenant General, Commanding, Third United States Army

Gen George S. Patton, commander of the U.S. Third Army

Dwight D. Eisenhower Library, National Archives and Records Administration

... Every one wanted me to get vodka for them to drink but I decided they could drink whiskey or nothing. The results were great the [Russian] gen. went out cold and I walked out under my own power ... I kept putting water in my Bourbon and he did not.

When I toasted Stalin and the 4th Guards Army, I ... then broke the glass. I think I will get a good medal as his aid said that I was the only man he had met with feeling (and an Iron stomach)

When I broke the glass he imbrased me.

They are a scurvy race and simply savages we could beat hell out of them....

From a letter by Gen George S. Patton, U.S. Army, to his wife, Beatrice, May 13, 1945

Russian automatic pistol, M1933 Presentation Tokarev given to General Patton "in honor of the victory over the German Fascist Barbarians 12 May 1945" by General Zaxbatayev

Patton Museum of Cavalry and Armor, U.S. Army

Island Hopping

In their projections as to how the war against the United States would unfold, the Japanese envisaged creating a defensive perimeter that ran through the central Pacific and was based on island bastions of the great oceanic groups. Some American planners had foreseen a straightforward drive toward Japan, culminating in one huge naval battle, but a more realistic assessment was for a staged advance, taking and consolidating one island, before moving on to the next.

This almost inevitably was what happened. Through much of 1942 there was raid and counter-raid, punctuated by great battles such as Midway and those around the Solomons. Then, gradually gathering momentum, the American advance began, led by carrier task forces that took on and destroyed the Japanese naval and air forces and followed by huge amphibious armadas. There were peripheral drives, such as up in the Aleutians, but the main thrust was in the central Pacific.

One by one, the Japanese islands fell: Tarawa, Eniwetok, the Solomons, Saipan, Iwo Jima. Others were left isolated to starve and surrender, as at Truk. The whole development of amphibious operations, and the highly sophisticated doctrine and technology to support it, was a peculiarly American contribution to the art of war. After World War I, military theorists had concluded an amphibious landing could not succeed; after World War II, they decided it could not be stopped.

Facing page:

Marine throwing a hand grenade

Life-size figure by Studio EIS, Brooklyn, New York

Photograph by Elliot Schwartz

Landing craft from the invasion fleet carry U.S. Marines to the beach of Iwo Jima and Mount Suribachi.

National Archives and Records Administration

It is 0430 19 February 1945, and we have just been fattened for the kill with a customary battle breakfast—steak and eggs.... Pistols and magazines are carefully being cleaned of excess oil and made ready for use. since I am to be in the first boat over the side, final preparations were made last night. All that can be done now is wait for the call "Shore Party free boat, stand by". Fully clothed, I crawl into my bunk ...

From the diary of 1st Lt Sven G. Carlson, U.S. Marine Corps

1st Lt Sven G. Carlson,
U.S. Marine Corps,
Woonsocket, Rhode Island

Mr. Sven Carlson

Men of the Fourth Marine Division prepare to attack from the black sand beaches at Iwo Jima.

National Archives and Records Administration

JACOBSON, DOUGLAS THOMAS

... Private First Class, United States Marine Corps Reserve, 3d Battalion, 23d Marines, 4th Marine Division. Place and date: *Iwo Jima, Volcano Islands, 26 February 1945.... Citation: ... Jacobson waged a relentless battle as his unit fought desperately toward the summit of Hill 382 in an effort to penetrate the heart of Japanese cross-island defense. Employing his weapon with ready accuracy when his platoon was halted by overwhelming enemy fire ... destroyed two hostile machinegun positions, then attacked a large blockhouse, completely neutralizing the fortification before dispatching the five-man crew of a second pillbox and exploding the installation with a terrific demolitions blast.... Moving steadily forward, he wiped out an earth-covered rifle emplacement and, confronted by a cluster of similar emplacements ... reduced all 6 positions to a shambles, killed 10 of the enemy, and enabled our forces to occupy the strong point.... he volunteered his services to an adjacent assault company, neutralized a pillbox holding up its advance, opened fire on a Japanese tank pouring a steady stream of bullets on one of our supporting tanks, and smashed the enemy tank's gun turret in a brief but furious action culminating in a singlehanded assault against still another blockhouse ... By his dauntless skill and valor, PFC Jacobson destroyed a total of 16 enemy positions and annihilated approximately 75 Japanese, thereby contributing essentially to the success of his division's operations ...*

From Medal of Honor citation

Pfc Douglas T. Jacobson, U.S. Marine Corps, Port Washington, Long Island, New York

Maj Douglas T. Jacobson, USMC (Ret.)

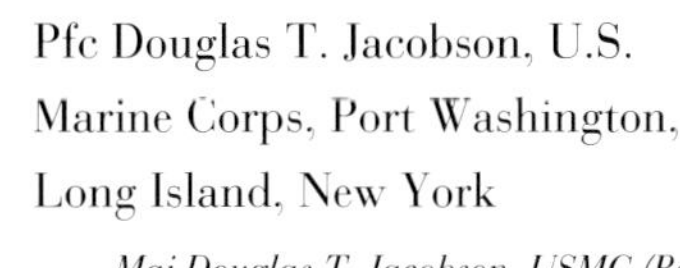

Medal of Honor

Marine Corps Headquarters, Military Awards Branch

Pfc DD Roche and Pfc Peter Sisoy, U.S. Marine Corps

Dear Pete!
... I'm plenty lucky to get off that Iwo Jima as easily as I did. The bullet that hit me was a twenty five cal. from a nambu. It didn't hit the bone. an awful lot of guys that we know were hit....

Remember that little kid from Det. that Walter used to run around with. His name was Sills. They brought him aboard the same ship that I was on with a bad stomach wound. He died a couple days after he got aboard.... These all happened in the first four days so you can imagine what the final list will be like....

Pete Never was such a battle in the History of the Marine Corps fought the Japs had the whole island staked off like a rifle range Every thing on that island had been measured off ... The barrage they laid was hedious not to mention the hundreds upon hundreds of rienforced bunkers with machine gun emplacements. They didn't have any open foxhols they were all rienforced with sand bags with tops on them coverd with sand. I have talked with guys here in the hospital who have been on The "Canal," Tarawa and Siapan and they say that this (Iwo) was worse than all of them put together

PS	*all for now*
I am in the	*Bus*
Marianas	*DD Roche*

Letter, Pfc DD Roche, U.S. Marine Corps, to Pfc Peter Sisoy, U.S. Marine Corps, March 7, 1945

Private Roche tells his previously wounded buddy how the Marines took Iwo Jima—and which of their mutual friends survived the battle.

Mr. Peter Sisoy

... A few hours after the initial landings, we began to take casualties aboard. At first I felt the sight touch my stomach, but I soon became hardened to it.... Everyone aboard took an interest in the welfare of our casualties. We tried to make them as comfortable as possible by giving them cigarettes, cheering them with our talk, and even writing letters for them.... The burial services that I witnessed were very solemn ceremonies. Our hearts were filled with the deepest reverence and our lips betrayed a silent prayer as we watched the weighted bodies slide from underneath the American flag and drop into the water....

From a letter by Lt (jg) William C. Bieluch, U.S. Coast Guard, to his wife, March 21, 1945

Lt (jg) William C. Bieluch,
U.S. Coast Guard,
Hartford, Connecticut

Mr. William C. Bieluch

A Japanese torpedo bomber bursts into flames after a direct hit by a five-inch shell from an American aircraft carrier.

National Archives and Records Administration

Overleaf:
Marines from the Fifth Division inch their way up a slope on Red Beach No 1.

National Archives and Records Administration

... OUR FUEL WAS VERY LOW AND WE WERE 255 MILES WEST OF OUR SHIP. WE HAD BURNED 200 GALLONS OF FUEL GETTING OUT THERE AND HAD BUT 120 GALLONS TO GET US HOME.... THE LEADER OF OUR GROUP FOR SOME UNKNOWN REASON BEGAN CHANGING HIS COURSE.... I RECHECKED MY NAVIGATION AND FOUND THEM TO BE 020° OFF COURSE. SOME POWER GAVE ME CONFIDENCE ENOUGH TO BREAK AWAY FROM THAT GROUP ALONE AND TAKE UP THE HEADING WHICH I BELIEVED TO BE CORRECT.... THE FUEL TANK I WAS ON RAN DRY AND MY ENGINE QUIT. QUICKLY I SWITCHED TO THE OTHER TANK AND THE ENGINE CAUGHT AND ON WE WENT.... I CUT DOWN MY MANIFOLD PRESSURE AND REDUCED MY ENGINE R.P.M. AS LOW AS I DARED. THE FUEL MIXTURE CONTROL WAS LEANED ALMOST TO THE POINT OF CUT OFF. MY ENGINE QUIT AGAIN - ALL THE GAS GONE FROM THAT TANK - I SWITCHED TO MY LAST TANK (75 GALLONS LEFT). THERE WAS STILL A LONG WAY TO GO....

I DECIDED THAT I WOULD TRY A WATER LANDING RATHER THAN BAIL-OUT AND LOSE OUR LARGE RAFT IN THE PLANE.... I KNEW THE WATER WOULD BE BLACK AND INVISIBLE. AT 50 FEET MY RADIOMAN WOULD FIRE A VERYS PISTOL FLARE AND I HOPED I WOULD BE ABLE TO DETERMINE MY TRUE HEIGHT ABOVE THE WATER AND LET DOWN ACCORDINGLY....

AT 2110 I SIGHTED A SMALL SEARCH LIGHT THROUGH A HOLE IN THE CLOUDS.... I LET DOWN TO 1000 FEET AND HEADED FOR WHAT I THOUGHT WAS A CARRIER SOME DISTANCE AWAY YET.... I HAD NEVER LANDED ABOARD A CARRIER BEFORE AT NIGHT BUT I WAS EAGER TO TRY. THE FIRST CARRIER I MADE AN APPROACH ON HAD ALL THE PLANES SHE COULD HOLD AND SO I PICKED OUT ANOTHER ONE. MY FUEL GAGE READ "O". I WAS WORRIED. ABOUT 15 PLANES WERE IN THE TRAFFIC CIRCLE AROUND THIS CARRIER AND I JUST MUSCLED IN AND MADE MY APPROACH.... WHAT LITTLE I COULD SEE OF IT SURE LOOKED SMALL FOR A PLACE TO LAND IN THE DARK.... I CONTINUED MY APPROACH AND LANDED ABOARD. I WAS ON HOME BASE AND VERY GLAD TO BE THERE....

I HAD A MECHANIC CHECK MY FUEL AND I HAD THREE (3) GALLONS LEFT. LESS THAN 2 MINUTES OF FUEL.... I WAS THE ONLY SB2C OUT OF 24 WHO GOT BACK ABOARD. THE REST RAN OUT OF GAS AND LANDED IN THE WATER ...

Diary, Lt (jg) Everett P. Fulton, U.S. Navy, June 20, 1945

The story of Lieutenant Fulton's return to safety after a raid on the Japanese main fleet is one of intelligent navigation and flying skill. Of all the planes that took off with him from the USS *Wasp*, Fulton's was the only one to maintain the proper heading on the return flight.

Mr. Everett P. Fulton

IN BIG WHITE LETTERS.
"THE INCREDIBLE" A
MOST FITTING NAME. (5)
AFTER LEAV-
ING THE FLIGHT DECK I
LEARNED THAT MY LANDING
WAS THE FIRST SB2C TO
LAND ON THAT CARRIER
THE U.S.S. ENTERPRISE. I ALSO
LEARNED THAT THE PLANE
WHICH I ALMOST COLLIDED
WITH WAS A LOST JAP
PILOT. HE WAS SHOT DOWN.
JUNE 21. I SPENT THE NIGHT
ABOARD THE ENTERPRISE
AND FLEW BACK ABOARD
THE WASP THE
NEXT MORNING. WHEN
I LANDED THERE WAS A
GENERAL SIEGE OF

JUNE 21

HANDSHAKING AND
CONGRATULATIONS FOR
ONLY THEN DID I LEARN
THAT I WAS THE ONLY
SB2C OUT OF 24 (7) WHO
GOT BACK ABOARD. THE
REST RAN OUT OF GAS AND
LANDED IN THE WATER
LAST NIGHT. LT. KANE
WAS PICKED UP O.K. -
DURING THE NIGHT. (9)

JUNE 22

WE RECEIVED WORD THIS A.M.
THAT OUR SKIPPER (LT. COMMAND-
ER J.D. BLITCH) HAD BEEN PICKED
UP BY A PATROL PLANE FROM
HIS LIFE-RAFT. (10)
LT. (JG) "MOOSE" AMUSSEN
AND ENS. BERG WERE PICKED
UP BY DESTROYERS AND

Lt (jg) Everett P. Fulton,
U.S. Navy, San Angelo, Texas

Pilot Everett P. Fulton and radio/gunner Larry Quinlan in a carrier-based SB2C Helldiver from the USS *Wasp* fly over Cebu Island in the Philippines on September 12, 1944.

Mr. Everett P. Fulton

The USS *Hornet* fires 40 mm shells toward Japanese positions as planes from Task Force 58 raid Tokyo.

National Archives and Records Administration

A marine throws a hand grenade at a Japanese position.

National Archives and Records Administration

Japanese ceramic hand grenade recovered from Iwo Jima

Private collection of Mr. Bradley J. Hartsell

Mark II fragmentation grenade

Dwight D. Eisenhower Library, National Archives and Records Administration

Marines use a flamethrower to reach inside fortified Japanese bunkers on Iwo Jima.

National Archives and Records Administration

A marine of the First Marine Division fires his Thompson submachine gun on Okinawa.

National Archives and Records Administration

U.S. Marines on Saipan

Harry Schmidt Collection, Hoover Institution Archives

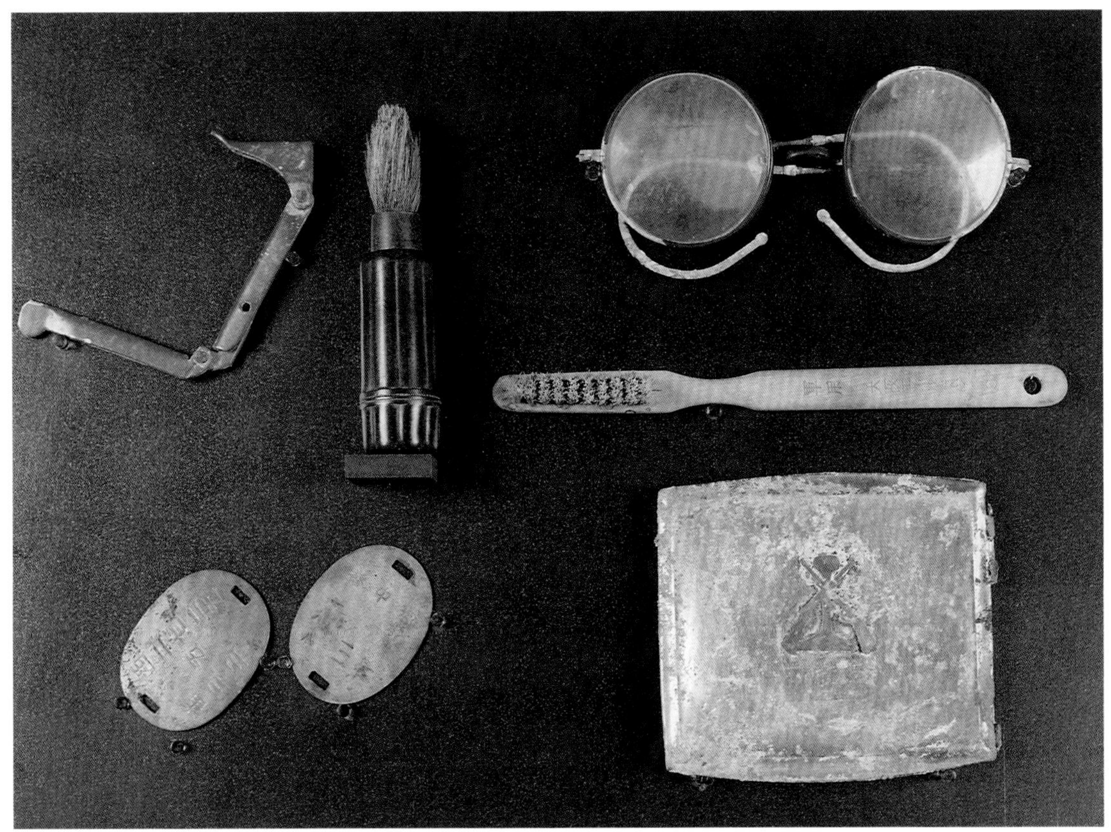

Razor, shaving brush, toothbrush, identification tags, eyeglasses, and cigarette case

These Japanese items were recovered from Iwo Jima.

Private collection of Mr. Bradley J. Hartsell

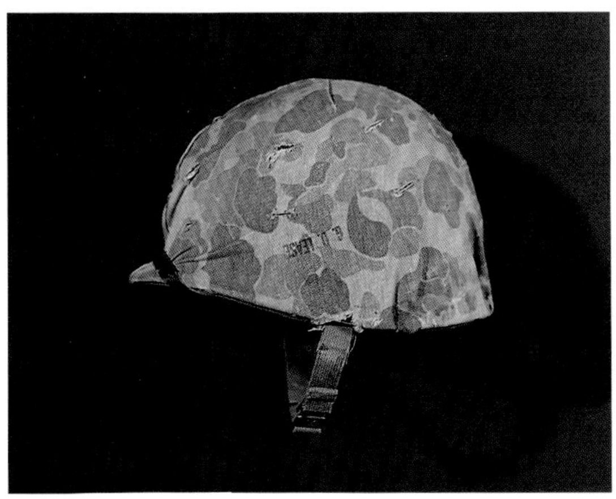

U.S. Marine helmet

U.S. Marine Corps Museums

Japanese helmet

Dwight D. Eisenhower Library, National Archives and Records Administration

Marine casualties on the beach at Tarawa attest to the savage fighting that took place there.

National Archives and Records Administration

Dead Japanese soldiers line the beach on Saipan.

Harry Schmidt Collection, Hoover Institution Archives

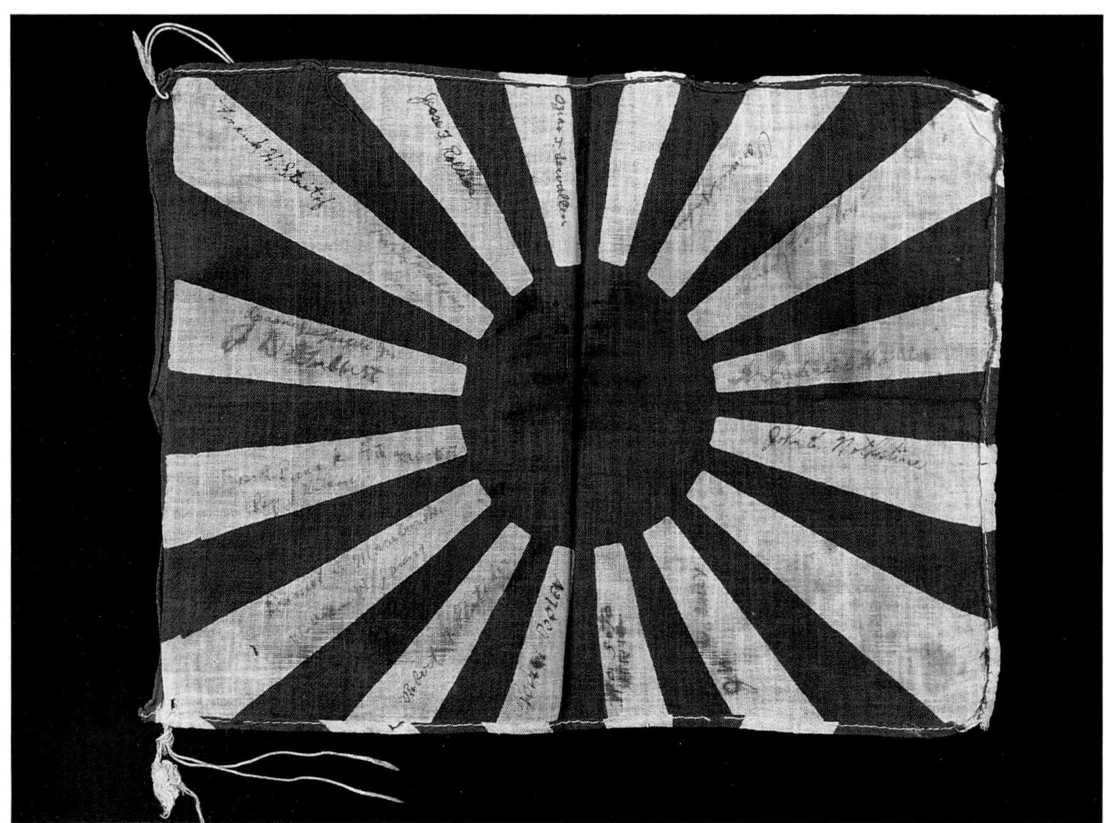

Japanese flag taken during the Battle of Saipan

Mrs. Catherine Warner Batey

... PFC Asa C. Warner, U.S. Marine Corps, and two of his buddies [Donald Carroll and Tom Price] promised one another that if anyone of the three came through the fighting he would visit the other's parents.... Asa was killed by a sniper.... the survivors of their company [Co E, 2nd Bn, 6th Marines, 2nd Division] signed their names to this small flag ... After the war, Tom personally delivered the flag to our parents ...

From the recollections of Mrs. Catherine Warner Batey

The bombsight at the beginning of World War II was heralded as a "secret weapon" ... and elaborate steps were taken to protect its secrecy, such as removing them from planes after missions and instructing bombardiers to destroy them in the event the plane went down behind enemy lines. Inevitably, some of the instruments were captured by the Germans, and security measures were relaxed.... Flying out of Saipan primarily, we bombed ... Iwo Jima, Chi Chi Jima, and Ha Ha Jima in the Bonin Islands ... and Mindinao, Luzon, Cebu and Mindoro in the Philippines.... we were able to place bombs on airfields, troop bivouacs, harbors, and even ships from altitudes over 20,000 feet thus avoiding enemy gunfire from any but long-range weapons....

From the recollections of 1st Lt Austen H. Furse, U.S. Army Air Force

1st Lt Austen H. Furse, U.S. Army Air Force, Eastland, Texas

Mr. Austen H. Furse

Norden bombsight, a gyroscopically stabilized synchronizing bombsight developed for accurate bombing from high altitudes

American Airpower Heritage Museum, Inc.

American soldiers set up a .50-caliber machine gun on Bougainville in the Solomon Islands.

Leonard Boyd Collection, Hoover Institution Archives

This soldier of the Twenty-fifth Infantry carries machine-gun ammunition to a forward area in action on Bougainville.

Leonard Boyd Collection, Hoover Institution Archives

Lt Russell Beegle, U.S. Army, Bedford, Pennsylvania, with his wife and son

Mrs. LaVerne Beegle

Lieutenant Beegle describes fighting the Japanese and being wounded during the battle of Attu, one of the Aleutian Islands in the Northern Pacific:

... When we were winning they wouldn't fight back. They'd watch us and when they got the chance they'd blow themselves up with grenades ... They are tricky and treacherous and many of these were seasoned fighters from Burma. They are poor shots. The fellow that got me had to fire eight times.... You can't order Americans, but they'll follow anywhere, into anything. I saw one fellow get three chest wounds before he'd quit....

... Did a show at Harmon Field. Today at the hospital we all got to pin the Purple Heart on some fellows, it was something & a wonderful expereince....

Diary by Shirley Rose Gray, USO Camp Shows, Inc., July 8 to 9, 1945

On Guam, Shirley Gray gets her first taste of the heady mixture of hard work, spare conditions, and congeniality with the officers and men, along with sobering moments such as hospital visits.

Dr. Gary Gallagher

Shirley Rose Gray, USO Camp Shows, Inc., Los Angeles, California, with Eddie Bracken entertaining troops in the Pacific theater

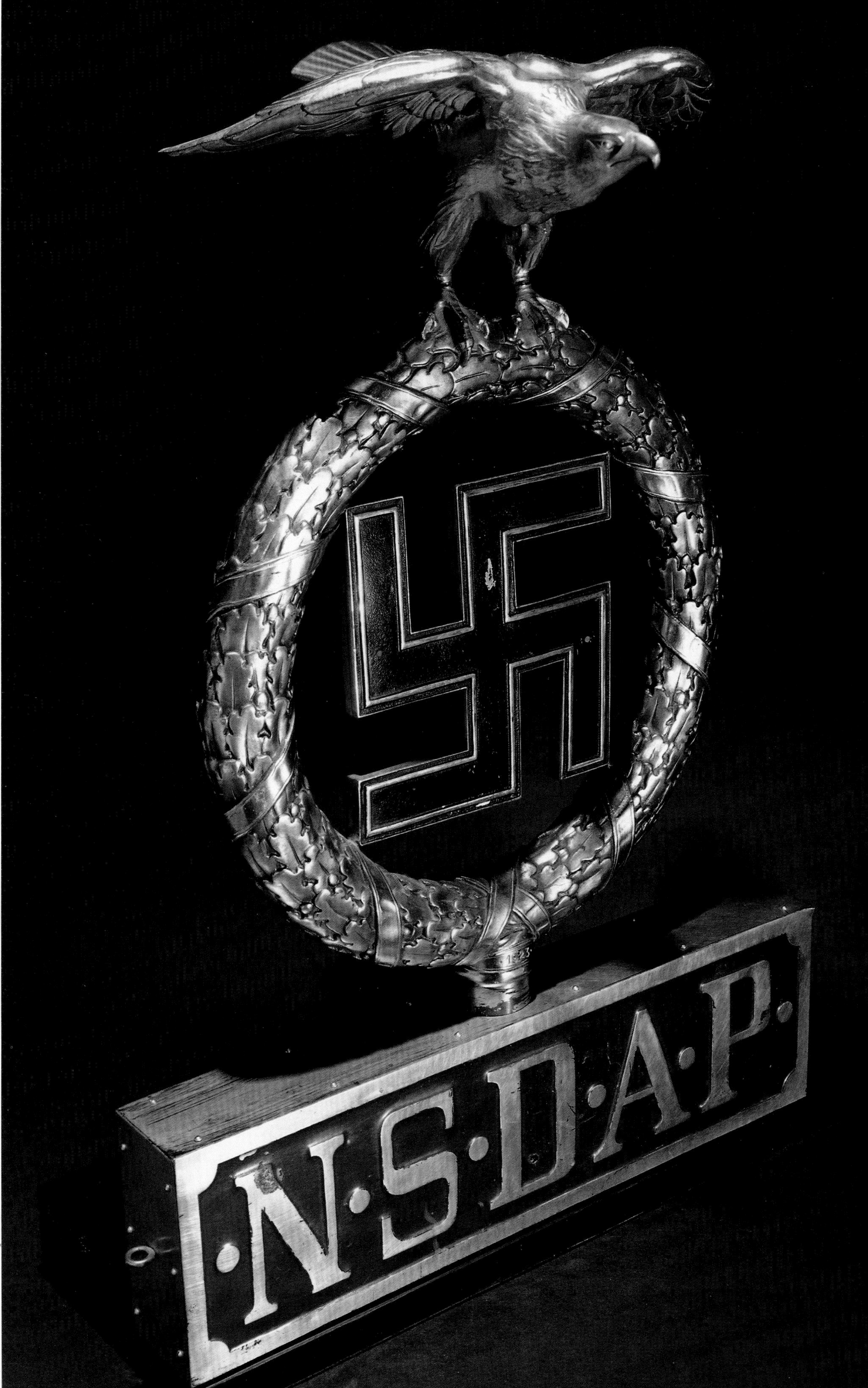
·N·S·D·A·P·

"My Private Will, My Political Testament"

From mid-1944 on, Adolf Hitler retreated farther and farther from reality; he insisted that time, space, and Allied superiority be met by "steadfastness and fanatical tenacity." He kept hoping for a miracle. But one by one his hopes were dashed; his empire crumbled, and his power to influence events grew ever smaller. All he could do was hold on and demand that Germany die with him, and that he did all too well.

As western Allied forces poured over Germany in April of 1945 and the Soviets battled for Berlin itself, Hitler and his personal entourage moved into the Bunker, a great underground complex beneath the Reichs Chancellery. After April 22 he issued few orders other than to denounce any of his commanders who tried to assume responsibility. Instead, he wandered about from room to room, while his followers wondered what to do.

On April 28 he married Eva Braun, his mistress of many years. Then he dictated his political testament, in the hallowed tradition of Frederick the Great and other German leaders. It started and ended with an attack on the Jews. Nothing was ever his fault: England had forced him to invade Poland. Germans should die rather than surrender, as he would do himself. From that he passed on to his private will, leaving his possessions to the Nazi Party, or failing that, to the state; then there were a few small, personal bequests. Such actions absorbed the last few hours of his life. Finally, he, with his new wife, committed suicide. It was all very banal; it would have been pathetic, had he not left behind him, as he once promised to do, a world in flames.

Facing page:

Nazi Storm Troop standard, dated 1923 (the year of the Beer Hall Putsch, the coup attempt that brought the budding Nazi Party to national attention) This standard was carried in parades, often in association with a banner inscribed, "Germany Awake!" The NSDAP stands for *National Sozialistische Deutsche Arbeiter Partei* (German National Socialist Workers Party).

Dwight D. Eisenhower Library; National Archives and Records Administration

Second from left, Field Marshal Wilhelm Keitel; Adolf Hitler; third from right, Secretary to the Führer Martin Bormann

From Eva Braun photograph albums, National Archives and Records Administration

The German army enters Paris, June 14, 1940.

From Eva Braun photograph albums, National Archives and Records Administration

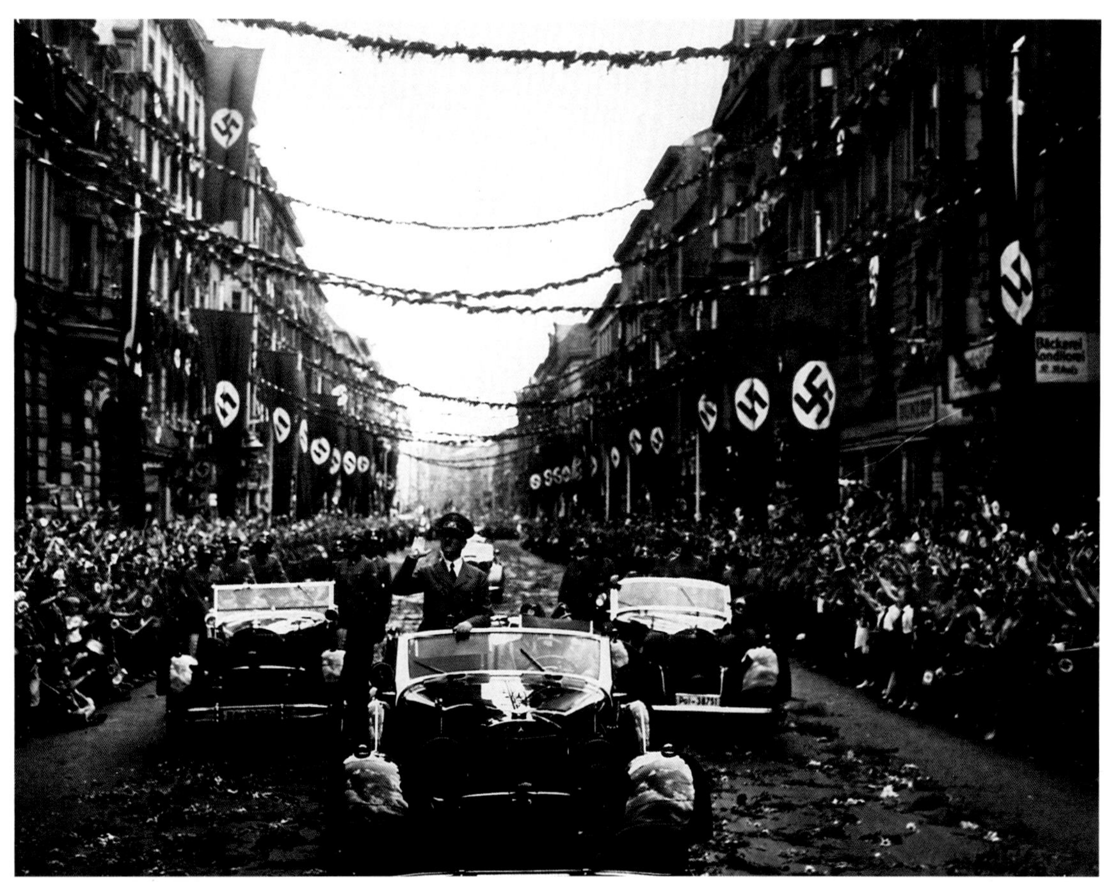

Hitler is given a hero's welcome in Berlin upon returning from Paris, June 1940.

From Eva Braun photograph albums, National Archives and Records Administration

The War Ends: V-E and V-J Days

For Germany and Japan, the last of the Axis powers, signing surrender documents was a necessary formality but not much more than that, for both states were utterly defeated. Total war had brought total destruction, and by the time the end came, the two states were barely functioning as such.

The German collapse came at the end of April and beginning of May, 1945. On April 29 German forces in Italy surrendered unconditionally, to take effect on May 2; the Soviets protested against what they regarded as a separate surrender. Hitler committed suicide on the night of April 30, and his successor, Adm Karl Dönitz, immediately moved to open negotiations. Over the next several days, German units in the field began laying down their arms independently.

On May 5, German representatives reached SHAEF (Supreme Headquarters Allied Expeditionary Force) in Rheims, France, and on the 7th, Gen Alfred Jodl signed the unconditional surrender document in the presence of representatives of all the major Allied states. Fighting was to end officially at 11:01 p.m. on May 9. President Truman and Prime Minister Churchill declared May 8 to be V-E Day, for "Victory in Europe." A second surrender document was signed on May 9 in Berlin.

The Japanese surrender, some three months later, was slightly less complicated. The Allies had again demanded unconditional surrender; on August 10, the day after the dropping of the second atomic bomb, the Japanese government announced its willingness to surrender if the emperor were left on his throne. The Allies replied on the eleventh that he must be subject to Allied authority. The next day Soviet troops invaded Korea, and on the thirteenth, sixteen hundred American planes bombed Tokyo. Japan agreed on the fourteenth to surrender unconditionally, and the Allies proclaimed August 15 V-J Day.

Through the rest of the month, there were various capitulations by Japanese units in the field, but it was not until September 2 that the final surrender documents were signed aboard the battleship USS *Missouri* in Tokyo Bay. Thus the war that officially began with Germany's invasion of Poland on September 1, 1939, officially ended with Japan's surrender on September 2, 1945.

Facing page:

A sailor and nurse on V-J Day

Life-size figures by Studio EIS, Brooklyn, New York

Photograph by Elliot Schwartz

READ THE TRUTH

THE CHICAGO SUN

FINAL

VOL. 4—No. 156 TUESDAY, MAY 8, 1945 Tel. ANDover 4800 THREE CENTS

LONDON SAYS V-E DAY IS TODAY; PRESIDENT BROADCASTS AT 8 A.M.

City to Mark Day in Spirit Of Humility

Two Premature Flashes Take Edge Off Gayety

By Charles Leavelle.

With two anticlimactic celebrations behind them, Chicagoans were prepared to observe V-E Day today in a spirit of thanksgiving and humility and with a determination that no time be lost in wiping out the enemy in the Pacific.

City's Plans for Day

U.S. Officers In Prague; Fight Still On

THIS IS HOW ARMIES WILL CONTROL GERMANY

Map shows where American, British, Russian and French forces will police conquered Germany. The control commission will have its headquarters in Berlin, which technically is in the Russian sector.

White House Plans to Tell Of Victory

Truman Delays Move, Adheres to Big 3 Agreement

Germans Told Of Surrender

King George and Churchill Ready to Address Britain

[Full page of maps, page 19; full page of pictures, back page. History of war on page 6. Other stories, maps and pictures, pages 1 through 8.]

By Peter Whitney.

LONDON, May 7.—Virtually all Germany surrendered unconditionally today—save for a diehard Wehrmacht garrison in Czechoslovakia—as the British government announced it would celebrate V-E Day tomorrow.

Prime Minister Churchill, the announcement further declared, will address the nation on this momentous occasion at 3 p.m. London time (8 a.m. Chicago time). King George VI will address the empire at 9 p.m. (2 p.m. Chicago time).

The Churchill announcement, it is expected, will be broadcast simultaneously with similar statements by President Truman in Washington and Marshal Stalin in Moscow.

The timing of the statements is in accordance with the three-power agreement.

The American broadcasting station in Europe (ABSIE) which is operated by the Office of War Information, broadcast the following announcement on the surrender:

"Germany has surrendered unconditionally. American, British and Soviet representatives have accepted the surrender of the German armed forces at General of the Army Dwight D. Eisenhower's headquarters near Reims, in France, where the official announcement was made.

3 Signed for Allies.

"The surrender took place at 0241 hours French time (7:41 a.m. Chicago time). Gen. Walter Bedell Smith, Gen. Eisenhower's chief of staff, signed for the supreme Allied commander. Gen. Ivan Susloparov signed for the Soviet Union. Gen. Francois Sevez signed for France.

Reich Faces Occupation For at Least Two Years

Britain's King Thanks Gen. Ike

48-Hour Week Curtailment Near

It's a Great Day For the President

Truman Gets Tart Reply From Stalin Over Poles

Secretary Killed As Train Hits Car

Remain on the Job, War Workers Asked

A.P. Ban Eased by Army; Surrender Writer Penalized

Police Veteran, Assailant Killed

Where It Is

The Weather

Chicago Sun, May 8, 1945

Lyndon Baines Johnson Library and Museum, National Archives and Records Administration

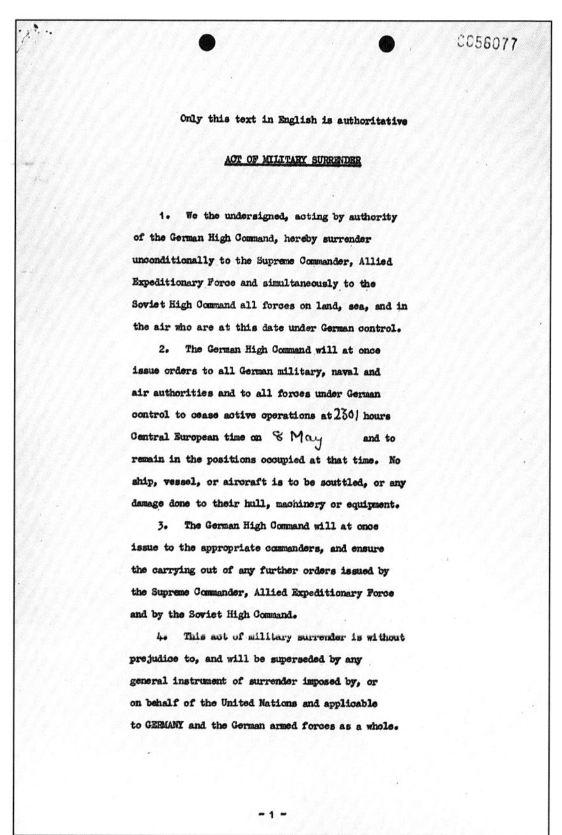

CC56077

Only this text in English is authoritative

ACT OF MILITARY SURRENDER

1. We the undersigned, acting by authority of the German High Command, hereby surrender unconditionally to the Supreme Commander, Allied Expeditionary Force and simultaneously to the Soviet High Command all forces on land, sea, and in the air who are at this date under German control.

2. The German High Command will at once issue orders to all German military, naval and air authorities and to all forces under German control to cease active operations at 2301 hours Central European time on 8 May and to remain in the positions occupied at that time. No ship, vessel, or aircraft is to be scuttled, or any damage done to their hull, machinery or equipment.

3. The German High Command will at once issue to the appropriate commanders, and ensure the carrying out of any further orders issued by the Supreme Commander, Allied Expeditionary Force and by the Soviet High Command.

4. This act of military surrender is without prejudice to, and will be superseded by any general instrument of surrender imposed by, or on behalf of the United Nations and applicable to GERMANY and the German armed forces as a whole.

- 1 -

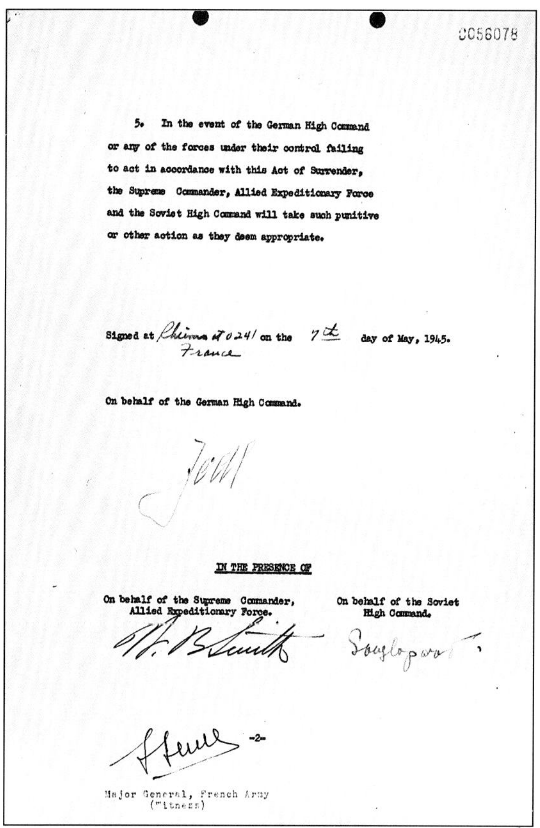

CC56078

5. In the event of the German High Command or any of the forces under their control failing to act in accordance with this Act of Surrender, the Supreme Commander, Allied Expeditionary Force and the Soviet High Command will take such punitive or other action as they deem appropriate.

Signed at Rheims France at 0241 on the 7th day of May, 1945.

On behalf of the German High Command.

IN THE PRESENCE OF

On behalf of the Supreme Commander, Allied Expeditionary Force.

On behalf of the Soviet High Command.

-2-

Major General, French Army
(Witness)

Surrender document signed in Rheims, France, on May 7, 1945

On May 7, 1945, the unconditional surrender document ending the war with Germany was signed in Rheims, France. Representing Germany was Col Gen Alfred Jodl, who was sent by Adm Karl Dönitz, Hitler's successor. Lt Gen Walter Bedell Smith signed the document as General Eisenhower's representative. Though the Soviet Union was represented at the Rheims surrender, they requested that an additional document be signed in Berlin.

Eisenhower had planned to attend the Berlin ceremony, but because the Russians sent Marshal Georgi Zhukov, a group commander of lesser rank, Eisenhower sent an equivalent officer, SHAEF deputy commander British Air Marshal Sir Arthur Tedder. The final document was signed May 9, 1945.

This document was written and signed in English, Russian, and German.

National Archives and Records Administration

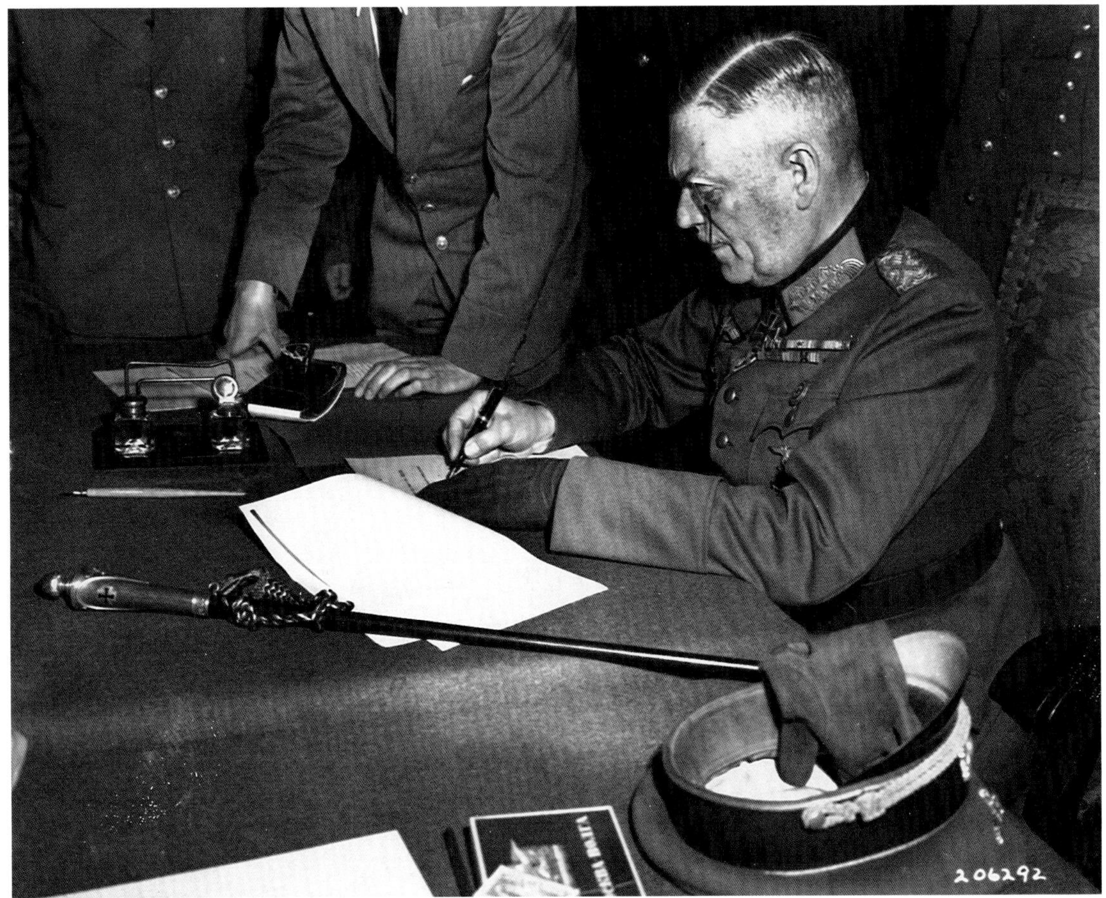

Field Marshal Wilhelm Keitel signs the ratified surrender terms for the German Army at Russian Headquarters in Berlin, Germany, May 9, 1945. Keitel was tried for war crimes by the Nuremburg Tribunal and hanged on October 16, 1946.

National Archives and Records Administration

Paris, 9 May 1945

My dear General:
At the time, when a complete victory over Germany has been won by the magnificent campaign waged ever since November 1942, by the Allied and French armies under your command, I am happy to thank you in the name of France.

The French Government prides itself on having placed under your high strategic command the French Forces operating in the European Theater of Operations. I can assure you that our officers and men will always remember you with respect and affection, which establishes a new and permanent link between the French and American Armies.

I have the great pleasure to inform you that the French Government has decided to confer upon you the Croix de la Liberation.

With my warmest felicitations, may I express to you my sincere personal regards.

C. de Gaulle.

Charles de Gaulle commanded the Free French movement after the collapse of France in 1940. He later became Prime Minister of France.

National Archives and Records Administration

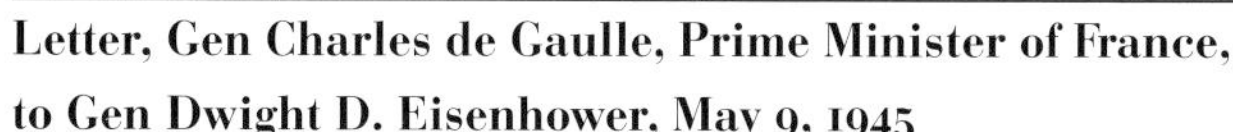

Letter, Gen Charles de Gaulle, Prime Minister of France, to Gen Dwight D. Eisenhower, May 9, 1945

The gratitude of the French nation is offered to the Supreme Commander of the Allied Forces in Europe.

Dwight D. Eisenhower Library, National Archives and Records Administration

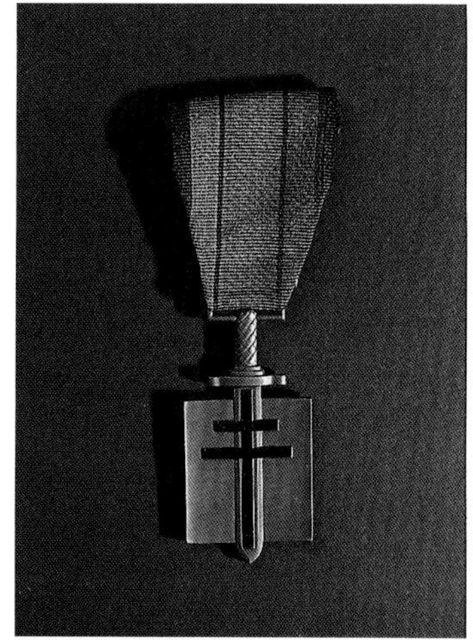

Croix de la Liberation awarded to Gen Dwight D. Eisenhower by the French government and presented by Gen Charles de Gaulle

Dwight D. Eisenhower Library, National Archives and Records Administration

Cpl William S. Dyer, U.S. Air Force, Salt Lake City, Utah

May 10, 1945

Darling,

The events of the past week finally burst into joyous song. Monday night was the night of celebration here, because ever faster than official channels, is the cafe grapevine, and before the radio had given out the news that the whole world was so anxiously awaiting, the plans for celebration were being rushed in every pub, bar, cafe, restaurant and bistro from one end of this little town to another. Monday night, everyone celebrated. I can think of no other place I'd rather have been in Europe than in a French or Belgian town or village. Paris, of course, was THE place to be, but never let it be said that this little spot on the map was ever caught short of gaiety, joy, or what-have-you. The people went mad. Mad with laughter and with happiness, mad with anything and everything. All up and down the streets the cheering populace let it be known that Hitler was KAPUT: once and for all....

Letter, Cpl William S. Dyer, U.S. Air Force, to Frances Wiggs, May 10, 1945

Corporal Dyer's letter to his wife-to-be gives a sense of the party spirit that prevailed in even the smallest villages when the word was out that "Hitler was KAPUT."

Mrs. Frances W. Dyer

Souvenir hunters display a Nazi flag and a portrait of Adolf Hitler.

National Archives and Records Administration

New Yorkers celebrate in Times Square after hearing the Associated Press report of Germany's unconditional surrender to the Allies.

National Archives and Records Administration

Disabled soldiers greet the skyline of New York on their return to the United States.

National Archives and Records Administration

At the club for Allied servicemen and women in New York City

National Archives and Records Administration

Prime Minister Winston Churchill, President Harry Truman, and Soviet Premier Josef Stalin outside the prime minister's residence in London

Imperial War Museum

Residents of Chicago kneel on State Street to offer prayers of thanks after hearing President Truman relay news of Germany's unconditional surrender and the end to the war in Europe.

National Archives and Records Administration

The royal family and Prime Minister Winston Churchill on the balcony of Buckingham Palace on V-E Day

Imperial War Museum

EXTRA! EXTRA!

THE AMARILLO GLOBE

TWENTY-SECOND YEAR, NO. 125 — AMARILLO, TEXAS, TUESDAY, AUGUST 14, 1945 — 12 PAGES — PRICE FIVE CENTS

PEACE

JAPAN ACCEPTS TERMS

FATAL ERROR

Dec. 7, 1941 . . . Pearl Harbor . . . Japs blast 86 ships of Pacific Fleet . . . destroy most of our planes on the ground. . . . it looked like utter disaster . . . but proved Japan's worst mistake. . . . America was aroused as never before in her history.

By The Associated Press

President Truman announced at 7:00 p.m. EWT tonight Japanese acceptance of surrender terms.

They will be accepted by General Mac Arthur when arrangements can be completed.

Mr. Truman read the formal message relayed from Emperor iHrohito through the Swiss government in which the Japanese ruler pledged the surrender on the terms laid down by the Big Three conference at Potsdam.

President Truman made this statement:

"I have received this afternoon a message from the Japanese gover ent in reply to the message forwarded to that government by the secretary of state on August 11.

"I deem this reply a full acceptance of the Potsdam declaration which specifies the unconditional surrender of aJpan.

In this reply there is n oqualification.

"Arrangements are now being made for the formal signing of surrender terms at the earliest possible moment.

General Douglas MacArthur has been appointed the supreme Allied commander to receive the Japanese surrender.

"Great Britain, Russia and China will be represented by high ranking officers.

"Meantime, the Allied armed forces have been ordered to suspend offensive action.

"The proclamation of V-J Day must wait upon the formal signing of the surrender terms by Japan."

Simultaneously Mr. Truman disclosed that selective service is taking immediate steps to slash inductions from 80,000 to 50,000 a month.

Henceforth, r. Truman said, only those men under 26 will be drafted for the reduced quotas.

The White House made public the Japanese government's message accepting that ended the war which started Dec. 7, 1941.

The text of their message which was delivered by the Swiss charge d'affaires follows:

"Sommunication of the Japanese government of August 14, 1945, addressed to the government of the United States, Great Britain, the Soviet Union, and China:

"With reference to the Japanese government's note of Aug. 10 regarding their acceptance of the provisions of the Potsdam declaration and the reply of the governments of the United States, Great Britain, the Soviet Union and China sent by American Secretary of State Byrnes under the date of Aug. 11, the Japanese government have the honor to communicate to the governments of the four powers as follows:

"1. His majesty the emperor has issued an imperial rescript regarding Japan's acceptance of the provisions of the Potsdam declaration.

"2. His majesty the emperor is prepared to authorize and insure the signature by his government and the imperial general headquarters of necessary terms for carrying out the provisions of the Potsdam declaration. His majesty is also prepared to issue his commands to all the military, naval, and air authorities of Japan and all the forces under their control wherever located to cease active operations, to surrender arms, and to issue such other orders as may be required by the supreme commander of the Allied forces for the execution of the above mentioned terms."

Japan has surrendered unconditionally, President Truman said.

The President made the historic announcement to a huge crowd of reporters who had been virtually living in the White House for days in anticipation of just such a development.

Smiling and surrounded by his staff, the President told the press that the Japanese had decided to accept unnocnditional surrender and mentioned that the reporters would not have to take any notes.

The President said they were entitled to a holiday tomorrow and Thursday with pay and only skeleton forces should be maintained.

Chinese Situation Is Grave

Roundup Is Problem

Idleness Is Facing Millions

Would End Draft Calls

WASHINGTON, Aug. 14 (P)—Chairman May of the House Military Committee today called for an immediate halt to further inductions once Japan falls and the earliest possible release of men already drafted.

Argues Petain Tricked Germans, But Never Allies

Hook and Eye Fasteners Are Given Priority

The Weather

Amarillo Globe, August 14, 1945

Lyndon Baines Johnson Library and Museum, National Archives and Records Administration

... When I was War Minister I issued, in compliance with His Majesty's wishes, the "Code of the Battlefield" (Senjin-kun) for the guidance of officers and men at the front. In short, the book was based on this idea: "Heroism must be sublime and impressive while kindness must be extended fairly and widely throughout the world. Even after the enemy is forced to her knees by superior Japanese fighting forces, the spirit of our moral victory would not be fulfilled unless we adhered to certain virtuous principles—stop all attacks once the enemy has surrendered and be kind to the obedient enemy." And we, throughout the China Incident and the Pacific War, constantly sought to achieve this idea through the Greater East Asia policy and also in our treatment and handling of prisoners of war, internees, and inhabitants in the occupied territories. However, judging from the evidence presented to the court it seems that the essential idea of my "Code of the Battlefield" was not carried out to the letter by those engaged in the actual tasks. I greatly regret this failure to follow my wishes, and I suppose that it was one of the most important reasons for our defeat....

Gen Hideki Tojo, former Japanese army chief of staff, war minister, and prime minister

Autograph manuscript, Gen Hideki Tojo, Japanese Army, no date

As army chief of staff, war minister, and prime minister simultaneously, General Tojo was virtual dictator in Japan during the war. In this statement he expresses regret for the failure of the Japanese to maintain the high moral stance he deemed essential to victory.

Dr. Carl Boyd

American soldiers and young English ladies parade through Piccadilly Circus on V-J Day.

Imperial War Museum

Americans of Italian descent in New York City on V-J Day

National Archives and Records Administration

Paris Post EXTRA

JAPS
QUIT

JAPS
QUIT
EXTRA

EPILOGUE

It began in 1939 with Nazi Germany's invasion of Poland and ended with the atomic bombing of Nagasaki in 1945. Military casualties, including both Allies and Axis, reached the staggering figure of 14,900,000 killed and 25,218,000 wounded. Civilian deaths on both sides totaled 38,600,000.

When it was all over, the world had changed beyond recognition. Europe and eastern Asia were devastated, and great empires lay in ashes, while the United States and the Soviet Union had emerged as superpowers. The results of this global war would dominate world politics for the next fifty years—and beyond.

♦ ♦ ♦

At the war's end, the individuals who survived their service on the front lines resumed their lives. Many went back to their homes and jobs or trained for a new career. Others remained in the military or assumed a leadership role at least partially as a result of their military experiences. For all, life would never be the same.

The following short biographical sketches follow the lives of eleven of the war's participants.

General Tadamichi Kuribayashi

As a lieutenant general in command of the Japanese 109th Division, Tadamichi Kuribayashi was posted to command the small island of Iwo Jima in May of 1944. Directly in the path of the oncoming American storm, Kuribayashi and his twenty-five- thousand-man garrison dug in furiously. The Americans began air and then naval bombardment in January of 1945 and landed on February 19. The battle for the island lasted until March 16. Japanese radio contact was lost after the twenty-third, and Kuribayashi, whose body was never found, is said to have committed suicide on the twenty-second. All but two hundred Japanese died, and there were twenty-four thousand American casualties.

Lieutenant (jg) Everett P. Fulton

Navy aviator Everett P. Fulton left the regular navy in 1945 but remained active in the reserves. He was employed by Wynn Oil Co. in San Angelo, Texas, until November 1, 1952, when he was called back into the navy for the Korean War. Fulton remained in the service, and in 1959 he retired with the rank of commander. He then returned to the oil business in Decatur, Illinois. He presently is retired and lives in New Braunfels, Texas.

Field Marshal Sir Bernard Law Montgomery

Bernard Law Montgomery was Britain's most successful field commander of the war, directing operations through North Africa, Sicily, Italy, France, and the Low Countries. After the war he was appointed Chief of the Imperial General Staff, then Deputy Supreme Allied Commander of NATO. His memoirs, published in 1958, remain a revealing and controversial classic. In 1976 Montgomery died at age eighty-eight in Isington, Hampshire, England.

National Archives and Records Administration

AMERICAN PRESIDENTS IN THE WAR

The lives of ten American presidents were directly touched by World War II. Two held the office during the war; the others experienced military service at levels ranging from Dwight D. Eisenhower's command of the Allied invasion at Normandy to the young Jimmy Carter's attendance at the U.S. Naval Academy at Annapolis.

The wartime story of each man is outlined in the following pages.

Franklin D. Roosevelt

Although he adopted a neutralist position when World War II broke out, President Roosevelt began to move more openly into the Allied camp when Germany attacked France and Great Britain. The Lend-Lease Act of March 1941, which provided fifty billion dollars in military supplies and equipment to Britain and the other Allies, represented Roosevelt's first major contribution to the Allied war effort. Further involvement came in August of that same year when he met with British Prime Minister Winston Churchill and signed the Atlantic Charter.

On December 8, 1941, following the Japanese attack on Pearl Harbor, Roosevelt delivered his famous "Day of Infamy" address to Congress. Another milestone in Roosevelt's role in the war occurred when he and Churchill met at the Casablanca Conference in January of 1943. It was at this meeting that plans for a massive aerial bombing program over Nazi Germany were drawn up, with the ultimate goal being unconditional German surrender. With Hitler's war machine rapidly disintegrating, Roosevelt and Churchill met with Soviet Premier Josef Stalin at Yalta in February of 1945 to make plans for postwar Europe. Roosevelt died on April 12, 1945, less than one month before Germany formally surrendered to end the war in Europe.

Franklin D. Roosevelt Library,
National Archives and Records Administration

Harry S. Truman

The German surrender and the end of the war in Europe greeted President Truman almost immediately after he was sworn into office. With the conflict in Europe behind him, he turned his attention to Japan. At the Potsdam Conference in the summer of 1945, Truman met with Churchill and Stalin to discuss Germany's future and to develop a plan that would force the unconditional surrender of Japan. The decision concerning the method for defeating Japan was an extremely momentous one for Truman because he had to choose between an invasion, which would result in hundreds of thousands of Allied casualties, or use of the newly developed atomic bomb. He chose to save Allied lives. On August 6, the *Enola Gay* dropped the first bomb on Hiroshima, inflicting 250 thousand casualties. When the Japanese failed to surrender, a second bomb was dropped on Nagasaki three days later. It was after this second bomb that the Japanese surrendered, and World War II reached a bloody and violent conclusion.

Harry S. Truman Library,
National Archives and Records Administration

Dwight D. Eisenhower

Dwight D. Eisenhower served as assistant chief of staff in charge of war plans almost immediately after the bombing of Pearl Harbor. Promoted to major general in March of 1942, he was appointed chief of the general staff's operation division. Later that year, in June, he was named commander of U.S. forces in Europe. Eisenhower also served as Allied commander in chief for the invasions of North Africa, Sicily, and Italy. President Roosevelt appointed him as Supreme Allied Commander in charge of Operation Overlord, the European invasion against Germany. In December of 1944 he became a five-star general and soon after directed the final assault against Germany. Eisenhower accepted the German surrender on May 7, 1945, closing his distinguished World War II career.

Dwight D. Eisenhower Library,
National Archives and Records Administration

John F. Kennedy

John F. Kennedy was commissioned in the navy in September 1941 and was shortly thereafter appointed as skipper of the assault boat PT-109. On August 2, 1943, the Japanese destroyer *Amagiri* struck Kennedy's boat in the Blackett Strait off the Solomon Islands. The collision snapped the PT boat in half, killing two navy seamen and throwing the others overboard into a blazing inferno of gasoline from the sunken vessel. Towing an injured crewman by a life jacket strap with his teeth, Kennedy landed on Olasana Island, where he and the crewman were discovered by natives and eventually reunited with Allied personnel. For his actions following the collision, Kennedy was awarded the Purple Heart and the Navy and Marine Corps Medal. The episode also worsened an already troublesome back condition, which required surgery. Kennedy was discharged from the service in April of 1945.

John F. Kennedy Library, National Archives and Records Administration

Lyndon B. Johnson

After joining the naval reserve in January of 1940, Congressman Lyndon Baines Johnson volunteered for active duty and began serving as a lieutenant commander in December 1941. While serving as an observer in Australia and New Guinea, Johnson's plane was attacked and nearly shot down by a Japanese aircraft. Following this mission, Johnson was awarded the Silver Star by Gen Douglas MacArthur. Despite the fact that Johnson was in the Pacific, he retained his seat in the U.S. House of Representatives throughout his service. In 1942 President Roosevelt ordered all congressmen in the armed forces to return to their legislative duties. Johnson complied by resigning his post and coming home to the states to resume his political career.

Lyndon Baines Johnson Library and Museum, National Archives and Records Administration

Richard M. Nixon

Lt Richard M. Nixon served as officer in charge of the South Pacific Combat Air Transport Command at Bougainville and Green Island from January to June of 1944. Vice Adm J. H. Newton cited Nixon for his service, commenting that "he established the efficient liaison which made possible the immediate supply by air of vital material and key personnel, and the prompt evacuation of battle casualties from these stations to rear areas." Recalled back to the mainland in August of 1944, Nixon ended his naval career in 1946.

Courtesy of President Richard M. Nixon

Gerald R. Ford

Following the attack on Pearl Harbor, Gerald R. Ford was commissioned in the navy as an ensign. After completing training at the Naval Academy in Annapolis and V-5 preflight school in North Carolina, he requested sea duty. Shortly afterward, he was assigned to the light aircraft carrier USS *Monterey* as gunnery division officer and later as assistant navigator. In addition to these duties, Ford served as the ship's athletic director. As a gunnery officer, he oversaw the firing of the ship's 40-mm antiaircraft gun. While aboard the *Monterey*, Ford participated in the assaults on Wake Island and Okinawa and in the Philippine campaign. As the war drew to a close, he returned to the states, where he served in the Naval Reserve Training Command at Glenview, Illinois.

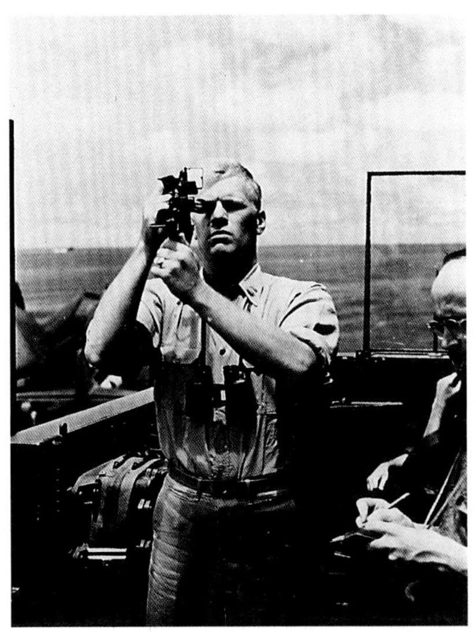

Gerald R. Ford Library,
National Archives and Records Administration

Jimmy Carter

In 1943 Jimmy Carter was admitted to the Naval Academy at Annapolis, where he graduated 59th in a class of 820 students. Carter excelled in gunnery class, naval tactics, and electronics at the academy and in 1944 served on the USS *New York* as part of the school's curriculum. After graduating, he served in the navy until 1953. His service included a stint as engineering officer under Adm Hyman Rickover aboard the *Sea Wolf*, which was one of America's first atomic submarines.

Jimmy Carter Library,
National Archives and Records Administration

Ronald Reagan

A second lieutenant in the army reserve, Ronald Reagan was called to active duty following the Japanese attack on Pearl Harbor. Defective eyesight prevented him from serving in a combat unit. He was assigned to Fort Mason in San Francisco, where he was in charge of the loading of convoys. He later worked in the Army Air Force First Motion Picture Unit as a narrator for preflight training films used to simulate what American flight crews could expect to see on their bombing runs over Tokyo. He also appeared in Irving Berlin's *This is the Army* during his time of service.

Ronald Reagan Library,
National Archives and Records Administration

George Bush

On his eighteenth birthday, George Bush enlisted in the navy to become a pilot. One year later, in June of 1943, he earned his wings and became the youngest aviator in the navy. He was assigned to the USS *San Jacinto*, an aircraft carrier in the Pacific. During the war Bush flew fifty-eight combat missions against Japanese positions in the Pacific theater including Wake Island, Guam, and Saipan. Downed twice, Bush won the Distinguished Flying Cross after his plane was hit by antiaircraft fire while on a bombing mission over the Bonin Islands. Even though his plane was burning, Bush attempted to hit his target before bailing out. He struck the tail on his bailout, which tore his parachute and lacerated his scalp. Shortly after touching down in the ocean he was rescued by the submarine *Finback*. In December of 1944, Bush returned to the mainland, where he completed his service in 1945.

The White House

THE EXHIBITION

Where It Came From

This exhibition began with an idea: Let the men and women who participated in the war tell the story, not in retrospect, but as it happened. Use their personal accounts as they wrote them fifty years ago in letters home and diaries. Limit the selection to correspondence and diaries from the actual battle theaters.

The search began with phone calls, letters, and eventually visits to institutional collections. A wealth of material was identified and later borrowed from several institutions.

At this point we had the means to mount an exhibition from the military leaders' point of view, but we still needed the voice of the enlisted man: the guy who carried the rifle, dug the foxhole, flew the bomber, manned the guns—the guy who actually carried out the strategic operations planned by generals and admirals. We wanted the stories of the average men and women who were drawn into the war.

To find this material, I appealed for help to the VFW and the American Legion. They were happy to comply, and both ran articles in their publication. The mail started coming in—a few letters a day, but steadily. The magazine of the American Association of Retired Persons, *Modern Maturity*, agreed to help by placing a small notice. A month later, I was getting a dozen or more letters and manuscripts a day, and they kept coming. Eventually we heard from over nine hundred individuals, many of whom had just what we were looking for. We found no shortage of good letters and diaries, but the response from women who had served overseas was very small. Had our exhibition concentrated on the home front, this situation would have been reversed.

In the early stages of planning this exhibition, I was reminded that World War II letters had been censored and that diaries had been forbidden by military order. I was told to expect that there would be no diaries and that the censor would have literally cut out anything of interest from the letters. Though I did see letters with parts of sentences removed, I discovered that American ingenuity had prevailed. Some letters had been written, kept, and mailed after the engagements. As for diaries, an interesting analysis of the situation came from Roger H. Tower, a marine who kept a diary. Transcribing his diary after the war in 1945-46, he added these comments:

> *In Navy Boot Camp I was told I could not keep a diary. My diary in Jap hands could help them. Violation of this rule would result*

in severe consequences. I had never thought about keeping a diary. I was too busy enjoying life to spend time writing about it. Suddenly the idea of a diary became attractive. I never smoked until my fooball coach told us we would be kicked off the team if we smoked.... Smoking was a mistake.

The selection process was cruel. So many excellent letters were edited out because of space constraints. This process especially hit home when my own brother's entry did not make the final cut. The exhibition could have easily tripled in size. The outpouring of letters and diaries brought great joy to all of us preparing the exhibition, but we were saddened each time the selection process eliminated another moving letter or excellent diary.

The authors of these letters and diaries had ringside seats to history—how could they not write about it and then carefully preserve it for their progeny? I am so very thankful that they did.

I am grateful to the veterans of World War II and their spouses, sons, daughters, and grandchildren who allowed us to include their personal stories in our exhibition. I also express my sincere appreciation to the institutions that made their collections available to us and to their staffs, who extended every professional courtesy.

Gary A. Yarrington
Curator of the Exhibition

ACKNOWLEDGMENTS

This catalog and traveling exhibition is the product of the collaborative efforts of many talented individuals. At the heart of all exhibitions organized by the Lyndon Baines Johnson Library and Museum is its staff:

Philip von Kohl, Exhibit Specialist
Patricia Partridge, Exhibit Specialist
Patricia Burchfield, Registrar
Char Diercks, Assistant Registrar and Copy Editor
Will Gallagher, Staff Assistant

♦ ♦ ♦

Other Johnson Library and National Archives staff members whose assistance proved to be invaluable:

Linda Brown, Assistant Archivist for Public Programs
Jill Brett, National Archives, Public Affairs Officer
Susan Cooper, National Archives, Public Affairs Specialist
Judy Davidson, Johnson Library Museum Education
Mike Gillette, National Archives Center for Legislative Archives
Ted Gittinger, Johnson Library Oral Historian and Research Assistant
Betty Hill and staff of the Still Picture Branch, Office of National Archives
Paula Megan, National Archives Office of Presidential Libraries
William T. Murphy and staff of the Motion Picture, Sound, and Video Branch, Office of National Archives
Sybil Roberts, National Archives Office of Presidential Libraries
Kathy Struss, Dwight D. Eisenhower Library
Pauline Testerman, Harry S. Truman Library
Doug Thurman, National Archives Office of Presidential Libraries
James Watson, Johnson Library Technical Services
Frank Wolfe, Johnson Library Technical Services

♦ ♦ ♦

Special acknowledgments for guidance and support:

Harry Middleton, Director of the Lyndon Baines Johnson Library
John Fawcett, Assistant Archivist for Presidential Libraries
Claudine Weiher, Deputy Archivist of the United States

♦ ♦ ♦

Photography: Patrick Keeley
Conservation: Carrabba Conservation
Catalog design: Heatly Associates Design
Catalog printer: The Whitley Company
Exhibit Fabrication: Design and Production Incorporated

LENDERS TO THE EXHIBITION

Albuquerque Museum
Albuquerque, New Mexico
Mr. James L. Moore, Director
Ms. Melissa Strickland, Registrar

American Airpower Heritage Museum, Inc.
Midland, Texas
Ms. Tami O'Bannion, Director
Mr. Larry Bowles, Curator of Collections

USS *Arizona* Memorial
Honolulu, Hawaii
Mr. Donald McGee, Superintendent
Mr. Bob Chenoweth, Curator

Dr. Paul L. Ashton
Santa Barbara, California

Mrs. Carol Barber
Rapid City, South Dakota

Mrs. Catherine Warner Batey
Cedar Rapids, Iowa

Mrs. LaVerne Beegle
Bedford, Pennsylvania

Mr. William C. Bieluch
Hartford, Connecticut

Mrs. Alfred F. Birra
Alexandria, Virginia

Dr. Carl Boyd
Norfolk, Virginia

Mr. Albert Buaas
Austin, Texas

Mr. Sven Carlson
Bloomfield, Connecticut

Mr. Richard E. Cole
San Antonio, Texas

Colorado Historical Society
Books and Manuscripts Department
Denver, Colorado
Stan Oliner, Curator

Mr. Donald W. Cortright
Monroe, Michigan

Mr. Clifford M. Dunn
Splendora, Texas

Mrs. Frances W. Dyer
Lafayette, California

Mrs. A. J. Ehlert
West Columbia, Texas

Dwight D. Eisenhower Library
Abilene, Kansas
National Archives and Records Administration
Dr. Daniel D. Holt, Director
Mr. Dennis Medina, Curator
Mr. Martin M. Teasley, Chief Archivist
Ms. Marion Kamm, Registrar

Mr. George M. Elsey
Washington, D.C.

Mr. S. Bruce Elson
Pueblo, Colorado

Mr. Willard H. Fluck
Quakertown, Pennsylvania

Mr. Arthur A. Fredette
Phoenix, Arizona

Mr. Everett P. Fulton
New Braunfels, Texas

Mr. Austen H. Furse
Austin, Texas

Dr. Gary Gallagher
University Park, Pennsylvania

Mr. Daniel M. Ganz
New York, New York

Mr. Walter G. Germann
Abilene, Texas

Mr. Raymond H. Geselbracht
Independence, Missouri

Mr. Nap Glass
Aventura, Florida

Mrs. Jean Fisher Hall
Abington, Pennsylvania

Mr. Peter C. Hand
Winter Park, Florida

Mr. Gordon Hansford
Kentville, Nova Scotia, Canada

Mr. Bradley J. Hartsell
Ann Arbor, Michigan

Mr. Vernon D. Hasley
Dimmitt, Texas

Mrs. Martha Commander Colvig Hildreth
Sarasota, Florida

Mr. Wesley Fay Hogue
Oklahoma City, Oklahoma

Hoover Institution on War, Revolution and Peace
Stanford University
Stanford, California
Mrs. Anne van Camp, Chief Archivist
Ms. Elena Danielson, Associate Archivist

Mrs. Bertl Humpert
Freiburg, Germany

Imperial War Museum
London, England
Mr. Robert Crawford, Assistant Director
Mr. Roderick Suddaby, Keeper of Documents
Mr. Philip Reed, Deputy Keeper of Documents
Ms. Suzanne Bardgett, Special Assistant, Directing Staff

Mr. Paul E. Ison
Fort Myers, Florida

Mr. Douglas T. Jacobson
Punta Gorda, Florida

Mrs. Lucy Wilson Jopling
San Antonio, Texas

Mr. Taro Kuribayashi
Tokyo, Japan

Library of Congress
Washington, D.C.
Mr. James H. Billington, Librarian of Congress
Ms. Tambra Johnson and Ms. Kathleen Tobin, Registrar's Office
Mr. Marvin Kranz, Specialist in American History

Mr. Charles F. Logue
Williamsport, Pennsylvania

Mr. Jose M. Lopez
San Antonio, Texas

The General Douglas MacArthur Memorial
Norfolk, Virginia
Mr. Edward M. Condra III, Director
Mr. Edward J. Boone, Jr., Archivist
Mr. Jeffrey Acosta, Curator

Mr. Jack A. Mack
Salt Lake City, Utah

Mr. Norman Maffei
Franklinville, New York

Mrs. Agnes J. Mangerich
Bethesda, Maryland

Mr. Hiram E. Mann
Titusville, Florida

Mr. John T. Moir
Austin, Texas

Mr. Bryan Moon
Frontenac, Minnesota

Audie L. Murphy Memorial Veterans Hospital
San Antonio, Texas
Ms. Amber L. Baldwin, Public Affairs Officer

National Archives and Records Administration
Washington, D.C.
Ms. Emily Soapes, National Archives Exhibits Branch
Ms. Lisa Auel, National Archives Exhibits Branch
Mr. James Zeender, National Archives Registrar
Ms. Catherine Nicholson, National Archives Document Conservation Branch

National Infantry Museum
Fort Benning, Georgia
Mr. Dick Grube, Director

National Park Service
Home of the Franklin D. Roosevelt National Historic Site
Hyde Park, New York
Mr. Duane Pearson, Superintendent
Mr. Greg Jessup, Museum Specialist
Ms. Betsy Calhoun, Museum Technician/Registrar

Mr. Marshall Nichols
Austin, Texas

Mr. Max L. Noe
Austin, Texas

Mrs. Jeanann Mariner Olds
Maumee, Ohio

Mrs. Patricia Partridge
Bastrop, Texas

Patton Museum of Cavalry and Armor
Fort Knox, Kentucky
Mr. John Purdy, Director
Mr. Charles Lemons, Curator

Col Henry A. Potter
Austin, Texas

Ernie Pyle State Historic Site
Indiana State Museum
Dana, Indiana
Ms. Evelyn Hobson, Curator

Mr. Howard M. Randall
Jonestown, Texas

Mr. Ralph R. Reber
North East, Pennsylvania

Mr. Kenneth W. Rendell
South Natick, Massachusetts

Lord Mayor Manfred Rommel
Stuttgart, Germany

Franklin D. Roosevelt Library
Hyde Park, New York
National Archives and Records Administration
Mr. Verne W. Newton, Director
Mr. Raymond J. Teichman, Chief Archivist
Mr. Wendell "Tex" Parks, Exhibits Specialist
Ms. Alycia J. Vivona, Museum Specialist

Mrs. J. Earl Rudder
Bryan, Texas

Mr. Earl M. Schaeffer
Assaria, Kansas

Mrs. Ernest L. Sheldon
Memphis, Michigan

Mr. Peter Sisoy
Detroit, Michigan

Mr. Angelo M. Spinelli
Hallandale, Florida

Col Blucher S. Tharp, Jr.
Austin, Texas

Mrs. Benjamin L. Thompson
Des Moines, Iowa

Mr. Leonard J. Travaline
Conshohocken, Pennsylvania

Harry S. Truman Library
Independence, Missouri
National Archives and Records Administration
Dr. Benedict K. Zobrist, Director
Mr. Clay R. Bauske, Curator
Mr. Mark L. Beveridge, Registrar
Ms. Pat Dorsey, Museum Specialist

Mr. Raymond M. Tufteland
Lemon Grove, California

Mrs. Mildred and Mr. Steven Turner
San Antonio, Texas

U.S. Air Force Museum
Department of the Air Force
Wright-Patterson Air Force Base, Ohio
Col Richard L. Uppstrom, Director
Mr. Jack Hillard, Curator
Mr. Scott Ferguson, Collection Management Specialist

U.S. Marine Corps
Marine Corps Air-Ground Museum and Museums Branch Activities
Quantico, Virginia
Mr. Kenneth Smith-Christmas, Curator

U.S. Military History Institute
Carlisle Barracks, Pennsylvania
Col Thomas Sweeney, Director
Lt Col Rick Eiserman, Assistant Director of Military History
Dr. Richard Sommers, Archivist

United States Military Academy
United States Military Academy Library
West Point, New York
Mr. Kenneth Hedman, Librarian
Mr. Alan C. Aimone, Chief Special Collections Division
Mrs. Judith A. Sibley, Manuscript Librarian

Mr. Peter Waligura
McKeesport, Pennsylvania

Mrs. Mildred E. Weeks
El Paso, Texas

West Point Museum
United States Military Academy
West Point, New York
Mr. Michael Moss, Director
Mr Pat Dursi, Registrar

Mrs. Eugenia Rutkowski Wilkinson
Bullard, Texas

Mr. Marcus H. Worde
Austin, Texas

CHECKLIST OF THE EXHIBITION

War Threatens the United States

Map, Malay Peninsula and South China Sea
Mr. George M. Elsey

Albuquerque Journal, November 27, 1941
Lyndon Baines Johnson Library and Museum, National Archives and Records Administration

Memorandum, Chief of Naval Operations to Commander-in-Chief, Pacific Fleet, February 1, 1941
National Archives and Records Administration

Pince-nez worn by President Franklin D. Roosevelt
National Park Service, Home of Franklin D. Roosevelt National Historic Site

Memorandum, Secretary of State Cordell Hull to President Franklin D. Roosevelt, September, 1941
Franklin D. Roosevelt Library, National Archives and Records Administration

Peacetime Pearl Harbor

Letter, Ens Thomas Ray Jones to his parents, April 8, 1941

Letter, Fireman First Class Edward Joseph (Bud) Heidt to Julia, November 24, 1941

Letter, Fireman First Class Wesley John Heidt to his mother, November 22, 1941

Letter, Pfc Richard Minear to his half-brother Frances A. Moore, December 2, 1941

Photograph, Ens Thomas Ray Jones, U.S. Navy, Tallulah, Louisiana

Photograph, Firemen First Class Bud and Wes Heidt, U.S. Navy, Los Angeles, California

Photograph, Pfc Richard Minear, U.S. Marines, Santa Clara, California
USS Arizona Memorial Museum, National Park Service

Recording "Hawaii Calls"
Courtesy of Hawaii Calls, Inc., Honolulu, Hawaii

Pearl Harbor

Photograph, Fireman First Class Edward Joseph (Bud) Heidt, U.S. Navy, Los Angeles, California

Photograph, Fireman First Class Wesley John Heidt, U.S. Navy, Los Angeles, California

Telegram, Rear Adm Randall Jacobs to Mrs. Genevieve Dunlap, December 21, 1941

Telegram, Rear Adm Randall Jacobs to Mrs. Genevieve Dunlap, January 24, 1942

Jumper, U.S. Navy, worn by Pharmacist's Mate First Class Path, Ford Island Clinic
USS Arizona Memorial Museum, National Park Service

Photograph, Mrs. Clara May Morse, Long Beach, California

Letter, Mrs. Clara May Morse to her son Francis Jerome, December 7, 1941
Colorado Historical Society, Books and Manuscripts Department

Maui News, December 8, 1941
Mr. John T. Moir

Draft of telegram, Maj Gen Emery S. Adams to all army commanders, December 7, 1941

Translation of statement of Ens Kazuo Sakamaki, December 14, 1941

Photograph, Maj Gen Emery S. Adams, Adjutant General of the Army

National Archives and Records Adminstration

Memorandum to President Franklin D. Roosevelt, December 7, 1941

Annotated draft of speech delivered to the Congress by President Franklin D. Roosevelt on December 8, 1941

Memorandum, President Franklin D. Roosevelt to Prime Minister Winston Churchill, December 8, 1941

Franklin D. Roosevelt Library, National Archives and Records Administration

Memoir, Pvt Earl M. Schaeffer, Jr., December 7, 1941

Photograph, Pvt Earl M. Schaeffer, Jr., U.S. Army Air Corps, Salina, Kansas

Mr. Earl M. Schaeffer

Photograph, Radioman First Class Raymond M. Tufteland, U.S. Navy, Lemon Grove, California

Diary, Radioman First Class Raymond M. Tufteland, December 7 and 12, 1941

Mr. Raymond M. Tufteland

Battan, Corregidor

Ampules of chlorine water purifer

Lens from a vision-testing set, used as a burning glass

Wooden "go-ahead" shoes

Photograph, Capt Paul Ashton, Medical Corps, San Francisco, California

Dr. Paul L. Ashton, M.D.

Photograph, Maj George Fisher, U.S. Army, Plumville, Pennsylvania

Letter, Maj George Fisher to his daughter Jean, September 19, 1941

Telegram, Adjutant General to Mrs. George Fisher, March 25, 1942

Mrs. Jean Fisher Hall

The *Daily Telegram*, March 17, 1942

Lyndon Baines Johnson Library and Museum, National Archives and Records Administration

Photograph, 2d Lt Lucy Wilson, U.S. Army, Tyler, Texas

Mrs. Lucy Wilson Jopling

Autograph manuscript, page from *Reminiscences* by Gen Douglas MacArthur, 1964

Autograph manuscript, page from *Reminiscences* by Gen Douglas MacArthur, 1964

The General Douglas MacArthur Memorial

Diary, Lt Gen Jonathan Wainwright, December, 1941

Radiogram, Lt Gen Jonathan Wainwright to the War Department, May 6, 1942

U.S. Army Military History Institute

Photograph, Col Clifford Bluemel, U.S. Army, Trenton, New Jersey

Letter, Col Clifford Bluemel to Mrs. Bluemel, February 7, 1942

Diary written on cigarette paper during Death March, by Col Albert Svihra, April 12 to April 31, 1942

Log of Events on Day of Surrender at Corregidor, Col Theodore Mosher Chase, May 6, 1942

POW tag worn by Col Theodore Chase, U.S. Army

Special Collections, United States Military Academy Library

Diary of prisoner of war 1st Lt Carl G. Weeks, May 23 to September 27, 1942

Photograph, 1st Lt Carl G. Weeks, U.S. Army, El Paso, Texas

Mrs. Mildred E. Weeks

Fragment of the American flag lowered on Corregidor by Col Paul Delmont Bunker before surrender flag was raised

West Point Museum Collections, United States Military Academy

The Doolittle Raid

Letter, 1st Lt Richard E. Cole to his mother, Mrs. Fred Cole, 1942

Letter, 1st Lt Richard E. Cole to his parents, Mr. and Mrs. Fred Cole, May 4, 1942

Letter, Brig Gen J. H. Doolittle to Mrs. Fred Cole, May 20, 1942

Time-distance computer

Ripcord and handle from parachute

Survival knife

Photograph, 1st Lt Richard E. Cole, U.S. Army Air Corps, Dayton, Ohio

Mr. Richard E. Cole

Replica of "Mark Twain" bombsight used by Doolittle Raiders

Reproduced by Lt Col Horace E. Crouch, USAF (Ret.), Columbia, South Carolina

Albuquerque Journal, April 18, 1942

Lyndon Baines Johnson Library and Museum, National Archives and Records Administration

Safety razor and officer's insignia recovered from one of the B-25 bombers that crashed in China after the crew had bailed out

Mr. Bryan Moon: Expedition Leader, 1990 Doolittle Raiders China Expedition

Flight jacket worn by 2d Lt Henry A. Potter, navigator on the lead bomber

Col Henry A. Potter, USAF (Ret.)

Memorandum, Lt Gen H. H. Arnold to President Franklin D. Roosevelt, April 22, 1942

Franklin D. Roosevelt Library, National Archives and Records Administration

Coral Sea, Midway

Life vest, Type B-4, popularly known as a "Mae West"

American Airpower Heritage Museum, Inc.

Photograph, Fire Controlman Clifford M. Dunn, Jr., Cisco, Texas

Diary, Fire Controlman Clifford M. Dunn, Jr., May 8, 1942

Diary, Fire Controlman Clifford M. Dunn, Jr., June 4, 1942

Mr. Clifford M. Dunn, Jr.

Photograph, Electricians Mate Second Class A. J. Ehlert, U.S. Navy, Bay City, Texas

Diary, Electricians Mate Second Class A. J. Ehlert, June 4, 1942

Mrs. A. J. Ehlert

Seaman's cap

Dwight D. Eisenhower Library, National Archives and Records Administration

Mason City Globe Gazette, June 5, 1942

Albuquerque Journal, May 8, 1942

Lyndon Baines Johnson Library and Museum, National Archives and Records Administration

Radio compass from a Japanese plane brought down in the Battle of Midway

Franklin D. Roosevelt Library, National Archives and Records Administration

Navy aviator's helmet

U.S. Air Force Museum Program

North Africa

Letter, Maj Gen George S. Patton, Jr., to Gen Dwight D. Eisenhower, November 15, 1942

Dwight D. Eisenhower Library, National Archives and Records Administration

Diary, Dr. Josef Goebbels, December 16, 1942

Josef Goebbels Papers, Hoover Institution Archives

Dog tags that belonged to L/Sgt H. J. Griffin

Letter, L/Sgt H. J. Griffin to his wife, May 28, 1943

Letter, Lt Gen Sir Bernard Montgomery to Tom Reynolds, November 1, 1942

Imperial War Museum

Sunday American-Statesman, November 8, 1942

Lyndon Baines Johnson Library and Museum, National Archives and Records Administration

Diary, Maj Gen George S. Patton, Jr., November 3, 1942

Diary, Maj Gen George S. Patton, Jr., November 9, 1942

Letter, Maj Gen George S. Patton, Jr., to his wife, January 25, 1943

Letter, Lt Gen George S. Patton, Jr., to his wife, April 17, 1943

Letter, Lt Gen George S. Patton, Jr., to Gen Omar Bradley, April 23, 1943

Library of Congress

Officer's identification card belonging to Maj Gen George S. Patton, Jr.

Patton Museum of Cavalry and Armor, U.S. Army

Letter, Field Marshal Erwin Rommel to his wife, January 17, 1942

Letter, Field Marshal Erwin Rommel to his wife, August 2, 1942

Compass owned and used by Field Marshal Erwin Rommel in North Africa

Herr Manfred Rommel

Cable, Prime Minister Winston Churchill to President Franklin D. Roosevelt, August 31, 1942

Franklin D. Roosevelt Library, National Archives and Records Administration

German canteen

Harry S. Truman Library, National Archives and Records Administration

Photograph, 1st Lt Eugenia Rutkowski, Detroit, Michigan (right), in group of U.S. Army Air Force nurses having lunch

Mrs. Eugenia Rutkowski Wilkinson, 1st Lt ANC, USAAF

Guadalcanal

U.S. Garand M1 semiautomatic rifle, .30 caliber

Japanese Type 38 rifle with bayonet, 6.5 mm

Dwight D. Eisenhower Library, National Archives and Records Administration

Albuquerque Journal, October 27, 1942

Lyndon B. Johnson Library and Museum, National Archives and Records Administration

Photograph, Pfc Jack A. Mack, U.S. Marines, Dixon, Montana

Diary, Pfc Jack A. Mack, November 2 to November 14, 1942

Mr. Jack A. Mack

Diary, unknown Japanese soldier, September 8 to September 16, 1942

Diary, unknown Japanese soldier, September 10 to October 11, 1942

National Archives and Records Administration

Photograph, S1C Richard Thomas Mariner, U.S. Navy, Toledo, Ohio

Diary, S1C Richard Thomas Mariner, October 31, 1943

Mrs. Jeanann Mariner Olds, former wife

Photograph, Electrician's Mate First Class George W. Beaver, U.S. Navy, Austin, Texas

Letter, Electrician's Mate First Class George W. Beaver to Frances, July 16, 1943

Mrs. Patricia Partridge

Photograph, Pfc Ralph R. Reber, U.S. Marines, Reading, Pennsylvania

Diary, Pfc Ralph R. Reber, August 12 to August 21, 1942

Mr. Ralph R. Reber

Draft message, President Franklin D. Roosevelt and adviser Harry Hopkins to Joint Chiefs of Staff, October 24, 1942

Franklin D. Roosevelt Library, National Archives and Records Administration

U.S. Garand M1 Bayonet

U.S. Marine Corps Museums

China, India, Burma

Photograph, Henry Mason Geselbracht, Jr., American Volunteer Group, Glendale, California

Diary, Henry Mason Geselbracht, Jr., January 4, 1942

Mr. Raymond H. Geselbracht

Hat with four stars

Musette bag

Army issue Hamilton wristwatch

Diary, Maj Gen Joseph Stilwell, February 9, 1942

Diary, Lt Gen Joseph Stilwell, February 21, 1944

Joseph Stilwell Collection, Hoover Institution Archives

"Allied POW Cemetery, Anganan 100KM Camp" by O. C. McManus, USN, pencil on paper

Portrait of Lt Col Blucher S. Tharp by Hoen, pencil on paper

Officer's identification card belonging to Lt Col Blucher S. Tharp, Texas National Guard

Diary, Lt Col Blucher S. Tharp, November 11 to December 13, 1941

Diary, Lt Col Blucher S. Tharp, December 29, 1943, to March 30, 1944

Japanese sword surrendered to Lt Col Blucher S. Tharp, Texas National Guard, by Japanese POW camp commander

Col Blucher S. Tharp, Jr.

Sicily, Italy, Anzio

Typewriter used by Ernie Pyle, Corona, 1917

The Albuquerque Museum, Gift of Don Bell

Photograph, Artilleryman Arthur A. Fredette, U.S. Army, Attlebord, Maine

Diary, Artilleryman Arthur A. Fredette, August 1 to August 7, 1943

1st Sgt Arthur A. Fredette, U.S. Army (Ret.)

Photograph, S Sgt Vernon D. Hasley, U.S. Army Air Force, Sudan, Texas

Mr. Vernon D. Hasley

Photograph, Lt Walter F. Commander, U.S. Army, Buffalo, New York

Letter, Lt Walter F. Commander, to his wife, June 3, 1944

Mrs. Martha Commander Colvig Hildreth

Albuquerque Journal, July 10, 1943

Lyndon Baines Johnson Library and Museum, National Archives and Records Administration

Bronze Star awarded to S Sgt Charles F. Logue

Photograph, S Sgt Charles F. Logue, U.S. Army, Williamsport, Pennsylvania

Letter, S Sgt Charles F. Logue to his parents, August 23, 1943

Letter, S Sgt Charles F. Logue to his parents, August 11, 1944

Mr. Charles F. Logue

"Grave of enemy soldier" by Pvt Norman Maffei, pencil on paper

Photograph, Pvt Norman Maffei, U.S. Army, Franklinville, New York

Mr. Norman Maffei

Photograph, 2d Lt Agnes A. Jensen, Stanwood, Michigan, with the 807th Medical Air Evacuation Squadron on board a boat in Italy

Mrs. Agnes Jensen Mangerich

Photograph, Lt Hiram E. Mann, a member of the Tuskegee Airmen, next to his P-51 Mustang

Mr. Hiram E. Mann

U.S. Army issue raincoat

National Infantry Museum

Hoosier Vagabond by Ernie Pyle, reprint, January 10, 1944

Ernie Pyle State Historic Site, Indiana State Museum

Letter, Gen Dwight D. Eisenhower to his wife, December 14, 1943

Private Collection of Mr. Kenneth Rendell

Memorandum, President Franklin D. Roosevelt to Gen Dwight D. Eisenhower, August 18, 1943

Franklin D. Roosevelt Library, National Archives and Records Administration

Photograph, Lt Randall Harris, U.S. Army, Pocahontas, Iowa

Letter, Lt Randall Harris to S Sgt Benjamin L. Thompson, December 15, 1943

Mrs. Benjamin L. Thompson

Photograph, Cpl Leonard J. Travaline, U.S. Army, Conshohocken, Pennsylvania

Mr. Leonard J. Travaline

Winter aviator helmet

U.S. Air Force Museum Program

Eastern Front

Photograph, Obergefreiter Kuno Schmitt, German army, Karlsruhe, Germany, with his sister

Letter, Obergefreiter Kuno Schmitt to his sister, November 7, 1943

Mrs. Bertl Humpert

German Mauser 98k rifle, 7.62 mm

Russian Mosin-Nagant 1891/30 rifle, 7.62 mm

Russian helmet

National Infantry Museum

Iron Cross, first class

German helmet

Harry S. Truman Library, National Archives and Records Administration

Normandy, France

Letter, Lt Col Alfred F. Birra to his wife, July 12, 1944

Photograph, Lt Col Alfred F. Birra, U.S. Army, Alexandria, Virginia

Mrs. Barbara A. Birra (Mrs. Alfred F.)

U.S. Army helmet found on the beach at Normandy

Clicker toy, used as an identification signaling device by the Allies during the Normandy invasion

U.S. waist-type life belt

Jacket owned and worn by Gen Dwight D. Eisenhower

Letter, Lt Gen George S. Patton, Jr., to Gen Dwight D. Eisenhower, November 11, 1944

Dwight D. Eisenhower Library, National Archives and Records Administration

Cloth Jewish star

Mr. Nap Glass

Letter, Capt C. T. Cross to his family, June 23, 1944

Memorandum, General Sir Bernard Montgomery to army commanders, spring, 1944

Imperial War Museum

Youngstown Vindicator, June 6, 1944

Lyndon Baines Johnson Library and Museum, National Archives and Records Administration

Letter, Lt Gen George S. Patton, Jr., to his wife, August 6, 1944

Letter, Lt Gen George S. Patton, Jr., to his wife, August 13, 1944

Diary, Lt Gen George S. Patton, Jr., August 14, 1944

Letter, Lt Gen George S. Patton, Jr., to his wife, September 16, 1944

Diary, Lt Gen George S. Patton, Jr., September 17, 1944

Letter, Lt Gen George S. Patton, Jr., to his wife, September 21, 1944

Letter, Lt Gen George S. Patton, Jr., to his son, George, October 4, 1944

Letter, Lt Gen George S. Patton, Jr., to his wife, October 8, 1944

Letter, Lt Gen George S. Patton, Jr., to his wife, November 12, 1944

Library of Congress

Watch owned and worn by 2d Lt Audie L. Murphy

Photograph, 2d Lt Audie L. Murphy, U.S. Army, Farmersville, Texas

Manuscript for *To Hell and Back*, by Audie L. Murphy, no date

Audie L. Murphy Memorial Veterans Hospital

Rank flag used by Lt Gen George S. Patton, Jr.

Patton Museum of Cavalry and Armor, U.S. Army

Photograph, Lt Col J. Earl Rudder, U.S. Army, Brady, Texas

Letter, Lt Col J. Earl Rudder to his family, June 15, 1944

Mrs. J. Earl Rudder

Photograph, 1st Lt Ernest L. Sheldon, U.S. Army, Johnston, Pennsylvania

Letter, 1st Lt Ernest Sheldon to his wife, August 25, 1944

Mrs. Ernest L. Sheldon (Ruth)

Photograph, Sgt Charles Easter, U.S. Army, Cincinnati, Ohio

Letter, Sgt Charles Easter to Marion Page Bunge, July 7, 1944

Special Collections, United States Military Academy Library

From the Bulge to the Elbe

Photograph, S Sgt Willard H. Fluck, U.S. Army, Quakertown, Pennsylvania (in group)

Memoir, S Sgt Willard H. Fluck, August, 1945

S Sgt Willard H. Fluck

Photograph, Craftsman Gordon Hansford, First Canadian Armored Brigade, Canadian Army Overseas, Wolfville, Nova Scotia, Canada

Letter, Craftsman Gordon Hansford to his mother, August 12, 1944

Mr. Gordon Hansford

Medal of Honor

Lyndon Baines Johnson Library and Museum, National Archives and Records Administration

Photograph, Sgt Jose M. Lopez, U.S. Army, San Antonio, Texas

Mr. Jose Lopez

Austin Statesman newsclipping, "On Gold Star List"

Letter, Mrs. Nichols to her son Seaman Marshall Nichols, December 17 and 18, 1944

The Marshall Nichols family

Dog tag worn by Sgt Max L. Noe in German prison camp Stalag IVB

Austin Statesman newsclipping, "Former Austin Postal Worker Missing in Luxembourg Action"

Purple Heart awarded to Sgt Max L. Noe

Postcard, Sgt Max L. Noe, prisoner in Stalag IVB, Muhlberg, Germany, to his wife, January 9, 1945

Telegram, War Department to Mrs. Caroline C. Noe, January 10, 1945

Mr. Max L. Noe

Russian automatic pistol, M1933 Presentation Tokarev given to General Patton "in honor of the victory over the German Fascist Barbarians 12 May 1945" by General Zaxbatayev

Campaign ribbons belonging to Lt Gen George S. Patton, Jr.

Patton Museum of Cavalry and Armor, U.S. Army

Photograph, 2d Lt Howard M. Randall, U.S. Army, Champaign, Illinois

Army boot top with a hole from the metal fragment that wounded 2d Lt Howard M. Randall

Dog tags worn by infantry 2d Lt Howard M. Randall

Meat can lid from the Krematorium Weimar stamped with the name of Hersch Zimmerman (No. 9593, 27 years old), who was exterminated at Buchenwald

Photograph, inmate at Buchenwald prison camp, photograph taken by 2d Lt Howard M. Randall

Letter, 2d Lt Howard M. Randall to his parents, March 3, 1945

Mr. Howard M. Randall

Photograph, Sgt Angelo M. Spinelli, U.S. Army Signal Corps, New York City, New York (left)

Roll call at Stalag III B, photograph by Sgt Angelo M. Spinelli

Red Cross parcels arrive at Stalag III B, photograph by Sgt Angelo M. Spinelli

Trading for food at Stalag III B, photograph by Sgt Angelo M. Spinelli

120-mm Voigtlander Bessa camera used to take secret POW pictures by Sgt Angelo M. Spinelli

Mr. Angelo M. Spinelli

Message, President Harry S. Truman to Prime Minister Winston Churchill, April 13, 1945

Harry S. Truman Library, National Archives and Records Administration

Oxygen mask

U.S. Air Force Museum Program

Letter, 1st Lt Earle C. Cheek to Doris Moellenberndt, February 28, 1945

Special Collections, United States Military Academy Library

Stars and Stripes, April 28, 1945

Mr. Peter Waligura

Island Hopping

Norden bombsight

American Airpower Heritage Museum, Inc.

Photograph, Ens Gaylord E. Barber, U.S. Navy, Bancroft, South Dakota

Letter, Ens Gaylord E. Barber to his family, April 20, 1945

Mrs. Carol J. Barber

Japanese flag taken during the Battle of Saipan

Mrs. Catherine Warner Batey

Photograph, Lt Russell Beegle, U.S. Army, Bedford, Pennsylvania, with his wife and son

Bead doll taken from Japanese soldier killed by Lt Russell Beagle during the Battle of Attu

Mrs. LaVerne Beegle

Photograph, Lt (jg) William C. Bieluch, U.S. Coast Guard, Hartford, Connecticut

Mr. William C. Bieluch

Photograph, Storekeeper Third Class Albert Buaas, U.S. Navy (Seabees), Austin, Texas

Dog tag made from fifty-cent piece

Mr. Albert Buaas

Photograph, 1st Lt Sven G. Carlson, U.S. Marine Corps, Woonsocket, Rhode Island

Mr. Sven Carlson

Mark II fragmentation grenade

Japanese helmet

Dwight D. Eisenhower Library, National Archives and Records Administration

Photograph, Lt (jg) Everett P. Fulton, U.S. Navy, San Angelo, Texas

Diary, Lt (jg) Everett P. Fulton, June 20, 1945

Mr. Everett P. Fulton

Photograph, 1st Lt Austen H. Furse, U.S. Army Air Force, Eastland, Texas

Mr. Austen H. Furse

U.S. Navy Certified Civilian Certificate of Identification for Shirley Rose Gray, Los Angeles, California

Photograph, Shirley Rose Gray and Eddie Bracken, USO Camp Shows, Inc.

Diary, Shirley Rose Gray, USO Camp Shows, Inc., July 8 to 9, 1945

Dr. Gary Gallagher

Photograph, Pvt Peter C. Hand, U.S. Marines, Boston, Massachusetts

Letter, Pvt Peter C. Hand to his parents, March 3, 1945

Mr. Peter C. Hand

Razor, shaving brush, toothbrush, identification tags, eyeglasses, and cigarette case recovered from Iwo Jima

Japanese ceramic hand grenade recovered from Iwo Jima

Pen that belonged to Lt Gen Tadamichi Kuribayashi, Japanese commander on Iwo Jima

Private collection of Mr. Bradley J. Hartsell

Letter, from Japanese schoolgirl Shihoko Katoh to kamikazi pilot Kanichi Horimoto, December 5, 1944

Mr. Wesley Fay Hogue

Photograph, Pfc Douglas T. Jacobson, U.S. Marine Corps, Port Washington, Long Island, New York

Major Douglas T. Jacobson, USMC (Ret.)

Photograph, Lt Gen Tadamichi Kuribayashi, Commander of Japanese troops on Iwo Jima, Tokyo, Japan

Letter, Lt Gen Tadamichi Kuribayashi to his wife, August 2, 1944

Mr. Taro Kuribayashi

Sunglasses owned and worn by Gen Douglas MacArthur

Corncob pipe owned and used by Gen Douglas MacArthur

Autograph manuscript, page from *Reminiscences* by Gen Douglas MacArthur, 1964

The General Douglas MacArthur Memorial

Medal of Honor

Marine Corps Headquarters, Military Awards Branch

Photograph, Seaman Marshall Nichols, U.S. Navy, Austin, Texas (right)

Letter to Seaman Marshall Nichols, July 6, 1945

The Marshall Nichols family

Photograph, Pfc DD Roche and Pfc Peter Sisoy, U.S. Marine Corps

Letter, Pfc DD Roche to Pfc Peter Sisoy, March 7, 1945

Mr. Peter Sisoy

U.S. Marine helmet

U.S. Marine Corps Museums

Lunch box, chopsticks, spoon, and cigarette holder

Photograph, Captain Marcus H. Worde, U.S. Army Air Corps, Morrison, Tennessee, (standing, second from left) with flight crew of B-29 "Sitting Pretty"

Photograph, maintenance crew of B-29 "Sitting Pretty"

Mr. Marcus H. Worde

My Personal Will, My Political Testament

Nazi Storm Troop standard, (*National Sozialistische Deutsche Arbeiter Partei*/German National Socialist Workers Party) dated 1923

Dwight D. Eisenhower Library, National Archives and Records Administration

Personal photograph album kept by Eva Braun, 1941-44

Signed typed document, *My Private Will, My Political Testament* by Adolf Hitler, 1945

National Archives and Records Administration

Adolf Hitler, *Mein Kampf*, Munich, 1936 edition

Special Collections, United States Military Academy Library

The Atomic Bomb

Letter, Technician Fourth Class Donald W. Cortright to his family, October, 1945

Photograph, Technician Fourth Class Donald W. Cortright, U.S. Army, Coldwater, Michigan

Photograph of Hiroshima taken by Technician Fourth Class Donald W. Cortright

Mr. Donald W. Cortright

Glass bottle that was found in Hiroshima by Cpl S. Bruce Elson, U.S. Army

Mr. S. Bruce Elson

Evening Star, August 7, 1945

Lyndon Baines Johnson Library and Museum, National Archives and Records Administration

Safety plug, one of two from the atomic bomb dropped on Nagasaki, Japan

Harry S. Truman Library, National Archives and Records Administration

The War Ends

Photograph, Gen Hideki Tojo, former Japanese Army Chief of Staff, War Minister, and Prime Minister

Autograph manuscript by Gen Hideki Tojo, no date

Dr. Carl Boyd

Photograph, Cpl William S. Dyer, U.S. Air Force, Salt Lake City, Utah

Letter, Cpl William S. Dyer to Frances Wiggs, May 10, 1945

Mrs. Frances W. Dyer

Croix de la Liberation awarded to Gen Dwight D. Eisenhower by the French Government and presented by Gen Charles de Gaulle

Letter, Gen Charles de Gaulle to Gen Dwight D. Eisenhower, May 9, 1945

Dwight D. Eisenhower Library, National Archives and Records Administration

Photograph, Chief Radioman Walter G. Germann, U.S. Navy, Abilene, Texas

Letter, Chief Radioman Walter G. Germann to his son, September 1, 1945

Chief Radioman Walter G. Germann, U.S. Navy (Ret.)

Chicago Sun, May 8, 1945

Boston Herald, May 9, 1945

Amarillo Globe, August 14, 1945

Williamsport Gazette and Bulletin, August 15, 1945

Lyndon Baines Johnson Library and Museum, National Archives and Records Administration

Surrender document signed in Rheims by Col Gen Alfred Jodl and Lt Gen Walter Bedell Smith, May 7, 1945

Surrender document signed aboard the USS *Missouri* by Gen Douglas MacArthur, Adm Chester W. Nimitz, Foreign Minister Mamoru Shigemitsu, and Gen Yoshijiro Umezu. Other signatures represented are from the Republic of China, the United Kingdom, the Union of Soviet Socialist Republics, the Commonwealth of Australia, the Dominion of Canada, the Provisional Government of the French Republic, the Kingdom of the Netherlands, and the Dominion of New Zealand, September 2, 1945

National Archives and Records Administration

Menu, written and voted on by sailors aboard ship for their long-dreamed-of celebration meal

Photograph folder from the restaurant "The Derby San Francisco's Finest" containing a group photograph of the sailors who imagined their menu

The Marshall Nichols family

Photograph, Lt Col J. Earl Rudder, U.S. Army, Brady, Texas

Letter, Lt Col J. Earl Rudder to his family, May 9, 1945

Mrs. J. Earl Rudder

Photograph, Cpl Robert E. Turner, U.S. Army, St. Paul, Minnesota

Letter, Cpl Robert E. Turner to Mildred G. Christianson, May 11, 1945

Mrs. Mildred Turner and Mr. Steven Turner

ADDITIONAL QUOTED MATERIAL

Courtesy of:

USS *Arizona* Memorial
Honolulu, Hawaii

Mrs. Catherine Warner Batey
Cedar Rapids, Iowa

Mrs. La Verne Beegle
Bedford, Pennsylvania

Mr. Henry Bethke
Hendersonville, North Carolina

Mr. William C. Bieluch
Hartford, Connecticut

Mr. Vic Brittain
Arlington, Texas

Bundesarchiv
Freiburg, Germany

Mr. Sven Carlson
Bloomfield, Connecticut

Congressional Medal of Honor Society
New York, New York

Mr. Richard Conn
Washington, D.C.

Mr. Clifford M. Dunn
Splendora, Texas

Mrs. A. J. Ehlert
West Columbia, Texas

Dwight D. Eisenhower Library
Abilene, Kansas
National Archives and Records Administration

Mr. S. Bruce Elson
Pueblo, Colorado

Mr. Austen H. Furse
Austin, Texas

Mr. Nap Glass
Aventura, Florida

Mr. Vernon D. Hasley
Dimmitt, Texas

Mr. Shiro Ishikawa
Tokyo, Japan

Mrs. Lucy Wilson Jopling
San Antonio, Texas

Mr. Arthur Kleppinger
Bethlehem, Pennsylvania

Library of Congress
Washington, D.C.

Mr. Jose M. Lopez
San Antonio, Texas

Mrs. Agnes J. Mangerich
Bethesda, Maryland

Mr. Hiram E. Mann
Titusville, Florida

National Archives and Records Administration
Washington, D.C.

Naval Historical Foundation
Washington, D.C.

Mr. Van Parker
Carmichael, California

Princeton University
Princeton, New Jersey

Mr. Howard M. Randall
Jonestown, Texas

Mr. Earl M. Schaeffer
Assaria, Kansas

Mrs. Murleen Self
Crosbyton, Texas

Mrs. Lee A. Shannon
Mesa, Arizona

Mr. Murray Shapiro
Chatsworth, California

Mr. Loren Tower
Tigard, Oregon

Mr. Leonard J. Travaline
Conshohocken, Pennsylvania

Harry S. Truman Library
Independence, Missouri
National Archives and Records Administration

Mr. Raymond M. Tufteland
Lemon Grove, California

U.S. Marine Corps Museums
Quantico, Virginia

U.S. Military History Institute
Carlisle Barracks, Pennsylvania

United States Military Academy Library
West Point, New York

Mrs. Eugenia Rutkowski Wilkerson
Bullard, Texas

PHOTOGRAPHS

From the collections of:

USS *Arizona* Memorial Museum, National Park Service, Honolulu, Hawaii
Bettmann Archives, New York, New York
Bernice P. Bishop Museum, Honolulu, Hawaii
Jimmy Carter Library, Atlanta, Georgia
Dwight D. Eisenhower Library, Abilene, Kansas
Gerald R. Ford Library, Ann Arbor, Michigan
Mr. Everett P. Fulton, New Braunfels, Texas
Mr. Daniel M. Ganz, New York, New York
Hoover Institution Archives, Stanford University; Stanford, California
Imperial War Museum, London, England

Mr. Paul E. Ison, Fort Myers, Florida
Lyndon Baines Johnson Library and Museum, Austin, Texas
John F. Kennedy Library, Boston, Massachusetts
Library of Congress, Washington, D.C.
National Archives and Records Administration, Washington, D.C.
President Richard M. Nixon
Ernie Pyle State Historical Site, Indiana State Museum, Dana, Indiana
Ronald Reagan Library, Simi Valley, California
Franklin D. Roosevelt Library, Hyde Park, New York
Royal Hawaiian Hotel, Honolulu, Hawaii
Harry S. Truman Library, Independence, Missouri
The White House, Washington, D.C.
Wide World Photos, New York, New York